THE ELECTRONIC
DAY TRADER

THE ELECTRONIC DAY TRADER

**MARC FRIEDFERTIG
and GEORGE WEST**

McGraw-Hill

New York   San Francisco   Washington, D.C.   Auckland   Bogotá
Caracas   Lisbon   London   Madrid   Mexico City   Milan
Montreal   New Delhi   San Juan   Singapore
Sydney   Tokyo   Toronto

Library of Congress Cataloging-in-Publication Data

Friedfertig, Marc.
    The electronic day trader / Marc Friedfertig and George West
      p. cm.
    ISBN 0-07-015808-8
    1. Electronic trading of securities.   I. West, George
    II. Title
    HG4515.95.F74 1998
    332.64'0285—dc21   97-45704
                                        CIP

McGraw-Hill

A Division of The McGraw·Hill Companies

   4 5 6 7 8 9 0   DOC/DOC   9 0 2 1 0 9 8

ISBN 0–07–015808-8

The sponsoring editor for this book was Stephen Isaacs, the editing supervisor was John M. Morriss, and the production supervisor was Suzanne W. B. Rapcavage. It was set in Times Roman per the IPROF design specs by Michele Betterman of the Hightstown McGraw-Hill Desktop Publishing Unit.

McGraw-Hill books are available at special discounts to use as premiums and sales promotions, or for use in corporate training programs. For more information, please write to the Director of Special Sales, McGraw-Hill, 11 West 19th Street, New York, NY 10011. Or contact your local bookstore.

This publication is designed to provide accurate and authoritative information in regard to the subject matter covered. It is sold with the understanding that the publisher is not engaged in rendering legal, accounting or other professional service. If legal advice or other expert assistance is required, the services of a competent professional person should be sought.

From a Declaration of Principles Jointly Adopted by a Committee of the American Bar Association and a Committee of Publishers and Associations.

This book is printed on recycled, acid-free paper containing a minimum of 50% recycled de-inked paper.

DISCLAIMER

Dedicated to Cameron, Cole, and Lindsay

CONTENTS

The classic *Reminiscences of a Stock Operator,* by Edwin Lefevre, originally published in the 1920s, tells the story of a stock operator (Livingston) and reveals valuable, timeless lessons of stock speculating. In his book, Lefevre describes bucket shops as very popular places where speculators could buy stocks and know instantly what price they would receive. They were places where speculators "could move like lightning" to get in and out of positions, enabling them to cut their losses or follow up on their luck in an instant. This was a game where a skillful speculator could profit handsomely and the average player would become a sucker.* It was a game that basically became extinct when the last of this style bucket shop closed in the twenties. The real brokerage firms, those that were members of the New York Stock Exchange, did business differently. They transacted their business on an exchange where both time and cost were factors that made trading the way Livingston (Livermore) did it in the bucket shop not feasible. Trading remained this way until now—but now day trading is back. It did not actually happen overnight. It took more like 30 years, and the combination of several major events and technological advancements (NASDAQ, competitive commission rates, DOT, SOES, and the Internet) for it to happen, but it has happened. Day trading is once again the hottest game on Wall Street, with speculators both making and losing fortunes.

The Electronic Day Trader is history repeating itself. You see *The Electronic Day Trader* brings back to Wall Street, just a few doors away from where Livingston operated, the ability to know right away the price at which you can buy and sell a stock. It has been nearly 70 years since the last bucket shops operated the way Lefevre describes them in his book. The instantaneous executions at the bucket shops, the type that made Livingston so successful in *Reminiscences,* is once again possible on Wall Street. The only differences are that the computer has replaced the blackboard, and today's technology makes this phenomenon available to anyone anywhere.

---

* Edwin Lefevre, *Reminiscences of a Stock Operator,* John Wiley and Sons, New York, 1923.

The Electronic Day Trader is unique in that it describes the A to Z's of becoming a modern-day stock operator. The book is divided into eight chapters. Each chapter has a distinct purpose, which, combined, describes a complete formula for success in a clear and lucid fashion. Chapter 1 reports on the allure of day trading—and the events that made it possible for day trading once again to become the hottest game in town. Chapter 2 gives the details of the methods of electronic day trading. Chapter 3 describes significant differences between the way NASDAQ and the New York Stock Exchange operate and the differences between the specialist system and the market-maker system they use. The chapter outlines advantages and intricacies one will encounter trading listed stocks versus trading in the over-the-counter market.

Chapter 4 explains how to gauge the strength of the market and determine which industry groups in the market are strongest. Chapter 5 describes the trading day and provides an in-depth look at interpreting the players in the markets. It also reveals the strategies that have made the authors successful in day trading. Chapter 6 discusses the psychology of day trading and offers advice on how to develop your own philosophy for day trading. Chapter 7 details the most advanced technology available today, including the advantages of this technology and where and how to inexpensively gain access to it and how to use it.

Chapter 8 ties the book together by summarizing the sections to present a complete approach to proceed with, along with the steps necessary to develop your own philosophy to enhance your success. Found throughout the book are many of the lessons a speculator will experience. Some of the lessons are very similar to the ones first pointed out by Lefevre in the twenties. Others are the authors' own rules of speculating. In addition, the authors share some novel strategies to apply to trading in today's market.

The Electronic Day Trader is the work of two highly successful day traders who prove the book's worth every day. Perhaps the most appealing part of this book is that the authors are accessible to anyone who would like to learn more. Their offices are open to the public, and they are willing to provide ongoing support for those who become their customers. On any given day you may find George West trading among others with similar goals, using the same skills described in this book. Typically, on the same day you may find Marc Friedfertig providing assistance to those who need guidance. For those who find their approach viable, it is still realistic to have the opportunity to trade in the same room with either Marc or George and others they have taught. Marc and George have shared their secrets with thousands. Both they and their customers have mutually benefited from the seminars they run, the books they have written, the trading facilities they provide, and the brokerage services they offer.

Marc and George originally decided to write this book to provide a detailed manual for those who wanted to learn their techniques. As they wrote it, the book evolved from a tutorial for their seminar into a broad book about day trading. The book now encompasses an understanding of the markets and a detailed description of interpreting the actions of the players, as well as an introduction to the most advanced technology available for day trading along with an understanding of how to use it effectively. Marc and George have succeeded in teaching many individuals to make exorbitant amounts of money day trading. Both are also quick to point out that this is not for everyone, and quite a few do not succeed. However, those who do succeed tend to be highly successful and truly love their work.

This book presents you, the reader, with everything you need to get started trading stocks and with the pertinent information to be a successful day trader. Even if you decide that day trading is not for you, you will still find portions of this book useful. The authors give you an inside look on how the markets and the players involved operate, as well as some useful philosophies for success. *The Electronic Day Trader* combines the ageless art of speculating with the cutting edge of today's technology to offer the reader an approach to succeed as a day trader in the twenty-first century.

Marc Friedfertig and George West

ACKNOWLEDGMENTS

We would like to thank our McGraw-Hill editor, Stephen Isaacs, for his confidence in our ability to write, as well as to trade. We would like to thank Dr. George Pieczenik for his insights, including the section on making money in random markets, as well as his invaluable input in helping us put it all together. We would also like to thank our wives and families for their perseverance during the long hours. And we would like to thank Jeff Wilson, Josh Levine, and Jeff Citron for the opportunity they gave us. Lastly, none of this would have been possible without all the students, traders, and staff who have helped us to develop, test, and prove the value of the techniques you are about to read.

The Reemergence of Day Trading

The art of speculating in one form or another has been around forever. When it comes to speculating, there are two things that you can be sure of—there will always be people willing to speculate, and history will repeat itself. Sure, the object of speculation may change, the rules may change, and the technology may change. However, what has happened before is sure to happen again. Whether it's tulip bulbs, precious metals, mutual funds, lottery tickets, football games, or penny stocks, human nature is human nature. Ignorance, greed, fear, and hope determine how people react and thus how prices move and markets behave. People have speculated on everything at one time or another. For the last hundred years and certainly into the foreseeable future, speculating on stock prices offers liquidity, combined with legitimacy and purpose. Stock speculation, trading, and investing have become an essential and vibrant part of both our economy and our lives. Trading is just another word for speculating, and investing is nothing more than speculating, except that it supposedly encompasses a longer time horizon and for some reason it implies less risk. Speculators speculate, traders trade, and investors invest to make money. Traders buy stock or any other object of speculation because they anticipate a price appreciation.

Speculation and gambling are similar, with a few important distinctions. One difference is the perception, sometimes true, that successful speculators profit due to their skill or an unseen advantage, while gamblers prosper due to chance or luck. Another distinction is that gambling in most forms has been illegal for the better part of our history, while speculating plays an essential role in our markets and thus our economy. These important distinctions make speculating an accepted occupation and gambling not accepted. Whether a gambler, a trader, or a speculator, in all cases the attraction is the same—the chance to make a lot of money in a hurry. It is the immediate measurable gratification of a win that makes theses games irresistible, and the unpredictable but significant reinforcement pattern that make them so addicting. Day trading appears so deceptively easy, yet in reality it is a never-ending challenge. It is a game, an opportunity to match wits against the majority and thereby prosper. Day-trading the stock market is the ultimate opportunity to speculate and the ultimate game.

HOW I GOT INVOLVED

Marc Friedfertig

Having been a member and a market maker of the New York Futures Exchange for 1 year and the American Stock Exchange for 8 years I assumed there were certain qualities that were common in all markets. These self-regulatory organizations (SROs) understood the importance of providing fair and orderly markets. They understood that fair, orderly markets bred investor confidence, which, in turn, fueled their volume, which ultimately filled their members' pockets. Members of these SROs recognized the importance of their reputation and saw fair and orderly markets as the ultimate way to enhance these reputations. On the American Stock Exchange, where I made markets in options, our quotes were always good for at least 10 contracts (equivalent to 1,000 shares). We made these sales sometimes against our better judgment. Sometimes, we even did more than we were obligated to, in order to defend the integrity of our markets.

As an option trader, trading options on both listed and NASDAQ stocks, I frequently relied on the markets in the underlying stocks to price and hedge my option trades. New York Stock Exchange stocks were generally easily accessible and always available at some price. I was able to access this market through my clearing firm's DOT system or through a floor broker, and both generally provided me with fair and accurate executions. NASDAQ stocks were accessible by using Instinet or by calling the market makers on the phone. I found the NASDAQ market fairly illiquid compared with listed stocks. Efforts to buy stock on Instinet at any reasonable price were frequently ignored. Phone calls to market makers frequently didn't prove fruitful. Market makers often refused to trade with me (a professional) at any price and typically claimed that there was an SOES order ahead of my request. This tweaked my interest in what seemed to be the only way to get executions in fast-moving, volatile, NASDAQ stocks. The following year I left a lucrative career as an option market maker to become an online day trader. Using an online system, I was able to get instantaneous executions in fast-moving stocks. I was able to get the executions I needed to profit in today's volatile trading markets.

WHY DAY TRADERS PLAY AN ESSENTIAL ROLE IN OUR ECONOMY

Day traders allow the stock market to put a price on the companies that are a constant, vital part of life. We know these companies, as they touch all of our lives in some way. They build our homes, produce our food, make our clothing, and build our cars. They broadcast the TV shows we watch and the radio programs we listen to. They provide jobs for our friends and families. As an integral part of our economic cycle, these are the companies that need capital to develop the products that will improve the quality of our lives in the years ahead.

The stock market allows day traders to put a price on these companies every second of the trading day. By actively trading, day traders provide the liquidity that is the cornerstone for our markets. Without liquidity, companies would not be able to raise the money they need to produce the goods and provide the services that we demand. Without liquidity, investors would not be able to commit capital. It is this capital that allows these companies to grow and prosper in our economy. And it is the day trader who plays a pivotal role in creating the markets that allow our economy to flourish.

Day traders add immense depth and liquidity to the markets. Liquidity enables any individual or institution to rapidly sell its stock for fair value, and that is a direct consequence of the large number of day traders providing an active market. **Liquidity does not just mean a rapid turnover; it means a rapid turnover at a fair value.** Anyone could immediately sell a Rolls Royce on the street for a dollar, but this would not constitute a fair price and therefore does not represent true liquidity. By the same token, real estate may sit for many expensive years before buyers appear who are willing to pay fair value. On the other hand, the stock market allows day traders to place a value on capital instruments and, most importantly, affords investors and traders the opportunity to enter or exit their equity positions efficiently. The economic functions of the market, coupled with unparalleled liquidity and a myriad of constantly arising new opportunities, makes the stock market the ultimate way to speculate.

WHY DAY TRADING IS THE HOTTEST GAME ON WALL STREET TODAY

While people have traded stocks for hundreds of years, recent changes in rules and technological advancements make the present the best time in history to become a day trader. Today, anyone, from anywhere, with a minimal amount of money can easily and inexpensively buy and sell stocks. Recent rule changes have leveled the playing field, while technological advancement allows individuals to buy and sell stock in an instant from a personal computer in their own home. Together, the rule changes, technological advancements, the low cost of doing business, and the globalization of markets have made the present the best time in history to day-trade—a time curiously reminiscent of the last turn of the century.

Bucket Shops

Starting in the latter half of the nineteenth century and peaking in the great bull market of the 1920s, bucket shops sprouted across the major U.S. cities. These shops were basically brokerage houses without licenses or for that matter without a true relationship with an exchange. Bucket shops were places where speculators or gamblers could go and buy or sell shares, or in some cases commodities, and speculate simply on the basis of changing prices. Anybody who could put up the required margin could buy or sell an unlimited quantity of a stock or a commodity without regard to intentions or ability to meet such obligations.* The margin was typically a small fraction of the true price. Bucket shops in many ways were more appealing to the masses than true brokerage firms. They were conveniently located, allowed for trading of small lots with little money, and charged lower commissions. They typically attracted both those who dealt in odd lots and those who were seeking entertainment and excitement. Bucket shops to the average person were

---

*Edwin Lefevre, *Reminiscences of a Stock Operator,* John Wiley & Sons, New York, 1923.

no different from real exchanges, and bucket shops meant action.* Comparing bucket shops with exchanges in the early 1900s is similar to comparing OTB (off-track betting) with the horse tracks today. They are more convenient and offer plenty of action. In many ways bucket shops are similar to the present-day trading firms that are flourishing across the country. However, the term "bucket shop" tends to have a negative connotation since it was generally used to describe unlicensed and in some cases illegal operations.†

Today's day-trading firms are generally licensed and transact their business on an exchange or through NASDAQ. There are many reasons that people are attracted to these places. Two of the most important reasons, which disappeared with the demise of the bucket shops (the crash of 1929), did not reappear until the rise of the legitimate day-trading houses of today. The first is instantaneous executions, and the other is the low cost of doing business. In the early 1900s a clerk posted symbols on a chalk quotation board as another clerk read the information off the ticker tape. Customers were able to buy or sell stocks instantly at the posted price while frequently posting as little as $1 per share margin. It was these two criteria that led to the profits of the famous stock operator (Livingston) described in *Reminiscences of a Stock Operator.* Livingston could not operate through legitimate brokerage firms that executed their trades on an exchange for the simple reason that he could not know the price he was getting until after the fact (3 to 15 minutes depending on the market). Livingston said that the execution methods of the bucket shops allowed him to "move like lightning. I could follow up my luck or cut my loss in a second."‡ The executions at the legitimate brokerage firms were much slower. Livingston's decisions were based on reading the ticker tape directly. However, the ticker tape typically lagged the market, and therefore stock purchases through real brokerage firms were executed by brokers on the floor several minutes after decisions were made. Economic conditions, market conditions, and new rules and regulations closed the day-trading brokerage firms, i.e., the bucket shops, of the previous era.

Present-day technology and low commissions now allow a day trader to get instantaneous executions and low-cost commissions on

---

*Ann Fabian, *Card Sharps, Dream Books and Bucket Shops—Gambling in the 19th Century,* Cornell University Press, Ithaca, N.Y., p. 189.
†Fabian, p. 191.
‡Lefevre.

legitimate transactions that are conducted on a major exchange. For the greater part of the middle of the twentieth century, day trading was a very difficult profession. Then, in the 1970s, the groundwork was laid, and now a quarter of a century later, as we write, the technology is still developing for what is today the hottest game on Wall Street—Electronic Day Trading!

Electronic Trading

On February 5, 1971, NASDAQ began. It became an electronic market, which allows one to buy and sell through a network of computers. It is a market where market makers electronically display their best bids and offers and where orders can be executed instantaneously through NAS-DAQ level 2 workstations. And as of January 1997, it became a market that allows customers' best bids and offers to be displayed and represented on NASDAQ by their brokers or through ECNs (electronic communications networks). ECNs allow customers to display their orders to other customers around the world and also allow customer orders to be paired, or traded with each other. This has the effect of providing more liquidity than at any other time in history. NASDAQ is currently the third largest stock market in the world, behind the New York Stock Exchange and the Japanese stock market. Most importantly, these factors have made NASDAQ the fastest-growing market in the last 20 years.

NASDAQ offers three levels of service. NASDAQ level 1 essentially displays the inside market—the highest bid and lowest offer that make up the best available price (also referred to as the quote). **NASDAQ level 2 displays a detailed quote that includes an actual list of market makers, or firms, and ECNs bids and offers, which make up this inside market. (*Note:* ECNs and market makers could be acting as agents and representing customer limit orders.) And it allows for order entry of SOES and SelectNet orders.** Lastly, NASDAQ level 3 permits all of the above and, in addition, allows market makers to adjust their bids and offers. Thus, NASDAQ was the first vital step forward toward making online day trading a viable profession.*

---

*Charles Allmon, ed., *Nasdaq—The Stock Market of Tomorrow—Today—The Nasdaq Handbook,*
   Probus Publishing, New York, p. 44.

May Day

In Communist countries May Day is celebrated as their "Labor Day." But on Wall Street May Day goes down in history as the day commissions were lowered. This major event of the 1970s occurred on May 1, 1975, or "May Day." May Day on Wall Street ended a 183-year-old tradition.* Fixed commission rates were a cornerstone of the U.S. markets for most of history. Exchange members were required to charge a minimum commission on every transaction based on the size and the dollar amount of the trade. The commission for a 1,000-share transaction typically cost hundreds of dollars (rates varied for quantity and price), making day trading extremely difficult because of the tremendous expense.

Mandated by the SEC, May Day was the culmination of a 5-year phaseout of fixed commissions and signaled the start of a new era. As with any major change to the established system, many of the most respected people on Wall Street made dire predictions that May Day would undermine the very structure of the industry. They said that brokerage firms would fail and the price of a seat (membership) on the exchanges would collapse.

Once the dreaded day arrived, changes began immediately. Some firms competed by offering "full-service" brokerage, which included research and other services and which were slow to adjust prices downward. But newer firms, the "discount brokers," competed strictly on price. The resultant cost to execute a trade plunged almost immediately and has continued lower until the present, making commissions a negligible factor in trading. Today some brokerage firms are willing to do transactions at next to no cost. One brokerage firm advertises commissions as low as $9.95 a trade for up to 5,000 shares, while another offers unlimited transactions for an annual fee.

In spite of these deep discounts, brokerage firms have become even more profitable. How is this possible? First, volume has increased a hundredfold. In the 1970s 5 million shares per day were traded on the New York Stock Exchange. Today, 500 million shares per day are the norm. Many of today's transactions are large-block orders. These trades are easier and less costly to execute than many small orders. In the 1970s orders on an exchange were typically executed through a series of steps. You called your broker, your broker called a trading desk, a trading desk called

---

*James E. Buck, ed., *The New York Stock Exchange—The First 200 Years,* Greenwich Publishing Groups, Essex, Conn., pp.204–205.

a clerk on the floor, a floor clerk gave the order to a floor broker, and the floor broker frequently gave the order to another floor broker or a specialist, who then executed the order; the process then reversed. These steps generally took several minutes, were very costly, and left a large amount of room for expensive errors.

Today, only a few orders are executed in this manner. The majority of orders on the exchanges are now done with fewer steps. A customer calls a broker, the broker gives the order to a clerk, who then plugs the order into a DOT (designated order turnaround) machine,* the DOT machine sends the order at the speed of light to the specialist, who typically fills the order and sends it back to the clerk, who tells the broker, who in turn tells the customer. This process typically takes under a minute. What used to be a many-step process has been reduced to only a few simple steps.

The increase in the number of shares being traded, along with the decrease in cost to the broker to execute each trade, has brokerage firms making more money than ever before. In addition, the rapid decline in commissions was an indispensable factor in making day trading a viable profession for the non-exchange member. This, in turn, increased trading volume, which helped bring down the cost of an execution.

SEC Rules Have Benefited the Market and the Day Trader

NASDAQ was a system primarily used to display competing bids and offers (quotes) to establish a market. Historically, most transactions were executed in-house (at the firm where the customer order was received) or over the telephone. NASDAQ was generally used to establish price but not actually to execute orders. Quotes drove the inside market where the best bid (highest price that will be paid) and the best offer (lowest price that a stock is offered for sale) created a market. Now market makers, and more recently ECNs, will post firm quotes (prices they will honor) that can be viewed by all those who have access to terminals that display this information. The inside market is generally available to all who have access to level 1 quotes.

NASDAQ introduced electronic executions when it developed the Small Order Execution System (SOES) in 1985 and subsequently the

---

*Buck, p. 209.

SelectNet system in 1990. SOES is an automatic execution system that allows customers to buy on the offer and sell on the bid up to a thousand shares at a time. This system was not fully implemented until 1988 when the SEC required all market makers to participate. The requirement was the direct result of the market makers' poor performance during the 1987 crash. At the time of the crash, market makers refused to answer the phones to honor their quoted prices, and customers could not get orders executed at any price. In response to an abundance of criticism, NASDAQ implemented an automatic electronic execution system for customers through SOES. This allowed customers to access and trade with market makers without having to call them on the phone. NASDAQ also implemented a system for market makers to communicate and to execute transactions electronically with each other through SelectNet.

Both SelectNet and SOES have experienced rapid growth in the 1990s. SelectNet's growth was largely tied to market makers' reluctance to communicate with customers over the phone and discuss and negotiate their orders. However, market makers used to talk to each other over the phone all day long. An investigation, implemented by the Justice Department in 1993, changed all that. This investigation, completed in 1996, concluded that market makers, for all practical purposes, were colluding to keep spreads artificially wide. As a result of this investigation the NASDAQ market changed forever and for the better. The NASD (National Association of Securities Dealers) in cooperation with the SEC implemented a host of changes designed to protect the public.

NASDAQ, when first developed, attracted illiquid stocks that did not meet the Big Board (New York Stock Exchange) or the American Stock Exchange listing requirements. NASDAQ market makers typically quoted wide spreads (the difference between the bid and ask), which was appropriate for illiquid stocks. These wide spreads were rationalized by market makers as justified, given the level of risk that they were taking to make markets in these stocks. Wide spreads, at the expense of the customer and traders, work to the market makers' advantage since they typically "make" this spread as a form of compensation for the risk that they are taking in providing continuous liquidity. ("Making" the spread refers to the market makers' ability to buy stock on the bid from one customer and sell it at a higher price on the offer to another.) In addition to the wide spreads, NASDAQ assured market makers the ability to earn the spread on every transaction. A market maker was always on the other side of every trade. This meant that customers were rarely allowed to trade with each other. Rather, they were forced to buy and sell stocks from a market maker who would benefit from wide spreads.

In fact, for most of NASDAQ's history, market makers rarely allowed customers to trade between the spread even if one customer was bidding higher than another customer who was willing to sell it. For example, it was very possible for a NASDAQ stock, with a market of 50 to $50\frac{1}{2}$, to have customers willing to pay $50\frac{3}{8}$ and customers willing to sell at $50\frac{1}{8}$ without a trade taking place. It was also possible for another customer to be bidding $50\frac{1}{4}$ while the firm representing the order was able to pay 50 to another customer for the stock and sell it to the bidding customer at $50\frac{1}{4}$. This could never happen on the New York or American Stock Exchange, where the specialist, whenever possible, pairs up customer orders (more than two-thirds of the time customer orders are paired up on these exchanges) and where customers are always given limit order protection. These original allowances in NASDAQ rules, which seemed appropriate for trading illiquid stocks, certainly did not belong in what was becoming one of the world's largest markets.

Many of these allowances continued to give the market maker advantages—until recently. The first change NASDAQ implemented was the creation of a customer limit order protection rule that made it illegal for a market maker to trade through a customer's order. For example, this eliminated the practice of market makers buying stock on their 50 bid while holding their unexecuted customer's $50\frac{1}{4}$ limit order bid. This change was followed by major changes on January 20, 1997 . On this date the Security and Exchange Commission mandated changes for which NASDAQ had neither the courage nor fortitude to make on its own. NASDAQ and its members fought these changes, but the Security and Exchange Commission implemented new order handling rules that leveled the playing field and brought NASDAQ to a new level. Ironically, it is these changes that are necessary if NASDAQ will become the "major market for the next hundred years." The SEC forced NASDAQ to adopt rules that were appropriate for the stocks that now trade on NASDAQ. These rules are the first step in transforming NASDAQ from a quote-driven market to an order-driven market such as the New York Stock Exchange.

The new order handling rules accomplished two critical steps toward ensuring a fair and orderly market, which allows customers to ultimately get the best price. The first step required market makers to fill or display any customer's limit order that improves on the inside price. This gives the customer limit order protection in the market, as opposed to just having a market maker execute the order when conditions were favorable to the firm. The second step forbade market makers to display prices better than NASDAQ's market in private markets such as Instinet unless these quotes were displayed and accessible to the public. This step opened the way for ECNs, such as Instinet (INCA), Island (ISLD), Spear, Leeds and Kellogg (REDI), Teranova (TNTO), and Bloomberg (BTRD) to be represented on the NASDAQ system, effectively creating one market with the best price. These changes have led to narrower spreads and fairer treatment for customer orders. Most importantly, these changes opened the way for NAS-DAQ to pair up customer orders where customers could trade with each other rather than solely with market makers. This allowed customers to potentially buy on the bid, sell on the offer, or trade in between the spread, as opposed to always paying the spread as they had previously. These steps made it possible for customers to trade with other customers, which can ultimately transform NASDAQ from a quote-driven market to an order-driven one. On the New York Stock Exchange orders drive the inside market, and the majority of the transactions are done customer to customer. The market is created by customer orders, not by market makers.

In 1997, another long overdue change was implemented. All of the major U.S. exchanges began allowing all stocks to trade in increments of sixteenths ("teenies") as opposed to eighths. This has resulted in narrower spreads, which in turn has decreased the market makers' and specialists' edge. The change has benefited all customers, because when they are forced to pay a spread to a market maker, there is a much tighter gap between the bid and the offer. In the next few years, it is highly probable that markets will switch to decimal pricing, potentially resulting in even narrower spreads.

Technology

The implementation of online access to the markets grew out of necessity. Markets could not continue to expand and serve our economy or the world's economy without online access. Online access to markets will continue to grow as the economy and markets become more global. The markets are changing rapidly. Companies and individuals from all over the world are interested in accessing the liquidity available in today's markets. This has made electronic access a staple of modern markets and ensures that this access will play an ever-increasing role in the markets of the twenty-first century.

For most of the past 20 years NASDAQ and other exchanges have been implementing changes to their technology in an attempt to stay ahead of the rapid growth of their markets. More recently, technological advances have made online access to markets possible for anyone from anywhere with a minimal amount of money. For as little as $3,000, individuals can enter orders through various online order entry systems designed to run on their personal computers. These online systems are able to provide individuals with the information they need to keep abreast of the markets and execute orders for extremely low commissions and get extremely fast executions. In fact, in some cases the executions are instantaneous. Customers who buy and sell stock online can do so without interacting with a broker. These systems have made it possible to get lightning-fast executions, for cheap commissions, from a personal computer. It seems that almost every day new online or Internet trading systems are being developed and offered to the trading public.

WHAT THE FUTURE HOLDS?

Every 50 to 100 years something happens that helps our economy to become more efficient and prosperous. In the mid-1800s it was the railroad, in the early 1900s it was the automobile, and in the late 1900s it is the personal computer. These advancements have paved the way to a more efficient, more national, and now more international economy. As our markets for goods become more global, our economy becomes more stable and more efficient. Global markets mean that recessions in one part of the world can be offset by expanding economies in other parts of the world. Furthermore, inflation in one part of the world can be tamed by supply from other parts of the world. Many individuals value our markets based on historical standards. Today, however, our companies can raise capital and grow faster and more efficiently than in any time in history. Personal computers can now do in minutes the work that a team of highly paid professionals once needed days to complete. Companies can now send mail (e-mail) to thousands of customers in seconds, and communication products have linked us closer together. As a result our companies are much more efficient, our economies are more stable, and our stocks are demanding much higher prices.

As these changes are taking effect, many respected members of the Wall Street community are once again making dire predictions for the future. As always, there are many who point the finger of doom at the over-valuation of our markets as they compare today's pricing to the pricing of a different era. Just as the Wall Street community thought that May Day would be the end of Wall Street, many feel that the new order handling rules and the narrower spreads will lead to very difficult times. What these naysayers must realize is that any changes that lead to more liquidity, and fairer pricing, will also lead to higher volume, which in turn will ultimately lead to higher profits for Wall Street. The volume of shares traded today has increased 100 times in the last 25 years. As the New York and NASDAQ markets attract more companies and more players from around the world, could volume possibly increase another 100 times in the next 25 years? This large increase in volume, or even a small increase, must be accompanied by the rapid growth of electronic trading. This may just be the beginning of a new era of more efficient and more sophisticated global markets—the start of an era of technology where billions of shares change hands each day and the beginning of the massive growth of online day trading.

CHAPTER 2

What Is Online Day Trading?

Whether you are currently trading in some capacity, or are joining us from another field, you are likely to find online day trading one of the most exciting and, it is hoped, rewarding experiences of your life. No other job can offer you both the flexibility and the profit potential that online day trading can afford. However, day trading is not for everyone. It requires the utmost in concentration as well as steadfast discipline. Here you are the master of your own fate. Nobody will ever tell you to be at work on time or ask for your vacation schedule. Yet it is very possible to earn in one month what it will take the average person to earn in a year.

Whether this is a new endeavor for you or you have a great many years of trading experience, this book will help make you a better trader. This book will bring you up to date on the cutting-edge technology available to day traders. It will present you with innovative trading strategies to allow you to take advantage of this technology. Reading about and employing the techniques in this book will not automatically make you a profitable day trader; however, the application of the techniques and ideas outlined in the following chapters have helped hundreds of online day traders yield consistently profitable returns. Day traders without the information presented in this book are clearly at a disadvantage.

This book is designed with several purposes:

- To introduce you to online day trading
- To explain the trading strategies being employed by a unique group of highly successful day traders

- To get you acquainted with the most advanced technology available, and explain how anyone can use this technology to put these strategies to work
- To provide you with an in-depth look at how to use this technology to interpret the actions of the players in the markets
- To explain the psychology and discipline it takes to be successful at this type of trading
- And finally, as you have already read, to explain why this is the best time in history to day-trade

There are four ways that day traders currently can get direct electronic access to the market: SuperDot, SelectNet, electronic communication networks (ECNs), and the Small Order Entry System (SOES). SuperDot is used strictly for trading listed stocks.* NASDAQ's SelectNet and SOES are used strictly to access the NASDAQ markets. ECNs are primarily used to access NASDAQ, but some ECNs may be used to trade listed stocks also. Recent technological advancements have made it possible to access these systems through online order entry terminals that are linked to networks of computers either through designated phone lines or via modem through regular phone lines or the Internet. These systems have been and will continue to be important as they become more widely used, more significant in our markets, and more efficient and more capable of handling this expansion. More efficient and reliable markets lead to greater investor confidence in our markets, and this confidence continues to fuel greater expansion.

SUPERDOT

SuperDot is a means of electronically accessing listed markets, and now executes more than 40 percent of the shares traded on the New York Stock Exchange each day. Furthermore, 80 percent of all orders entered on the New York Stock Exchange come through SuperDot. SuperDot can handle orders for up to 99,999 shares at a time. It was introduced in 1984 as an improved version of DOT.

SuperDot is an electronic order delivery system that links member firms directly to specialists who can rapidly execute their orders and send them a report. The specialists then manually pair up orders, fill the orders

---

*Buck, p. 209.

from their inventory, or place the orders on their limit order book. The limit order book allows the specialists to organize the orders to help them establish a market and to execute these orders when the orders become marketable. This system has substantially increased the efficiency of the listed markets. This makes it possible to execute orders quickly and inexpensively. In normal market conditions orders are typically filled in seconds. However, in extremely busy times orders can take several minutes to fill. As a result, third markets, such as the Chicago Stock Exchange, have been competing for orders by guaranteeing to fill some marketable orders at the best available price, as displayed by the New York Stock Exchange. This effectively creates an automatic execution system for those firms that route their orders to these third markets.

SuperDot gives individual investor orders of less than 2,100 shares priority over all larger institutional orders and allows brokerage firms to offer their customers online access to stocks traded on exchanges. SuperDot, coupled with low commissions, has made day-trading listed stocks (those traded on an exchange) viable.* It is our belief that the SuperDot system is likely to become more and more automated over time as the New York Stock Exchange attempts to maintain its dominance in this market. However, SuperDot is not easily available to individuals. But Internet systems, such as Datek Online, offer similar access to the markets and similar executions to those offered by SuperDot—and in some cases better executions.

ELECTRONIC COMMUNICATIONS NETWORKS

An electronic communications network was the first concept to be implemented for electronically executed trades. **An ECN allows market makers' and customers' bids and offers to be displayed on national systems to others who can fill these orders.**

Instinet

Instinet, the first ECN, was introduced in 1969 as a way for institutions to display bids and offers, in both listed stocks and NASDAQ stocks, to other institutions. Instinet also gave the institutions on its network the ability to

---

*Buck, p. 26.

execute transactions through its system. Originally, Instinet catered only to institutions that wanted to trade with other institutions. Later it allowed brokerage firms to use its network also. The major drawback to the widespread use of Instinet is that it has attempted to limit its users to a select group of institutions and brokerage firms. Instinet is not generally accessible to most individual investors. This seems at odds with the spirit of current regulations. **The SEC order handling rules (implemented in January 1997) were designed to provide the customer limit order protection and to eliminate private markets with better prices.** The SEC rules were intended to force the NASD to ensure that customer limit orders are filled at the best possible price. The order handling rules have been a big step in the right direction. However, ECNs are only required to display orders entered by market makers, and ECNs are *not* required to display block orders (those over 10,000 shares or worth more than $250,000). These two exceptions are inconsistent with the SEC's intention and should be eliminated in order to ensure that customers have access to the best available price.

Instinet has not made all of its bids and offers available to the public, but a substantial amount of Instinet's orders are now being included in NASDAQ's quotes and are represented by the four-letter symbol INCA. These orders have added substantial liquidity to the NASDAQ's markets. A large percentage of NASDAQ's volume is executed through Instinet (it has been estimated to be as high as 50 percent in the past), and 80 to 90 percent of these orders are being entered by market makers. Instinet is regarded as the best available system for institutions and market makers to trade large blocks of NASDAQ stock. Even though Instinet is generally not available to individuals, the SEC order handling rules have for the most part given individuals access to the liquidity that was previously only offered to a select group by forcing Instinet to display the majority of its orders on NASDAQ.

Island

Island, introduced in February 1996, has been the fastest-growing ECN. Represented on NASDAQ level 2 quotes as ISLD, Island is inexpensive, easy to use, and available to just about anyone. Institutions, market makers, and practically anyone from anywhere can enter orders on Island in a variety of ways. For example, customers can enter orders on Island by using Island order entry terminals, Datek Online, or Watcher. All Island bids and offers that are not immediately executed will be displayed on NASDAQ throughout the world. This allows individuals to actually establish bids and offers and, in effect, make the market in NASDAQ stocks. This was not possible until January 20, 1997. Before this date only a market maker could do this. The introduction of Island has given the individual the ability to access the markets the same way that the market makers do without incurring the cost and without having to fulfill the rigorous requirements of becoming a member of NASDAQ and/or being a market maker.

Institutions and brokerage firms can access Island through an Island terminal or can establish a direct link to Island with their own order entry system. Individuals who would like to access Island and would like the added flexibility of being able to enter SOES orders can do so through an online trading system called Watcher. Individuals who would like access to Island in a simple, efficient, inexpensive way can do so through Datek Online, an Internet system. All three of these trading systems, Island, Watcher, and Datek Online, can be easily accessed from almost anywhere. Specific information on how you can access Island can be found on the World Wide Web at: www.electronicdaytrader.com or can be obtained by calling the Broadway Consulting Group in New York City.

Island's easy access makes these systems the most liquid trading vehicles available to anyone, and liquidity is the ultimate engine that drives our markets. Their liquidity, coupled with speed, reliability, and efficiency, has made these systems ideal for those that want to electronically day-trade. More information on these systems can be found in "Watcher and Datek Online" in Chapter 7.

Other ECNs such as Bloomberg, represented as BTRD on level 2 quotes, and Teranova, represented as TNTO on level 2 quotes, have not experienced the recent growth that Island has, and are not as easily accessible as Island. Bloomberg, Teranova, and Instinet all charge additional fees to third parties who attempt to fill orders displayed on them. Island is free. This makes orders entered on Island the most likely to get executed. All ECNs are accessible to anyone with access to level 2 through NASDAQ's SelectNet System. ECNs must be accessed through preferencing.

SELECTNET

SelectNet allows traders to negotiate price through NASDAQ, as opposed to over the phone. This gives traders (order entry firms or other market makers) the ability to enter an order in between the quoted prices and to potentially fill the order. SelectNet orders are similar to orders entered on ECNs except for two very important distinctions. SelectNet orders are only broadcast to market makers, and they do not afford limit order protection to the trader entering the order. Both of these distinctions are not consistent with the SEC order handling rules and may be changed in the future. Both SelectNet orders and orders entered on ECNs are only executed at the contra parties' option. These orders are not executed automatically like an SOES order.

SelectNet orders may be displayed to all market makers or may be displayed to a specific market maker through "preferencing." Preferencing is used when a trader, who either is not eligible to use SOES or does not want to use SOES, would like to trade at the quoted price. Preferencing is a way for a trader to say, "You are offering at 50, and I am willing to pay 50." If a trader preferences a market maker, then that market maker is theoretically obligated to fill at least part of the order. If the trader does not fill the order, he or she is "backing away" and thus is in violation of NASDAQ's firm-quote policy rule. However, if the market maker can demonstrate that he or she just filled an order at that price (perhaps a SOES order), and was in the process of updating the quote, then he or she is not obligated to fill the order. Like SOES, a market maker is obligated to fill a preference order if it is at a price he or she is advertising. Unlike SOES, where an order is executed automatically, a market maker must initiate the execution of a preference order. A preference order is generally used by a trader who is willing to pay the advertised price. A SelectNet order is generally used by a trader who wants to trade at a price better than the price advertised. A SelectNet order is only filled if another party chooses to execute the order.

SelectNet and preferencing are actively used by market makers to communicate with each other. Both SelectNet and preferencing have helped market makers to avoid using the telephone. By negotiating their orders through these methods, market makers have been able to save time, cut down on errors, and avoid saying things on the phone that are confidential, which may be construed as collusion (see the two accompanying articles). Prior to the new rules that permitted ECN quotes to be displayed on NASDAQ, day traders who wanted to trade between the spread did so by entering orders into SelectNet. Now that traders can enter orders on an ECN, they can broadcast their orders to a larger audience and have the added advantage of limit order protection. Day traders can still benefit from the use of preference and are using this tool.

Nasdaq Dealers Weigh $900 Million Settlement

NEW YORK – More than two dozen Nasdaq dealers are in talks to reach a $900 million settlement with investors in a class-action lawsuit alleging that the firms rigged prices in past years on the Nasdaq Stock Market, according to people familiar with the matter.

At the same time, the Securities and Exchange Commission is preparing civil

> By Wall Street Journal staff reporters Deborah Lohse, Scot J. Paltrow and Patrick McGeehan.

charges against dozens of traders in its own investigation of alleged price manipulation in the past on Nasdaq, according to people familiar with the SEC probe.

The possible class-action settlement—which would bring the total settlements

The Penny-Stock Sting

The SEC charged 55 promoters, brokers and small-company officers in a crackdown related to the FBI sting of 14 months ago. Small Stock Focus, C9.

agreed to by Wall Street firms to $1 billion, one of the largest civil-antitrust payouts in history – arises from a highly publicized lawsuit filed in U.S. District Court in Manhattan in 1994 against 37 firms, including giants Merrill Lynch & Co.; Goldman, Sachs & Co.; Bear Stearns Cos.; and the firm then known as Smith Barney Inc., which is now the Salomon Smith Barney unit of Travelers Group Inc.

The investors alleged that market makers at the firms conspired from 1989 to 1994 to keep the trading "spreads" between the buy and sell price of 1,659 Nasdaq stocks overly wide. In a separate case, two dozen of the firms settled similar charges with the Justice Department last year, agreeing to beef up compliance and tape-record a small percentage of their trading-desk calls, though they neither admitted nor denied the allegations.

The SEC has largely completed its latest phase of its own probe, including interviews with traders, though it hasn't yet sent out "Wells notices" formally notifying that charges are likely to be filed, say lawyers familiar with the inquiry. It remained unclear whether the SEC also will file charges against securities firms for which the traders worked.

Earlier this week, brokerage firm PaineWebber Group Inc. announced it was reorganizing its over-the-counter, or Nasdaq, trading operations under new co-heads, William Heenan and Patrick Davis, with PaineWebber President Joseph Grano citing "the significant challenges faced by over-the-counter firms in the

The Nasdaq-Dealer Saga

■ **May 1994:** Study from two finance professors suggests Nasdaq dealers "tacitly collude" on prices.

■ **July 1994:** Investors file civil lawsuits against more than 30 dealers.

■ **October and November 1994:** The Justice Department and the SEC launch probes into Nasdaq dealers and their self-regulator, the National Association of Securities Dealers.

■ **July and August 1997:** 24 firms and NASD settle with regulators agreeing to beef up oversight of Nasdaq desks.

changing competitive and regulatory environment."

PaineWebber officials declined to say whether the changes were connected to the SEC's investigation. But after announcing the changes, Mr. Grano told Bloomberg News that "hundreds of [Nasdaq] traders on the Street, including ours, are under some sort of inquiry." People familiar with the inquiry say only several dozen are likely to face charges. Mr. Grano added in the same interview, "Because of the inquiries, because of the changes in economics, the old ways weren't appropriate." A firm spokesman said Mr. Grano was quoted accurately.

Meanwhile, the possible class-action settlement, which is still under negotiation but could be announced by year end, would bring the total amount settled in the suit to around $1 billion, people familiar with the matter say. Since April, six brokerage firms, including Montgomery Securities and Jefferies Group Inc., have settled individually for a total of $100 million.

Garret Rasmussen, a Washington antitrust lawyer with Patton Boggs who is unaffiliated with the case, said the settlement would be the largest for any civil antitrust class action. Many antitrust lawyers say that until now, the largest such settlement pool was paid by companies in the corrugated-box industry that settled a price-fixing lawsuit for a total of around $550 million, including interest.

Arthur Kaplan, co-lead counsel for the plaintiffs, said he wouldn't discuss the negotiations, nor would Robert Skirnick, another co-lead counsel for the plaintiffs. An attorney for the Wall Street defendants, Jay Fastow, didn't return calls. Spokespeople for Goldman Sachs, Salomon Smith

Please Turn to Page C20, Column 5

Nasdaq Dealers Seek Settlement

Continued From Page C1

Barney, Merrill Lynch and Bear Stearns each declined to comment.

It is unclear whether all 31 of the firms that haven't settled individually will join the global class-action settlement. Some people close to the issue say one or two smaller firms were considering opting out of the deal. Smaller firms might find it more debilitating to pay multimillion-dollar settlements than giant brokerages that are experiencing record profits this year.

While every firm is likely to deny wrongdoing in settling the issue, there has been pressure to get this lawsuit settled by year end, people close to the firms say.

For one thing, record profit levels, estimated at $12 billion before taxes across all Wall Street firms, make a big settlement easier to absorb this year, say some people close to the firms. Moreover, many of the firms named in the class action are involved in mergers or merger discussions and don't want the uncertainty of a jury trial hanging over their heads.

Before investors get their hands on any of this $1 billion, members of the class must be notified, possibly through mailings in their account statements or over the Internet, that they may have a claim. The court must approve the settlement after a hearing in which class members can object to the settlement if they wish. All that could take a year or more, some antitrust lawyers say.

The good news for investors is that with a settlement this large, the lawyers' fees may represent well under 10% of the total, Mr. Rasmussen estimated. How to distribute the remaining funds to investors who can prove they have claims, and how much will go to each, will be worked out over the next year or more, he estimated.

A global settlement has been under discussion since Sherwood Securities became the first firm to opt to settle the case in April, people familiar with the matter say. As five other firms settled individually, it increased the pressure on the other firms to settle together or singly, since under antitrust rules defendants who don't settle may face liabilities incurred by those who do, according to Mr. Rasmussen.

Last year, capping the first phase of its investigation, the SEC censured Nasdaq's parent, the National Association of Securities Dealers, for allegedly failing to police the market. Among the SEC's findings: that Nasdaq dealers colluded to keep spreads artificially wide, thus boosting their profit margins. The SEC also concluded that dealers failed to honor their publicly quoted prices and deliberately delayed reporting trades until after the end of the trading day.

The SEC also ordered sweeping rule changes meant to prevent manipulation of spreads and to put small investors on a more equal footing with brokerage firms and institutions in getting access to the best available prices. Firms have complained that the new rules have significantly eroded their profits from acting as dealers, or market makers, in Nasdaq stocks.

Once the rule changes were put into effect, the SEC turned to investigating specific instances of allegedly illegal acts that came to light in thousands of hours of audiotapes the agency and the Justice Department had subpoenaed from the firms. Many Nasdaq dealer firms had routinely taped traders' phone conversations to use as a reference if a trade was disputed.

Several PaineWebber traders were heard on tape discussing the manipulation of prices of stocks traded on Nasdaq, people familiar with the firm said. But PaineWebber officials declined to say whether any of six departing traders were among them.

The firm said the longtime head of its OTC desk, Richard Bruno, retired at the age of 51 but would remain a consultant. PaineWebber also said the six OTC traders were leaving the firm "to pursue other opportunities." They are Peter F. Comas, Robert D. Coppola, Gerard Kane, Joseph J. Palma, Arthur Raiola and Joseph H. Raiola.

Joseph Raiola declined to comment on the reasons for his departure from Paine-Webber. None of the others could be reached for comment.

MARKET WATCH
FLOYD NORRIS

Comeback Player Of 1997: Nasdaq

The movements of stock markets are often ephemeral, on the front page one day and forgotten the next as prices fluctuate. We remember the 1929 crash because it foretold disaster, but the 1987 one, which did not, is already fading from memory.

Thus it is that the enduring news made in the financial markets in 1997 will probably not prove to be any of the items that sent prices soaring or falling. It will not be the extraordinary gains of the year or the brief plunge brought on by Asian concerns.

Instead, it is likely to be the reforms made at the National Association of Securities Dealers, which runs the Nasdaq stock market and licenses stockbrokers. It is well on its way to being the first-class stock market that its advertisements used to say it already was. And its regulatory arm has made real progress in cleaning up the sleazy side of the brokerage business.

The N.A.S.D. should be honored as the Wall Street organization of the year.

Not all the credit for that goes to the association, of course. Change came only after the Feds cracked down in 1996 on trading practices that assured profits for market makers at the expense of investors. Credit should go to Arthur Levitt Jr., the chairman of the Securities and Exchange Commission; to Richard Lindsey, the S.E.C.'s director of market regulation, and to Anne Bingaman, who headed the antitrust division of the Justice Department.

Still, the people who took over top posts at the N.A.S.D. have done a magnificent job in turning around an organization that once appeared to be more responsive to the interests of its brokerage-firm members than it was to the interests of the investing public. Frank Zarb, the new head of the N.A.S.D.; Mary Schapiro, the boss of its regulatory arm, and Al Berkeley, the head of the Nasdaq stock market, all deserve praise.

On the regulatory front, Ms. Schapiro has moved to discipline not only the brokerage firms that routinely rip off customers, but also the brokers that used to go from one sleazy firm to another. Crooks now have good reason to fear the N.A.S.D.

But it is at the Nasdaq stock market that the most far-reaching changes are being made. Investors are much more likely to get a good price — defined as a higher price if they are selling or a lower one if they are buying — than they ever were before. It may or may not be as good a market as the New York Stock Exchange, but until this year it was impossible to make the comparison without snickering.

A Better Deal
Average change in quoted spreads between bid and asked prices on Nasdaq, Jan. 1997 to Nov. 1997.

Large stocks	-33.5%
Medium stocks	-23.7%
Small stocks	-23.1%

Those savings for investors come from the brokerage firms that make markets and that used to dominate Nasdaq. There have been forecasts of widespread withdrawals by market makers, and publicity has been given to some big firms that cut back on the number of stocks they trade. But the statistics show that there are more market makers, not fewer, than before the reforms.

That may change. There probably were more market makers than were needed in many stocks, and some will find it hard to compete in the new environment. Also, the jury is still out as to how much liquidity will be available in a prolonged bear market.

The Nasdaq market grew out of the old over-the-counter market, a dicey place in which customers were often treated badly. And it was slow to change even as classy companies were listed.

One can argue that improvements should have been made years ago. But the important thing is that the market is better. Frank Zarb and his colleagues deserve investors' thanks.

NASDAQ SelectNet is actively used by all traders to preference ECNs. If a trader or a market maker or anyone else chooses to trade with an ECN, he or she must do so by preferencing the ECN. The exception to this rule is if the order entry system has a direct link to the ECN. For example, online trading systems such as Watcher and Datek Online offer a direct link to Island. This allows customers of Watcher and Datek Online to access Island without using NASDAQ's SelectNet system, saving these customers both time and money. SelectNet is available to anyone with access to level 2.

NASDAQ'S SMALL ORDER EXECUTION SYSTEM (SOES)

What is SOES trading? NASDAQ's Small Order Entry System, commonly referred to as SOES, has become the primary vehicle for day traders that like to trade 1,000 shares of a NASDAQ stock at a time. SOES is an execution vehicle that is designed for the small, individual investor and that allows direct access to the NASDAQ national market and its constituency of market makers. The system was fully implemented after the 1987 crash in an attempt to provide liquidity for the public customer, and has become a popular method of day trading since its inception. SOES simply allows the individual to electronically trade NASDAQ stocks with institutions that are currently advertising to buy or sell these securities at specified prices. Traders that use SOES are restricted by the following rules:

1. SOES trades are executed in lots up to but not in excess of 1,000 shares. For stocks that trade with low volume a SOES trader may be limited to as little as 200 shares per SOES execution.

2. A 5-minute time restriction is placed on all orders executed by the customer on each side of the market in the same security. For example, a day trader who buys 1,000 shares of Intel using SOES must wait 5 minutes before he is allowed via the SOES system to purchase Intel again. This time restriction does not prohibit the trader from buying additional stock through NASDAQ's SelectNet system or from an ECN.

3. Registered representatives and NASD broker-dealers cannot trade SOES for their own accounts.

4. Selling short on SOES must be done on a plus-tick bid, in compliance with all applicable short sales rules.

5. SOES trading is a mandatory execution system. This means that a market maker who is advertising to buy or sell a stock must trade at least the amount he or she is advertising.

6. Small-capitalization stocks are the exception to rules 4 and 5. There is no plus-tick rule for short sales. Furthermore, SOES is not mandatory for these stocks. Small capitalization stocks are noted by the letter *s* on the NASDAQ system.

NASDAQ's Small Order Execution System gives the small investor, or day trader, electronic access to the markets it displays.

Why Is SOES Controversial? Shouldn't All Markets Have to Honor Their Quote Prices?

Market-maker participation in SOES became mandatory for all NASDAQ stocks in 1988, as a regulatory response to the widespread inability of retail customers to access market-maker quotes during the October 1987 market crash. Before that time, brokers had to call market makers on the phone to execute their customer orders. During the market break in October 1987, market makers were very difficult, or in some cases impossible, to reach, leaving many customer marketable orders unexecuted. The SOES policy was implemented to assure customers access to the posted markets and to bolster investor confidence in the NASDAQ market. Market makers are given numerous privileges and, in turn, are responsible for providing depth, liquidity, and continuity in the market. However, market makers have generally viewed this policy as adopted at their expense and have opposed SOES since it was first introduced.

This became more apparent after the Justice Department began to openly criticize the NASDAQ market and its members' policy. The Justice Department did a study that concluded that NASDAQ market makers colluded to keep spreads artificially wide, at the expense of the customer. As a result of this study, in 1996 the Justice Department began to bring antitrust actions against many of the NASD market makers. To combat the negative press on how the NASD market makers engaged in price fixing and how it cost individual investors money, the NASD and its constituents counterattacked. They claimed that their markets were friendly to the small investor and that the NASDAQ Small Order Execution System gave the customers fair and, in some cases, more than fair access to their markets.

They claimed that the NASDAQ market makers were burdened with a flood of customer SOES orders that forced them to trade at their advertised limits. As a result of this, NASDAQ provided more than adequate liquidity for its customers, and NASDAQ market makers were entitled to make the spread on these transactions. Not only were they doing their job, but they were being taken advantage of by a group of traders they labeled "SOES bandits." SOES bandits are the group that the NASD and market makers claimed abused the system by taking advantage of stale or outdated quotes that SOES forced them to honor.

The newspapers, which depend on the large investment houses for a constant flow of stories, have generally bought into the negative picture that market makers have painted of the day traders sitting at terminals waiting for their markets to be out of line and then using the SOES system to execute trades at these inaccurate prices. In reality, nothing could be farther from the truth. SOES traders put capital at risk and rely on current accurate prices for their executions. In fact, NASDAQ has a rule that prevents SOES traders from taking advantage of incorrect pricing or bad quotes. This rule, and a poorly defined one at that, allows "clearly erroneous" trades to be broken. NASDAQ generally breaks all trades that take place outside of the current market on the basis that they are "clearly erroneous." Also, a trade can be broken at any time after the trade, even weeks later. There are no numerical definitions for "clearly erroneous," nor are there any time limits.

For many years NASD and its dealers attempted to curtail SOES trading. They made rules that said that SOES traders who did more than two trades a day, or more than 500 shares in a trade, were professional traders and therefore were not eligible to use the SOES system. In some cases, the NASD prevented new firms from gaining access to SOES. Many of these attempts to curtail SOES trading were eventually eliminated, although some are still in effect and were outlined previously. Recent attempts decrease the exposure that market makers have from 1,000 shares to only 100 shares.

Why is all this effort being expended to curtail SOES trading, which came about as a result of market makers improperly handling customer orders in the first place? Market makers are expending a lot of effort to block day traders because day traders have been able to exploit a small portion of the short-term trading profits that previously only the market makers were able to exploit.

NASDAQ market makers are required to do no less or no more than market makers on other exchanges or markets. And SOES traders are doing nothing more than anyone else who invests, trades, or speculates. They are buying in anticipation of price appreciation and selling in anticipation of price depreciation. **Automatic execution forces NASDAQ market makers to trade at their advertised price. This is a basic premise of any market.**

CHAPTER 3

The Markets, the Specialist, and the Market Makers

THE MARKETS

The primary purpose of this section is to discuss the fundamental differences between the listed securities markets (NYSE and ASE) and the over-the-counter (OTC) market. By exploring the rudimentary elements of these two types of market, the day trader should gain valuable insight into the inherent nature of stocks and their subsequent behavioral patterns. Thus, understanding the differences between the way the listed-securities markets and the OTC markets conduct transactions is a critical function in the day traders' comprehension of movement and mannerisms of NASDAQ and listed stocks.

As a general premise, listed securities (or those traded on the New York Stock Exchange) are large-capitalization companies that have a historical record of earnings and financial accountability. These securities are generally household names, such as General Electric, Ford, Alcoa, Aetna, etc. These companies are usually representative of the more stable or solid issues traded in the American financial arena. Further, listed securities are also a prominent bellwether of the American economy. The Dow Jones Industrial Average, the most widely known and followed indicator of market valuation, is composed of 30 NYSE listed issues. Stocks traded on the American Stock Exchange are also considered listed securities, although their market capitalizations are generally significantly lower than those traded on the NYSE.

On the other hand, stocks traded on the NASDAQ national market are usually companies that exhibit more volatile earnings growth and thus have more sporadic patterns of financial histories and accountability. It should be of no surprise that a great deal of technology stocks fit into this category. Most were started less than 30 years ago and have financial histories that have proved explosive and sometimes erratic.

Also traded on the NASDAQ are biotechnical, communication, Internet, and a myriad of other issues that have, or have yet to, become the great companies of America's future. A few household-name issues now traded on NASDAQ are Microsoft, Intel, Netscape, Cisco, and Amgen. These corporations all experienced explosive earnings growth as sales of their products or services expanded with the world's insatiable appetite for new technologies. Subsequently, many up-and-coming companies involved in these sectors remain listed on the NASDAQ exchange because it is associated with such phenomenal success stories as the aforementioned enterprises. Thus, issues on NASDAQ can certainly represent large-capitalization companies as well as other smaller issues that might trade at significantly higher-earnings multiple as investors speculate on future growth rates.

The New York Stock Exchange

The most fundamental difference between the listed-securities and NASDAQ markets is the manner in which each provides liquidity to the public. The NYSE is an auction market. It is a place where a specialist maintains and oversees all transactions in his specific security. If you want to buy a stock on the NYSE, your broker can either enter your order onto a DOT system or give the order to a floor broker. A floor broker will literally walk into a crowd where the stock is traded on the floor and ask for a market. It is then the specialist's responsibility to consolidate all the various interests in the crowd, and on the electronic DOT system, and then announce the current best price at which the security can be bought or sold. The specialist must also announce the "size" of the market that lets the broker determine how much stock (by number of shares) is currently offered for sale at the best price and how much stock is wanted to buy. It is important to remember that in this market the specialist will represent only the current bids and offers that have been presented to him or her by the interested parties in the crowd.

For example, a broker from Salomon Smith Barney might be bidding for 10,000 shares of GE. This bid, along with all others at the same price, will be represented in the specialist's market. However, a Smith Barney broker who has 1 million shares of GE to buy will not announce his intentions since others in the stock might "run it up," forcing the broker from Smith Barney to pay higher prices. After the specialist has announced the price and size of the current market, the broker may then announce his intention to buy stock by either bidding at the best price with other buyers in the stock, establishing a new improved bid, or paying the asking price. In a great deal of situations, the buyer will attempt to buy the stock "in the middle," thus getting a better price for the customer.

For example, the current market given by the specialist in GE is $62^1/_8 \times 62^3/_8$, size $5,000 \times 10,000$. This means that there is a buyer, or buyers, of 5,000 shares who is willing to pay $62^1/_8$, and 10,000 shares are for sale at $62^3/_8$. The broker, at his or her discretion, or at the discretion of the customer, depending on the type of order, will bid $62^1/_4$ for the stock. Obviously, the intention is to purchase the stock at a lower price than the asking price. The hope is that the seller will come down in price. This strategy sometimes results in the buyer getting a better price, but the broker also runs the risk that others will buy the stock for sale at $62^3/_8$ and the broker will be forced to pay an even higher price. Further, when the buyer announces his or her intention to pay higher than the current bid in the stock, the specialist then changes the market to reflect the new buyer in the stock. The price of the new market will now read $62^1/_4 \times 62^3/_8$.

When there are no current bids or offers in the market, the specialist is required to provide liquidity for public customers. Thus, in stocks where there is not a great deal of volume, or there is a lack of current buyers or sellers in the crowd, the specialist must provide the public customer a fair market. For example, the current market in Pep Boys (PBY) is $43^1/_2 \times 43^7/_8$, size $2,000 \times 500$. If a broker, representing a public customer, enters the crowd and wants to buy 1,000 shares at the current offered price but there are only 500 shares for sale, the specialist is expected to sell the additional 500 shares out of his or her own account.

Thus, the specialist is, essentially, a natural buyer of stock on the way down and a natural seller on the way up. This privilege is afforded to the specialist because he or she is also willing to take the inherent risks associated with providing liquidity in the market during large moves in stocks; i.e., he or she will buy great amounts of stock during sell-offs and likewise become short in uptrends. A New York Stock Exchange specialist is also required to maintain a fair market. A fair market, in turn, protects the interests of the public customer as well as all other parties currently expressing interest in the specialist's stock.

The Specialist

A specialist is awarded the privilege of making a market on a stock in an exchange for assuring that he or she will be a buyer or seller of last resort. The specialist is responsible for assuring continuity and liquidity in the market. This means that markets should generally appear to be orderly. If a stock typically trades in eighth-wide increments and the stock moves $1, then some stock should trade at every eighth of that move. Specialists are judged by how well they perform this job. Specialists who receive good ratings are rewarded with additional listings. These listings can be extremely valuable, especially when major companies such as America Online and Gateway decide to move from NASDAQ to the NYSE, or stocks like AT&T decide to spin off pieces such as Lucent.

On stock exchanges there is only one specialist per stock. A stock exchange holds its specialist accountable to assure that the market in his or her stocks is fair and orderly. As just noted, if a specialist does a good job, then he or she is rewarded with new valuable listings. If a specialist does a poor job, he or she is reprimanded by the exchange board. An exchange may not give new listings to a specialist who is not fulfilling his or her responsibilities. An exchange may fine a specialist who is not providing liquidity. And an exchange may actually take stocks away from a specialist who is abusing his or her privilege. The specialist system works so well because it is easy to measure a market maker's performance when that market maker is the only one. As a result of this system, specialists generally do a great job of making markets. And as a result of their monopoly, specialists have certain advantages that market makers on the NASDAQ do not. In particular, since all orders in a stock must go through a single specialist, that specialist has the distinct advantage of knowing all the orders in a stock. This helps the specialist determine at what price there are buyers and at what price there are sellers.

The NASDAQ

The NASDAQ national market relies on individual market makers rather than a single specialist to provide liquidity in over-the-counter securities.

These market makers combine their efforts in each stock to collectively provide a market. All those participating are required to be both buyers and sellers. This is referred to as "honoring a two-sided market." Essentially, if a market maker is willing to sell a stock at one price, there must be a reasonable price at which he is willing to buy it back.

The constituency that forms this community of traders in each stock is made up of institutional market makers, such as Merrill Lynch (MLCO), Smith Barney (SBSH), and Goldman Sachs (GSCO). At each of these firms, traders are given the responsibility of making markets in a "list" of NASDAQ securities. These lists typically consist of 20 to 30 stocks that customarily contain several very active issues as well as several low-volume securities. Thus, for a popular stock such as Intel, of which millions of shares are traded every day, there will be many firms who will seek to represent themselves. However, for a stock such as DNA Plant Technologies, of which only a few thousand shares are traded daily, there will be fewer market makers. Therefore, in heavily traded stocks, no one market maker can dominate the marketplace. However, in smaller, less liquid securities, one or two dominant players usually can control the market.

Operationally, trading in listed securities is substantially different from trading in over-the-counter securities. Rather than there being an auction market, where traders verbally announce their intentions, market makers place their names on a list of buyers and sellers. This list is electronically posted by NASDAQ. The number of market makers participating in these listings may vary anywhere from 3 to as many as 30 or greater, depending on the volume in the stock. A market maker will be listed on either the buy or sell side, depending on customer orders, feelings regarding future movement of the stock, or the responsibility to provide a two-sided market. Trades are initiated either over the phone by market makers or on one of several online execution systems sanctioned by NASDAQ. A market maker who is advertising has an obligation to be either a buyer or a seller of 1,000 shares in a particular stock. After fulfilling his or her obligation, he may then leave the market and reinstate a new bid or offer in an attempt to make a profit.

For example, suppose Goldman Sachs is currently willing to sell stock in Altera Corp. (ALTR). The market is $48^3/_4 \times 49^1/_8$. If GSCO sells 1,000 shares at $49^1/_8$ where the market maker is listed on the offer, he may leave the list of other market makers attempting to sell stock there and instead bid for the stock. This bid may be lower than the current market, i.e., $48^5/_8$, or GSCO may create a new market by bidding $48\frac{7}{8}$. Usually, if a market maker is ful-filling the duty of providing a two-sided market and not acting as agent for a customer, that market maker will place his name on the current list of buy-ers. If the market maker is successful at repurchasing the stock at this price, he has "made the spread," and netted a profit of $\frac{3}{8}$, or $375 on 1,000 shares.

Institutions trading in these securities are involved for two primary reasons. The first reason is to provide their customers with access to the NASDAQ market and subsequently to execute transactions for which they receive a commission. When acting in this capacity, the market maker is essentially acting as an agent through which orders are execut-ed. Generally, the market maker will attempt to execute a customer's order at the best possible price. The market maker can do this by adver-tising his or her intentions to other market makers or by simply purchas-ing stock that is currently for sale in the marketplace. The second reason institutions trade is to actually own or be short the stock, in a proprietary fashion. Ownership may yield substantially more profit. When acting in this respect, the market maker is usually attempting to purchase stock on the bid side of the market and sell it on the offer. By taking advantage of the inherent spread in these securities, the trader hopes to reap numerous small profits without a great deal of risk. On some occasions, the market maker will establish a long or short position, which varies with the risk parameters of his firm, in an attempt to speculate on future price move-ments. In either event, the market maker's primary function is to provide a liquid market in which the public can trade. As is the case with the spe-cialist in listed securities, the market maker essentially ends up selling stocks on the way up and buying them on the way down.

For the online day trader, it is extremely important to realize the inherent differences between listed securities and NASDAQ. Whereas the intentions of traders in listed securities are usually masked and not easily obtainable, market makers on NASDAQ are constantly adding their names to markets as buyers or sellers of stocks. **Profits will come easily to the day trader who can determine whether these specific market makers are simply fulfilling their responsibility to provide a two-sided market or are actual buyers or sellers of stock.**

The Role of a Market Maker

Firm traders on NASDAQ have several responsibilities that are relevant to price fluctuations in the over-the-counter market.

Market makers are supposed to:

1. Attempt to execute orders for their firms' customers.
2. Trade for their "own" accounts.
3. Make a two-sided market.
4. Make money!

The primary purpose for a NASDAQ market maker is to execute orders for his firm's customers at the best possible price. There are several ways to do this.

A trader can advertise the intention to buy stock in ABCD by placing his or her name on a current list of other marker makers who are also "bidding" for stock at a specified price. You will see these names listed in the NASDAQ level two quote windows. Current buyers, at the specified price, are listed in the left-hand column and current sellers on the right. By placing his name on this list, the market maker is showing the rest of the marketplace his "intentions." Other market makers or traders can call him (yes, on the phone) and tell the market maker that they would like to sell him stock, and a transaction would occur at that price. The market maker can also call other market makers who are advertising to sell stock and trade with them. (*Note:* At this time, market makers are still allowed to call each other on the phone in order to consummate trades. However, because of the SEC's investigation that concluded that market makers colluded to keep spreads artificially wide, their phone calls are now monitored. This has resulted in most market makers accessing each other electronically via SelectNet in order to avoid any phone discussions regarding customer bids and offers which might be interpreted as collusion.) A marker maker who is advertising to buy or sell stock is expected to trade at least the number of shares he is quoting at the advertised price. The seller of stock is responsible for reporting the transaction so that it is listed with all other sales on the "tape." Failure to trade at the advertised price is known as "backing away," and the market maker can be fined as well as lose status among fellow market makers, who will ostracize the offender.

Furthermore, by placing himself on this NASDAQ level 2 list, the market maker becomes eligible for executions on NASDAQ's SOES system. Here, the order can be filled electronically, 1,000 shares at a time, by day traders who have access to NASDAQ level 2. Once the market maker has executed an order on SOES, the market maker has two options:

1. The market maker can refresh the bid/ask and essentially restate his intentions to buy/sell the stock and become eligible for SOES again.
2. The market maker can adjust the quote.

The other means to fill orders is SelectNet, which is also available to anyone with access to NASDAQ level 2 or through an ECN accessible through some order entry terminals. These systems are "nonmandatory," meaning that the orders will only be filled if a contra party chooses to trade at the advertised price. ECNs are useful when trading stock "in the middle," between the current bid/ask, or on the bid or the ask advertised by market makers. Unlike SelectNet, ECNs, if represented on level 2, provide limit order protection.

Thus, four primary vehicles are available to the market maker for executing customer orders:

1. The phone (known as ACT trades)
2. SOES (a mandatory execution system that can be used on behalf of customers)
3. SelectNet (a system that allows market makers to trade with other market makers)
4. ECNs (third-party execution systems that anonymously display limit orders)

The second primary purpose of a market maker is to trade for his "own" account. Each major firm usually has an extensive list of NASDAQ stocks in which it is willing to make a market. Each trader is given a "list" of roughly 30 stocks for which the trader and a clerk are responsible. In addition to filling orders for customers, these traders are also trying to generate proprietary revenue by trading the stocks on their respective lists. When examining price fluctuations on a NASDAQ level 2 quote, you will frequently notice that once a market maker has either bought or sold stock in the marketplace, he will frequently flip to the other side of the market. As an example, take Netscape (NSCP) and the "window" displaying the market makers and their respective quotes. There may be an up arrow near NSCP showing it is trading on an uptick. The quote window will show that the inside market is 52×53, for example, and that there is one market maker on the bid (WEED) willing to pay 52 for stock. Six market makers (AGIS, JPMS, OLDE,VOLP, PWJC, TSCO) are willing to sell at the ask price of 53. Assume AGIS has sold 1,000 shares to a SOES trader, and he moves to the bid. Now you will see AGIS and WEED bidding 52, where AGIS will attempt to buy back the stock. If AGIS succeeds, he will have made a point on the spread. These movements represent an attempt by a trader to take advantage of the inherent spread of each stock (see Figure 3-1).

For another example, assume the market in stock ABCD is $49^3/_4 \times 50^1/_4$. After purchasing stock on the bid at $49^3/_4$ either from another market maker or on the SOES system, the trader will immediately offer to sell stock at 50 or $50^1/_4$ in order to make a profit. This simple buy-low, sell-high strategy is an integral part of a market maker's repertoire of profit generators.

Depending on market conditions, market makers will also take positions in certain stocks where they are speculating on future price movements. Each firm has certain risk parameters that limit the exposure a market maker can take, but most major houses have experienced traders who are used to taking risks and can subsequently "move" stocks as they speculate.

The most important aspect to remember regarding market makers trading for their own accounts is that they are active in stocks for one reason—**profits!**

FIGURE 3-1

The quote area shows an active quote window for a stock symbol NSCP (Netscape). The up arrow indicates that NSCP is trading on an uptick. The quote area shows that the inside market is 52×53 and that there is one market maker on the bid (WEED) willing to pay 52 for stock. Six market makers (AGIS, JPMS, OLDE, VOLP, PWJC, TSCO) are willing to sell at 53, the ask. This stock is an SM10 stock, which means the customer could, at most, buy or sell 1,000 shares per order on SOES. NSCP is down 2, from yesterday's close.

Level 2: Quote Window

NSCP	↑	52×53	(136)
L 49	H	53−2	SM10
WEED	52	AGIS	53
MSCO	51	JPMS	53
SHWD	51	OLDE	53
DMGL	51	VOLP	53
MONT	51	PWJC	53
SBSH	51	TSCO	53
LEHM	51	GSCO	54

The third responsibility of a market maker, and hence the origin of the name, is to literally make a two-sided market. If a market maker is advertising to sell stock a certain price, then he must also be willing to buy that stock at a lower price. Usually, this price is lower than the current bid, but it must be within a reasonable discount to the stock's current price. There is no lawful requirement that determines the distance between bid/ask prices, but the system has become somewhat self-policing within the fraternity of traders.

For example, if the market maker has just sold stock ABCD at $49^1/_8$ and the spread in ABCD is usually a $^1/_4$ wide—or $48^7/_8 \times 49^1/_8$— typically the market maker will advertise to buy the stock at a lower price—$48^5/_8$. Houses that back away, that do not adhere to the customary spread differentials inherent in each specific stock, are often ostracized by the other market makers and even reported to the authorities at NASDAQ for reprimand. Backing away is heavily discouraged. Offenders are subject to punishment by disciplinary action or fine. Thus, the primary purpose of a market maker, according to the letter of the law, is to provide liquidity in the marketplace. To do this, each market maker **must** provide a two-sided market within a reasonable distance from the current bid/ask, where he is responsible for trading stock.

Market makers, regardless of laws or responsibilities, are really involved in their respective stocks for two reasons.

1. To make their customers happy, to retain their business, and to generate commission dollars (for which they receive a percentage)
2. To make money trading in a proprietary capacity for their firm so that they can get a big fat bonus

Trading with these market makers is somewhat analogous to playing poker. There are a great number of bluffs, fake-outs, antes, etc., that occur every day in every single stock. Sometimes, it is easy to read the other guy's face and take his money. Sometimes you can read him wrong and get burned. The point is, there is no easy money in the market. Market makers need to take money out of the market in order to keep their jobs and get paid. They are not stupid and will steamroll you in their quest for profits. As a trader once said "The only reason there is money in the markets is that other traders put it there....**The money you want to make belongs to other people who have no intention of giving it to you.**"

ADVANTAGES OF TRADING ON THE NYSE

The New York Stock Exchange was built on the main principle of assuring that orders are handled in a fair and efficient fashion. This is an integral part of its culture. The American Stock Exchange follows similar principles. On both of these exchanges, the specialist is responsible for ensuring that customer orders are handled in the proper manner in accordance with strict applicable rules and regulations on the exchange. The specialist is monitored by the exchange and its members, who scrutinize and rate the specialist based on his performance in providing liquidity in the market as well as how he executes trades on behalf of the exchange's customers. A specialist who does a poor job of making a market is a poor reflection on the entire exchange, and the members make it a point to police each other.

For listed securities, all orders must go through the one and only specialist in that particular security. There are two ways an order can be delivered to a specialist. The primary, and most conventional, method is delivery by a broker. Sixty percent of the volume on the New York Stock Exchange is handled by brokers. The secondary way is through the DOT system. Eighty percent of all orders on the New York Stock Exchange are sent to the specialist through DOT.

As you may have deduced from the above paragraph, brokers usually handle the larger orders on the New York Stock Exchange. Brokers tend to handle orders that require a little extra attention to fill (see "NYSE Prints, Crossing, and Techniques" in Chapter 5). The firm with the orders calls its brokers on the floor of the exchange and tells them which stock to buy or sell, along with the quantity, price, and any other special instructions that may accompany the order. The broker then physically walks (or sometimes runs, if he is willing to break the rules) the order to the location on the floor where the stock is traded. The broker asks for a market in the stock, price, and size, and the specialist provides a market. For example, a conversation between a broker and the General Motors specialist may sound like this:

Broker: "How's Motors?"

Translation: The broker wants a market and size in GM.

Specialist: "A quarter, a half, fifty!"

Translation: "You can sell 50,000 at $61^1/_4$, or you can buy 50,000 at $61^1/_2$.

Broker: "I can pay a half for a hundred."

Translation: *"The broker can pay $61\frac{1}{2}$ for a 100,000."*

Specialist: "Who are you?"

Translation: *"What firm do you represent?" The specialist wonders if there will be more to buy behind it.*

Broker: "Solly."

Translation: *"Salomon Brothers."*

Specialist: "You bought 50 at a half, 20 to the book, 10 me, 20 to the crowd, the balance at three quarts immediate."

Translation: *"You bought 50,000 at $61\frac{1}{2}$, 20,000 from customers on the book, 10,000 from me, and 20,000 from brokers in the crowd, and you can fill the rest of your order at three-quarters if you're quick."*

The broker calls the customer: "You bought 50,000 at a half, the balance at three-quarters immediate."

Solomon: "Buy 'em!"

Broker: "I'll take 'em."

Specialist: "You bought 20 from the book, 10 me, 20 out."

Translation: *Specialist fills all orders, including those with a $\frac{5}{8}$ low at $61\frac{3}{4}$.*

The broker calls his or her firm back and reports that the order has been executed. If the order has parameters that do not allow it to be executed at that particular time because of the current market price and size, the broker may leave the order on the specialist's book and call the firm to let it know at what price its order can be filled. The order may be time-stamped and placed in the book where the specialist will ensure that, pending market conditions, the order is executed in a fair manner according to the time it was received and any other stipulations outlined by the customer.

The broker may choose to stay in the crowd and personally represent the order. As long as the specialist is aware of the broker's stated intentions and will honor those intentions, the specialist will allow the broker to participate in any transactions that take place at the price the broker indicated he is willing to buy or sell at. This is called "matching" and may give the broker an opportunity to get an execution faster than if the broker "dropped the order on the book." A broker "working" a customer order may not fill the order out of his own inventory. This would be called "dual trading"; and although not allowed here, it is permitted in many of the commodity markets. A similar practice is followed on NASDAQ, where market makers frequently fill their own customers' orders. A broker who is bidding "in the crowd" (representing a customer's order) will be privy to the order flow. The broker will be able to hear other brokers state their intentions and witness the specialist as he restates the market to reflect both new interest from brokers and new orders through the DOT. The broker can reflect this interest to his customer and frequently aid the customer in deciding at what price to pay or at what price to sell. Since the broker is not able to fill the order from his own inventory, it is in that broker's best interest to get the best possible price for the customer. A job well done will surely lead to more orders and, thus, more commissions the broker can bill. A firm may even be willing to pay a higher rate for a broker who is willing to work its orders. The broker has a fiscal interest of getting the customer the best possible price.

The New York Stock Exchange is a relatively small community, and most brokers have good relationships with at least some of the specialists. Brokers who openly state their intentions are generally rewarded with accurate information and good executions from specialists. **Specialists can state whatever they want as a market, as long as they honor it. The posted market may be representative of the true market in the stock, or it may be representative of that which the specialist wants the public to perceive.** With this in mind, take another look at the same situation, only this time Solomon Brothers has asked the broker to find out where he can buy 100,000 shares of General Motors, but has not yet given the broker an order:

Broker: "How's Motors?"

Translation: Again, the broker wants a market and size in GM.

Specialist: "A quarter, a half, ten up!"

Translation: "The market is $61^{1}/_{4} \times 61^{1}/_{2}$. You can buy or sell 10,000."

Broker: "Where can I buy a hundred?"

Translation: "Where can I buy 100,000 shares?"

Specialist: "At a half immediate."

Translation: "You can buy one hundred thousand shares at $61^{1}/_{2}$."

The specialist turns to his clerk and says: "Show the offer!"

Translation: The special is requesting that his clerk displays his offer to the public.

Before we go forward, let's take a closer look at what is happening. This time the specialist quoted only a 10,000-share market. The broker indicated he was a buyer, and the specialist showed him a fill on his current offer. He then instructed his clerk to post the new market: $61\frac{1}{4} \times 61\frac{1}{2}$ $10,000 \times 100,000$. Why did he do this?

The specialist, knowing that there is a buyer, is attempting to bring in sellers. Speculators and day traders seeing size offered may be tempted to lower their offers, and some are likely to be scared into hitting the specialist's $61\frac{1}{4}$ bid. As the broker tries to get the order, the specialist manages to pick up 20,000 from weak hands whom he is "shaking out." The specialist buys all stock coming in; quarter sellers get filled at $61\frac{5}{16}$ while $\frac{3}{8}$ sellers get filled too. The specialist is attempting to accumulate stock to fill a potential buyer. He made a great offer and is willing to run the risk that the broker can get the order. If the broker comes back with an order, the specialist will pick up eighths and quarters on the stock he bought, but will still have to sell size to fill the order. If the broker does not come back, the specialist is left holding the bag. Another broker in the crowd, who is offering 5,000 at a half, sees the scenario developing. His customer calls to tell him to hit the quarter bid, but the broker tells the customer to stay at a half for now and eventually earns his pay.

Brokers cost a little more, but have a strong incentive to get a "good fill" for the customers. Inexpensive DOT executions have forced the brokers to generally concentrate on servicing only "size" orders for customers who provide them with a lot of business. Small orders are generally better serviced by the DOT.

The DOT is cheap and fast and can handle orders up to 99,000 shares per order. DOT can deliver an order from a broker's fingers to the specialist in an instant. While the specialist generally does a great job filling these orders, the order is not represented by a broker who will protect your order. Your order is only protected by the integrity of the specialist and the New York Stock Exchange. Specialists generally fill an order in seconds, but they are allotted a 2-minute window to do it or to place it on their book to be represented in their quote. This 2-minute window generally comes into play during hectic market periods. Traders frequently complain about this, as they believe they have not gotten a fair execution. During chaotic periods it may be difficult for a specialist to always post an up-to-date market. Brokers sometimes do better during these periods, but they are generally expected to fill an order in 3 minutes. Overall, the DOT is a quick and easy way to get executions.

Another advantage to trading listed securities versus OTC stocks is that in a centralized market, where all orders must go through one market maker—the specialist—the specialist frequently pairs customer orders; i.e., it is common for customers to trade with other customers. In NASDAQ securities, the market maker more frequently can take advantage of the customer by constantly being on the other side of the order and making the spread whenever possible. The new order handling rules and the inclusion of ECNs in the NASDAQ marketplace have enabled customers to access each other without having to direct their orders through a market maker. New rules have drastically reduced the market maker's advantage, but it is still much more likely for a specialist to fill an order that he would prefer not to fill than a market maker filling such an order.

On the New York Stock Exchange, when a buyer and seller wish to trade stock at the same price, the specialist will simply pair off the orders and will receive a small fee from the executing firms for performing this service. Orders on the NYSE are executed in this fashion approximately 70 percent of the time. Thus, buyers and sellers are truly trading with each other, rather than allowing someone else to directly profit from their order flow. The remaining 30 percent of the time, the NYSE specialist will take the other side of customer orders to provide liquidity in the absence of orders on the book. As listed securities tend to be less volatile than OTC issues, the specialist will usually fill these orders at the current quote.

Far fewer restrictions exist for trading listed securities than for trading on NASDAQ. Most importantly, there are no rules governing how long you must wait before executing a trade. This is obviously a significant advantage to day traders as they are not limited when entering and exiting positions. When a trader enters to "sell market" on the NYSE, the specialist is responsible to provide liquidity and fill the order. By contrast, if the trader has made a sale on SOES in a NASDAQ security, that trader must wait 5 minutes before using SOES again. For example, if the trader is long 3,000 shares of INTC and wants to sell, he or she is only allowed to sell 1,000 shares every 5 minutes using SOES. Although it is highly unlikely, it may take 10 minutes before traders can sell out their position.

NYSE stocks as a whole represent larger and more stable companies than NASDAQ. As a result there is less chance for a surprise announcement than there is in non-NYSE stocks. Generally speaking, there is one major exchange (regional exchanges account for about 15 percent of volume). In turn, there is only one true market maker in listed stocks, and all orders must go through this market maker; this market maker has the privilege of seeing all the order flow. Order flow gives the specialist an inside look at the supply and demand in a stock. It is a tremendous aid to the specialist in formulating trading strategy.

In summary, the advantages of trading listed versus OTC stocks are many. There are fewer restrictions, tighter spreads, and greater liquidity for the large majority of the stocks. In addition, there is one specialist who is likely to match your order with another customer order and takes responsibility for executing your order fairly. An added protection for customers is that floor brokers cannot trade in those stocks for which they handle customer orders. The NYSE also tends to be less volatile than NASDAQ since stocks on the NYSE represent companies tending to be larger and more stable. Specialist are better informed of the true interest in their product since all orders go through them. As a result, they're more confident in the markets they make and ultimately more likely to provide liquidity than their less informed counterparts on NASDAQ. Since there is only one specialist per stock, the liquidity that the specialists are ultimately solely responsible for is in their stock. Specialists fill many orders, and specialists ultimately prosper handsomely. Well-informed traders generally make good traders, and specialists tend to have a good rapport with many brokers who rely on them for an accurate market picture. The New York Stock Exchange is a highly liquid market and less volatile than the NASDAQ.

ADVANTAGES OF TRADING ON THE NASDAQ

Orders in NASDAQ stocks are handled by numerous market makers who are neither expected nor required to provide as much liquidity as the specialist. Market makers are usually privy only to the orders of their customers. The market-maker system is generally a bit chaotic because no one really knows the complete picture. Day traders can now have simultaneous access to all the same information that market makers have, with the exception of the market maker's internal order flow, and perhaps the block orders (over $250,000 or 10,000 shares). Instinet has found ways to conceal these block orders from the general market. While the market makers have a fiduciary responsibility to their customers, they will, whenever possible, profit from their customers' orders. Customer orders can be neglected. On the other hand, multiple market makers on NASDAQ control prices and vie for business. No one market maker is entitled to all the order flow, and those who provide the most liquidity tend to attract the most orders. This phenomenon allows day traders greater opportunity, as they may capitalize on the agendas of multiple market players in a stock rather than compete in an arena where the dealer holds all the cards, as on the NYSE. Thus, while the specialist on the NYSE determines how stocks will trade and also determines the depth and liquidity of the market in the absence of orders, multiple market makers with different agendas regarding order flow and liquidity essentially define the parameters of OTC markets. The added chaos created by multiple market makers also adds volatility to the market, something that is not usually prevalent in listed securities. Subsequently, this volatility adds to the profit opportunities for the agile day trader, as well as adds additional risk.

There is a good deal of difference between the way an order is executed on the NYSE and the way it is executed on the NASDAQ. For example, assume there is a large buy order in a listed security. In this case, the specialist will allow the sell orders on his book to provide the initial liquidity and then sell the balance of the order out of his personal inventory. The specialist will trade the tail end of the order at a price at which he feels that he will be able to make a profit. He will push the stock up to a price that he chooses, sell the stock, and attempt to repurchase it at a lower price. He may be able to achieve this by trading the stock and then adjusting his market downward by lowering the ask price of the stock. The momentum buying that was created when the stock was going up has essentially been stopped by the specialist, and as a result selling pressure, or profit taking, may ensue. All the buyers who were attempting to "piggyback" the original buy order must now decide if they wish to remain in the stock. The specialist may bid for a small amount of stock, let it trade, and again adjust his market downward by lowering the ask price and bid price at the same time. Now the previous momentum buyers are starting to get nervous and send their sell orders to the specialist. The specialist, once again, only buys a small amount of stock and readjusts his market even lower. Now, all the previous buyers want to get out, and a large wave of sell orders is being sent to the specialist. He lowers his price once again, and then suddenly buys all the stock that is for sale in the marketplace, thereby netting a tidy profit.

This entire scenario might entail the stock moving $\frac{1}{2}$ to $\frac{3}{4}$ of a point from its genesis until the specialist's final purchase. Thus, in the absence of liquidity in the listed marketplace the specialist decides where and when he will provide markets, and the day trader is essentially at his mercy.

Now, look at how the same order may work on NASDAQ. A buy order in a NASDAQ stock will produce a much different scenario. Since market makers are only required to sell 100 shares at every level (or at each subsequent spread price), a large buy order could drive the price significantly higher since no one entity is required to provide liquidity. It should be noted that although NASDAQ market makers are only required to honor their quotes for 100 shares, they usually trade in 1,000-share increments. A single market maker may elect to step into the marketplace and fill, or sell to, the buyer as he has a sell order or believes that the stock may not continue higher; however, he is not required to do so. Furthermore, the market makers may not have any idea which of their peers holds the buy order, and so although they wish to make a sale, they do not know whom to contact. Even if they do find out who holds the order, they may call and find out that the buying firm has no intention of trading with any other firms. The buying firm may not want to give up business to its competitors. The firm that holds the order will most likely sell the stock to its customer out of firm inventory and attempt to buy the stock back lower.

One must also consider that other traders have most certainly tried to anticipate the advance of this stock. What are their positions now? Will they sell as the stock begins to retreat, or will they hold their long positions in anticipation of the same or a new buyer returning to the marketplace? The answer is probably a little of both. Also, now that the stock has gone up, it is likely that many of the market makers are notifying their customers who may wish to make a sale that this might be an opportune moment. The same scenario could also be witnessed on the downside as the stock trades lower. It is also possible the original buy order was filled immediately by the firm that held it. Maybe the trader thought the market was about to sell off, or maybe he owned the stock from a lower price and wanted out of his position.

Regardless of what happens as a result of a trade, it is important to note that there are as many possibilities as there are players in the OTC market, as opposed to the NYSE where one specialist handles all orders. It would not be uncommon for a stock to move $2 or $3 as a result of this order, whereas the same order would cause a listed stock to move only $\frac{1}{2}$ to $\frac{3}{4}$ of a dollar. The bottom line is that the day trader never knows when one or several market makers will decide to provide liquidity in the marketplace—or if they will provide liquidity at all. If they do not have sell orders from their customers on their desk, then they are required to provide liquidity as a group. However, if the market makers choose to only honor 100 shares at each price, a large order could drive up a stock price significantly. Because the market maker holding the original buy order probably has no intention of letting other market makers help fill the order, as he wants to retain the business for himself, the markets may remain chaotic as day traders and other market makers jockey for position in anticipation of the order being completed.

The good news is that as a result of a marketplace where most of the players do not know exactly what is going on, there will be opportunity. Furthermore, because the moves in these OTC stocks tend to be more swift and severe, there is not only a greater number of situations in which to enter a trade, but also greater profit potential when a trader enters a position. If the day trader deduces that Goldman, Sachs has the buy order, then he may go out and purchase the stock from Merrill Lynch or Salomon. Since these market makers are required to provide liquidity in these stocks, they may be making sales in stocks when they do not want to. They might have also deduced that Goldman has a buy order and feel that the stock will trade much higher. Yet they are required to make sales because of their responsibility to provide liquidity and depth in the marketplace. On the other hand, a specialist on the NYSE knows exactly where to trade the stock and has a significant advantage over market makers who do not know the specific agenda of their competitors.

The second major advantage of trading OTC securities is that online access to this market provides guaranteed executions, whereas listed trading only has a means to electronically deliver an order to the specialist. Furthermore, technology has made executions virtually instantaneous on NASDAQ. In an instant, a trader can know whether or not he or she has purchased a stock. On the NYSE, the specialist has a 2-minute window from the time he or she receives an order in which to **attempt** to execute it. It is, therefore, not uncommon to have "just missed buying or selling" a listed stock at the price you wanted, or get filled on stock at a price you probably do not want. This phenomenon is one of the biggest complaints from listed traders as they feel they are constantly missing the boat when a specialist determines the fate of their order. Although specialists on the NYSE are bound by certain obligations and rules, remember they are attempting to make money and are not likely to give anything away they don't absolutely have to give.

By contrast, if a NASDAQ market maker is advertising to buy or sell stock at a specified price, he is subject to automatic execution. The first person to electronically access the market is automatically entitled to the trade. This access is undeniable and irrefutable. The ability to get guaranteed executions with blazing speed is a great advantage to the day trader. By instantly knowing his position, the day trader can react to situations that have the potential for quick profits. A trader in listed securities may have to wait up to 2 minutes to know where he stands, and this time can mean the difference between capitalizing and not capitalizing on opportunities— or, in essence, the difference between making and losing money.

Thus, SOES has provided the trader with the ability to access an efficient marketplace. In the past, the only way a public customer could trade OTC stocks was to place the order with a market maker who used his "best discretion" when executing the order. This would commonly result in the customer receiving fills at prices that enabled the market make to profit from the order. For example, the customer would only be able to purchase the stock if the market maker was able to purchase the stock at a lower price and then mark it up and sell it to the customer at a higher price. Now the customer/trader has direct and efficient access to the best prices in the marketplace and receives better executions as a result. This phenomenon has resulted in a great number of traders who wish to speculate in a market where they alone are responsible for how their orders are handled. No longer can a market maker "game" their order and attempt to profit as a result of customers receiving inadequate fills.

The third advantage of trading is common to both the NASDAQ and the NYSE. They are available to most anyone from anywhere. Technological advancements have enabled direct access with a computer and a phone line. You simply need to open an account with a firm that provides these services, and you are immediately placed on a level playing field with other participants. There are relatively little or no barriers to entry, and you can get started with as little as a few thousand dollars. As described in this book, there are several access systems that are available, and individuals must decide which system is best for them. This ease of access is certain to provide explosive growth to day trading, which, in turn, will only serve to increase liquidity and continuity in the marketplace.

CHAPTER 4

Gauging the Strength of the Market

STANDARD AND POOR'S

Perhaps the most significant factor in making money in day trading is not fighting the overall trend of the market. The direction of individual stocks strongly correlates to the direction of the market. In a weak market, traders should be extremely selective or else turn their focus to shorting. In a strong market, traders can be much more aggressive and consider substantially more opportunities. In this section, we will focus on understanding the Standard & Poor's (S&P) 500 futures and why it is the key to determining the overall strength of the market.

The Standard & Poor's 500 Futures

The best indicator of market direction is the S&P 500 futures. This index represents a broad base of stocks (500) in a wide variety of industries. The index is the most widely used gauge to measure money managers' performance. In addition to stocks, there are actively traded futures contracts on the S&P 500, and they are extremely liquid. Futures are leading indicators. On the other hand, cash indexes, such as the Dow Jones Industrial Average, the Philadelphia Semi-Conductor Index, and the OEX (S&P 100), are lagging indicators. There is a reason why the S&P 500 futures leads the market rather than lags it. The S&P 500 futures is the most efficient and effective way for money managers' to put money to work. After the money managers' bullish or bearish sentiment is reflected in the futures market, the arbitrageurs sell the overvalued assets and buy the undervalued assets. This forces the stocks to reflect the additional funds put to work in the futures market. Take a closer look at the causal mechanism to see why this is true.

What Are Futures?

First, you must understand what futures are. An exchange-traded futures contract is nothing more than an agreement between two parties in which one agrees to buy and the other agrees to sell a specified quantity and quality of an underlying commodity on a specified date. (In the simplest of terms, a future could be equated to paying the milkman for delivering a certain number of gallons of milk at a future date for an agreed-upon price. No matter what the price of milk is on that day, the milkman has agreed to sell and you have agreed to buy at the predetermined price.)

Futures generally fall into two categories, financial futures and commodities, i.e., orange juice, soybeans, precious metals, etc. There is an important distinction between the two. If you sell or buy a commodity future and fail to close out your position before expiration, you must either deliver the commodity or take delivery of the actual commodity. (In the simple example above, you would have to accept delivery of the milk and then sell it in the marketplace or drink it.) Financial futures are settled in cash. If you purchased an S&P futures contract, at expiration you don't actually have to buy the stocks you have agreed to purchase. Instead, you would just make or lose the difference between what that basket or group of stocks is worth at expiration and what you agreed to pay for the basket when you entered into the agreement.

Another important point is that you can calculate a fair value for the S&P futures contract by understanding the difference between the future and the underlying index. Two factors determine the fair value of the future. The first is the interest one can earn on money between the time a futures contract is entered into and the time it expires. The second factor relates to the dividends lost that the futures holder would have received had he actually owned the stocks. If the interest saved by forgoing the purchase of the stocks is greater than the dividends that would have been received if the stocks were purchased, then the futures should trade at a premium equal to this amount. If the future trades at any other amount than the fair value (as it very frequently does), then there is an arbitrage situation; and arbitrageurs will step into the market and buy the undervalued asset and sell the overvalued asset, bringing the markets into line. The arbitrageurs with the lowest transaction costs will have most profitable opportunities.

Now that you understand the basic idea about futures, take a closer look at how this whole process works. In most mutual fund prospectuses and frequently in advertisements for mutual funds (especially for the few that outperform the S&P), you will find the fund's performance compared with the S&P performance. Mutual funds and their managers are most commonly measured relative to the performance of the S&P. Knowing this, think of ways you might consider beating the S&P if you were a fund manager. Perhaps the most obvious approach is to find some way of picking a distinct group of stocks that is representative of the best stocks in the S&P.

You might consider stocks with the lowest price-to-earnings ratio; or stocks with the highest book values in relation to price; or ones with the most growth potential; or those with the lowest debt, or the highest free cash flow, or the highest dividend yield; or perhaps stocks of the biggest companies, or the smallest companies, or maybe the best managed companies. How about considering industry groups rather than companies? One suggestion would be to buy only the stocks in the industry groups that, you think, will perform well given the current economic climate. A second idea is to buy the groups that outperformed last year; or for that matter, maybe you want to buy the groups that underperformed, i.e., "the Dogs of the Dow." You get the idea.

Money managers will buy stocks that meet their criteria. When money managers have substantial assets that have to be put to work in a hurry, frequently it is much faster, much less expensive, and in many ways less risky for them to purchase futures contracts rather than individual stocks. Equally important, if money managers have already reached their goals for the year and now they choose to cut their exposure to the market, it is a lot more efficient and cost-effective to sell futures than to sell out their stocks. These are the stocks they probably will just want to buy back again at the beginning of the following year.

Sentiment about the market is quickly and efficiently reflected in the futures market. The fair value of the S&P futures is equal to the price of the index plus the interest saved less the dividends forgone. If the fair value of the future is $1 over the price of the cash index, and buyers come into the futures market forcing the futures to trade $2 over, then arbitrageurs will step in and sell the overvalued futures and buy the underlying stocks. This will drive the price of stocks higher and force the market back into line. If sell orders come into futures market pushing the futures price down, then arbitrageurs will step in and buy the cheap futures and sell the over-valued stocks, driving prices down. **Why does this occur? Stock prices follow futures prices. They have to, because if they did not, there would be free money (arbitrage profits) left in the market. Someone will always find ways to exploit such quick-profit opportunities.** In fact, this "index arbitrage," as it is better known, is done by selling or buying the future, and doing what is referred to as a "program trade," where at one push of a button a program electronically sends orders through DOT, buying or selling the exact number of shares of all the stocks to duplicate the index, thereby locking in profits.

Other Indicators—The Dollar, CRB Index, Oil, Gold, and 30-Year Bond Futures

Any short-term technical approach to gauge the strength or the "trend" of the market should revolve around the S&P futures. However, the S&P futures, at times, can be extremely volatile. To supplement this approach, one might consider other indicators to avoid being shaken out by intramove gyrations. One approach might be to determine what factors are influencing the S&P futures. Sometimes the market has appeared to key on the dollar, the CRB Index (indicator of price of commodities), or occasionally oil or gold prices. When the prices of commodities are on the rise, economists are fearful that inflation will stunt economic growth and squeeze corporate profits. Rising interest rates will produce flight from capital markets to the debt markets as investors search for higher and safer yields. Investors may, at times, also look to the metals markets, as rising prices in the past have been a result of "flight to safety." When investors become fearful that debt issuers will be unable to fulfill their obligations to repay their notes, they consider buying metals (generally considered a stable value). Most of the time, however, the S&P futures seem to follow the 30-year bond futures.

Bond futures are a good indicator of the direction of interest rates. If bond prices are rising, yields are dropping; when yields drop, money tends to flow from lower-yielding bonds, certificates of deposit, and savings accounts into the stock market. In addition, lower rates of interest make it cheaper for companies to borrow and expand and for consumers to borrow and consume. Both behaviors lead to higher growth. However, while S&P futures and, therefore, stock prices will follow the bond market more often than not, they will sometimes go in opposite directions. This reversal can be explained by the fact that, in a rapidly expanding economy, many businesses and consumers are competing for limited funds, thereby forcing rates higher. However, the economy is being fueled by a demand for goods. This leads to higher earnings, which, in turn, fuel the stock market.

Additional Ways to Gauge Strength—Advance Decline Line and Market Leaders

In addition to the S&P futures, you may consider a few other indicators. They can help you to determine the probability of a rally or a sell-off. We usually take into consideration the advance decline line and the performance of market leaders. The advance decline line tells you how many stocks are up for every stock that is down. If more stocks are down than up, then we would be wary of any attempted rally. We also find that a good indicator of the overall strength of any movement is the direction and strength of market leaders such as IBM, T(AT&T), MSFT (Microsoft), and INTC(Intel). There will rarely be a powerful upward move without solid gains in the leaders.

There are many approaches to gauge the strength of the market, but as we said before, the S&P 500 futures is the most effective approach for short-term trading. Traders should be aware that there are a limited number of OTC stocks in the index and that the S&P 500 is heavily weighted with large-capitalization issues. There are futures on other indexes, such as the Russell and the NASDAQ 100 Index. However, because of the tremendous liquidity of the S&P futures, it is the first place that reflects market sentiment.

TECHNICAL ANALYSIS

Technical analysis is the study of price movement. Technicians attempt to recognize patterns that they believe are likely to repeat. They do this by studying historical data and focusing primarily on price and to a lesser extent on volume and other factors. Other factors can range from the obvious, such as sentiment, money flow, market cycles, and seasons, to more obscure ideas, such as following the stars or letting the winner of the

Super Bowl determine the direction of the market. Academics tend to dismiss technical analysis. They claim that prices are random and markets are efficient. But the academics who make this claim, obviously, do not make a living trading. Many traders would like to prove them wrong (see "Can You Make Money in a Random Stock Market?" in Chapter 6). However, they cannot, because whenever they do, academics can always claim this is an anomaly, or an exception. Or they change their definition of "efficient markets" to allow for professionals to earn something for providing liquidity.

On the other hand, this does not mean that we believe that the winner of the Super Bowl will help you to determine the direction of the market. It is supply and demand that determine prices. Specialists, market makers, and professionals act repeatedly in similar ways to reflect changes in supply and demand (see Chapters 2, 3, and 5). Some technical rules can help you to recognize changes in supply and demand and, in addition, prove very useful, even if they are not always absolute indicators.

RELATIVE STRENGTH

For day traders, technical analysis can be very appealing and, if used correctly, potentially rewarding. The areas of most interest to online day traders are the ones that concentrate on changes in very short price runs, and the timing of these changes. Rules that help to anticipate or determine trends are useful. While there are many different theories and approaches to technical trading, we chose to focus on what we found to be the two most simple, consistent, and effective approaches. The two technical indicators we believe all traders should be familiar with are (1) relative strength and (2) trends.

Looking for Strong Groups

An effective approach to day trading is to identify strong industry groups and play stocks from these groups. Identifying strong groups is much simpler than identifying a strong market. All you need to do is pick some measure of the market, such as the S&P 500, and compare the strength of your industry group with it. For example, if the S&P 500 is currently trading at 600 and is up 3 points on the day, then the S&P is up $\frac{1}{2}$ of 1 percent. If you're looking at the SOX (the Philadelphia Semi-Conductor Index) and it's trading at 200 up 2 points, then it's up about 1 percent on the day. The SOX, for this particular day, is outperforming the S&P's. Another term for this is relative strength. The SOX is relatively strong compared with the market, and, therefore, may be a good place to look for stocks that are acting well and might follow through.

Relative Strength and Stocks

The concept of relative strength is used to determine the strength of an individual stock compared with a group of stocks, or a group of stocks with a larger group of stocks or with the market in general. For instance, you might want to determine the strength of INTC compared with the strength of a technology index such as the SOX (the Philadelphia Technology Index). Or you may try comparing the strength of various industry groups with a broader market index like the S&P 500. This can be very easy to do by comparing the percentage changes for a period of time. For instance, if INTC was trading 70 and is now trading 77, INTC is up 10 percent. If during the same period the S&P 500 went from 600 to 630, this would only represent a 5 percent increase. INTC would be considered to be twice as strong as the broader market—and thus exhibits good relative strength. For another example, say Microsoft (MSFT) is strong and the S&P 500, the Dow, and the SOX are weak; then when the market rallies, MSFT is a potentially good long candidate.

Relative strength can be used in many ways. Some traders like to use it for a very short duration, such as an hour. Others like to use it over much longer periods of time, such as weeks or months. Some like to calculate relative strength; others just like to look for characteristics of stocks that exhibit relative strength. We have found relative strength, in some form, extremely useful. Both stocks that are up strong early and stocks that close strong are worth following. Strong stocks are strong for reasons. And what is strong tends to get stronger.

Relative Strength in the Morning

Stocks with excessive demand (large unmatched buy orders) in the morning are worth watching. CNBC and Bloomberg frequently give a recap of the most active stocks and greatest point gainers and losers during trading days. But do not buy them just yet. Rather, place them on your ticker to watch. *The reason you do not want to buy them right away is that many of these stocks that are up strong early, i.e., within the first 15 minutes, will pull back. This happens because the professionals that made sales on the opening to meet their imbalances will attempt to bring the stocks back in order to cover their shorts. The stocks that cannot pull back, or only pull back a little, tend to be worth keeping an eye on.* It is likely that if the market makers, the specialist, and other traders who got in on the opening cannot pull them back, then they were not able to cover their shorts. If this is the case and the buyers return, the market makers and the specialist will be very reluctant to make more sales unless they can receive a substantially higher price. They will also be forced to cover their shorts, which will make stocks go up. Thus, potentially, a stock can move substantially higher in a short time. On the other hand, if and when some selling comes, the shorts can absorb some of the stock, thus making the path of least resistance higher. (See "The VWAP" in Chapter 5.)

Trend Reversal

Another stock pattern that often accompanies intraday relative strength is reversal of the trend. Look for stocks with small percentage declines relative to the market on sharp down days. When the market rallies, look for these stocks to reverse. **Stocks that are down on the day and reverse, and turn positive on the day, are frequently good buys when crossing from minus to plus.** Before buying, make sure that the stock actually makes it plus on the day. This is because yesterday's close may also form a resistance level. This resistance level is created by traders who came in long, who now have an opportunity to get out even on the day, and who may be willing to do this at yesterday's closing price. Again, make sure the stock actually trades above the closing price before buying. Another variation on this theme are stocks crossing back through the opening price. ABCD closes at 50, opens at 49, and trades down to 48. Next, it turns and rallies back above 49. This pattern frequently leads to higher prices. The reverse of these patterns also holds true. Stocks that go from plus to minus tend to make good shorts.

Strong into the Close/Gap in the Morning

A third pattern that often works well is buying stocks that go out strong into the close of the market. This tends to work the same way that stocks that are up early do. If a stock goes out strong, this means that the market makers or specialists are likely to be short, since they probably have to meet the buyers' demand (if there were real sellers to meet the stock demand, then it wouldn't go out very strong). Buying in the morning will squeeze the short sellers, and they will open the stock as high as they can in an attempt to average out. If they have to sell more, then they are going to demand a good price. On the other hand, if there is selling in the morning, then the shorts are natural buyers and can cover. There is built-in demand to absorb selling pressure. **Therefore, strong stocks that close near their highs are more likely to go higher than lower the next morning.** Note: Refer to the "The VWAP" in Chapter 5 for additional support for this strategy.

Relative Strength and Volume

Relative strength can be used in many ways, and, in one form or another, it is extremely important to momentum traders. An added variable when using relative strength is to look for relative strength accompanied by more than average volume. This can be a way of measuring the actual increase in demand. Strong prices and strong demand can be a powerful indicator of future movement. However, one word of caution: Extreme moves or extreme volume generates attention, and this tends to bring in supply to offset demand. **Stocks trading 2 to 4 times average volume and up 5 to 10 percent will continue to go up and follow through.** However, stocks up 25 percent on 20 times average volume tend to make headlines, attract supply, and become vulnerable to pullbacks.

Relative Strength, Volume, and Groups

Traders frequently ponder buying weak stocks in strong groups as they antic-ipate that if the group is acting well in general, then eventually the buyers will get around to buying the laggards of the group. While this may or may not be true, reality is that this stock has not rallied because there is a seller. It is not uncommon for money managers to buy one stock in a group while selling another as they readjust their portfolio. It is also not uncommon for other money managers to buy entire groups of stock. Volume may provide a useful key here. A large print can be a good indicator both that a buyer has "taken out" the seller and that a stock is about to strengthen.

Traders who are interested in quickly identifying stocks that meet criteria similar to those mentioned above can use "Insight." Insight is a useful day-trading tool that allows traders to write queries to identify stocks that meet certain patterns in real time. More information on Insight is available at: www.electronicdaytrader.com.

Anticipating Relative Strength

While relative strength is easy to recognize after the fact, successful traders need to identify which groups or stocks are acting well early in a move. Day traders should find measures of the economy and inflation useful in anticipating which groups may be strong.

Every Saturday Barron's lists which statistics will be released by the Department of Commerce in the week ahead. Economic indicators such as gross domestic product, new home construction, and unemployment are generally interpreted by Wall Street as indicators of economic strength and weakness. Wall Street interpretation of these numbers will be reflected in the bond market. If Wall Street believes that the numbers indicate that the economy is stronger than previously believed, bond prices are likely to fall, as strong economic reports are a precursor of higher interest rates. In this case, the market is likely to do one of the two obvious things: go lower as people pull their money out of stocks and invest in higher-yielding bonds, or go higher in anticipation of higher earnings. The S&P futures are likely to tell which is going to happen. In either case, stocks that have cyclical earnings are likely to outperform stocks that have earnings that are more sensitive to changes in interest rates.

Cyclical stocks, such as technology, automobiles, and retailers, tend to do well in strong economies. Firms are more likely to update their PCs during times of strong growth; individuals are more likely to have more disposable income to buy computers, cars, and clothes during these periods.

Interest-sensitive stocks, such as banks and home builders, tend to do poorly on days when the bond market performs poorly. Bank margins tend to get squeezed when rates rise. Banks tend to lend at fixed rates (mortgages, credit cards) and borrow at variable rates (savings accounts, certificates of deposit). Thus, bank profits are directly related to the spread between what the banks make on lending at one rate and what they must pay to attract funds to lend. Furthermore, no matter what rate they lend money at, when their cost to borrow this money goes up, their profits suffer. As rates rise and money becomes more expensive, people are less likely to buy new homes and home builders such as Toll Brothers (TOL) and Kaufman Broad (KBH) also tend to suffer.

The 30-year bond is generally the most followed and should be watched closely. On days that the S&Ps are strong and the bonds are weak, cyclical stocks are likely to outperform. On days that bonds are strong and the S&Ps are strong, interest-sensitive stocks are worth following. On days of weak S&Ps and weak bonds, interest-sensitive stocks are likely to be good short candidates. On days of weak S&Ps and strong bonds, cyclical stocks are likely to be the first to turn north when the market turns back up.

The technology group is typically one of the most volatile of the cyclical groups. There are various measures of this group, including the SOX and the Morgan Stanley Technology Index (MSH). These indexes are a good measure to use versus the S&P to measure relative strength. Those who day-trade will find the technology stocks are frequently where they want to focus their attention.

Another statistic of interest to this group is the monthly book-to-bill ratio. This is basically a ratio of new orders to shipments. For example, a book-to-bill ratio for computers of a number over 1 indicates that more new orders are coming in than computers are being shipped out. This is obviously a sign of a robust economy as well as a good indication of future earning in the technology sector. (A number of 1.25 would indicate that for every 100 computers shipped there are 125 new orders.)

Other Indicators

Oil prices can be a good indicator for airlines and for oil stocks. Oil stocks such as Mobil and Exxon tend to do well when prices are rising, as rising prices lead to higher profit margins. This is because the oil companies can charge a higher price for their goods while their cost to produce those goods remains stable. Airline stocks such as Delta and American tend to do poorly since the airlines' largest expense, jet fuel, is increasing sharply while their prices are less elastic.

A strong dollar bodes well for companies that produce overseas and sell in the United States. When the dollar becomes stronger than another country's currency, the price of goods produced in the other country goes down in relative terms to the dollar. This essentially makes goods from other countries attractive in price, and so Americans buy more imports. This, in turn, increases the profits of foreign companies. At the same time, the cost of buying American goods becomes more expensive, and exports from the United States may suffer as a result. Nike, Toyota, and some technology stocks may benefit here, while stocks such as beverages and drugs may not fare as well. Furthermore, companies that produce goods that face competition from overseas can be affected. The earnings of companies such as electronics makers or car manufacturers will come under pressure; for example, Chrysler has to cut prices to stay competitive with Nissan, and General Electric has to cut prices to stay competitive with Sony.

Volatile gold and silver prices can lead to volatility in mining stocks. Higher precious metal prices lead to higher profit margins for stocks such as Newmont Mining and Barrick Gold.

An extensive list of stocks and industry groups is given in Appendix C. Traders should find this list a good reference to help determine which companies and which symbols fall into which group of stocks.

UNDERSTANDING KEY PATTERNS

A good trader will buy stocks because they meet certain criteria. As long as those criteria have not changed and the amount the traders were willing to risk has not been lost, they will stick with the stock. Charts and trends can be useful in choosing the right stocks to play, determining the right time to play them, and anticipating when the trend may reverse. Figure 4-1 shows a graph that represents typical stock patterns. You can see from the figure that there are three main sections: A, B, and C.

Figure 4-1

Typical Stock Patterns.

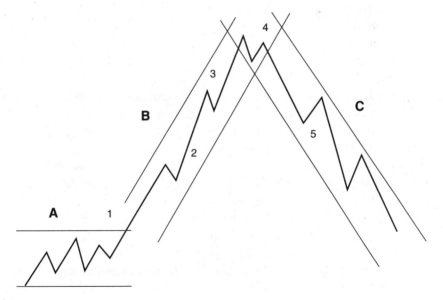

Stocks rarely move in a straight line. Stocks tend to ratchet up for periods of time, move sideways for periods of time, and ratchet lower for periods of time. These are the three basic patterns that all traders should be familiar with: a trading range, an uptrend, and a downtrend. These patterns are very simple, yet extremely important.

Section A is a trading range. The stock price is gyrating in a narrow range, unable to trade at a higher price than it did on the previous move up, and also unable to trade at a lower price than it did on the previous move down. This is generally good for market makers. However, astute traders who are willing to take small profits can make money in these trading ranges, too. It is important not to give up the spread on both sides of a trade when a stock is in a tight trading range. This happens when a trader is constantly buying stock on the offer and selling it on the bid. Rather, the trader should attempt to buy stock on the bid or sell it on the offer using limit orders when opening positions. This way the trader is "gaining the spread" by acting as a market maker or specialist would, on one side of the trade. In tight trading ranges there is generally not enough of an edge to pay the spread on both sides of a trade. An active trader who typically does 50 round-trip trades a day can save a significant amount of money by using limit orders on one side of the trade. For example, if a trader trading 1,000-share lots with an eighth-wide spread can gain the spread on just 25 percent of those trades, the trader could save $3,125 a day:

$$100 \text{ trades per day} \times \tfrac{1}{8} \text{ point per trade} \times 25 \text{ percent of trades}$$
$$\times 1{,}000 \text{ shares per trade}$$

This can easily be the difference between being successful and not being successful.

When a stock is in a trading range, astute traders and market makers are less likely to panic and pay up than they would be when a stock is in a strong trend. The longer the trading range, the more traders that are likely to recognize it and the more likely it may be to continue and potentially narrow. This is a result of more players trying to buy on the low end of the range and sell on the high end of the range. Traders should also beware that if more traders have recognized the range, then more traders are likely to need to cover when the stock ultimately breaks out of this range.

Point 1 in Figure 4-1 is the point that a chartist would call a "breakout." The breakout point is the point at which a stock moves out of the trading range and into section B. The longer the trading range, the more short covering there will likely be when the stock ultimately breaks out. Traders that sold what was previously the high end of the range will ultimately need to buy back the stock they shorted or will want to buy into the uptrend now unfolding.

Section B is what is defined as an uptrend. An uptrend can be recognized by identifying a series of higher highs and higher lows. Point 2 is the point where many chartists would look to buy. This is the pullback to the breakout. Point 3 represents one of several pullbacks in the uptrend. Stocks, generally, do not go straight up. This is because market makers who are providing liquidity for buyers try to force the stock lower whenever they can in order to buy back the stock they are selling. In strong stocks, pullbacks are generally shallow and short-lived. This is because the lower prices generally bring the buyers back as they perceive potential value. In strong stocks, the buyers return long before the average market maker has had an opportunity to buy back the supply that they provided. Market makers sometimes sell from their inventory, but frequently sell short. Market makers that are shorting stock to provide the buyers with stock will demand ever-higher prices as they assume greater and greater risk. Each time the buyers return, stocks are forced to higher highs onward and upward until point 4. At this point no higher high was made. This is a sign of the end of the trend and often allows the trader to anticipate a potential reversal, leading to section C.

Section C is a downtrend. It started when the stock failed to make a higher high at point 4. This is confirmed when it made a lower low than the previous low at point 5. The thing to keep in mind about downtrends is that they can be violent and that they frequently take place faster and are sharper than uptrends. This is so because more people play the market from the long side than the short side. When prices are going up, most investors are making money and are happy. When prices are going down, people are generally losing money. The paper profits they were counting on—and, perhaps, had already planned how to spend—are lost. People panic when they are losing money. This tends to accelerate price movement toward the downside. Just as people rush for the exits of a burning building, people tend to dump stocks in a hurry too.

Some day traders use charts extensively where they identify much more sophisticated patterns. Some common names of patterns used by technical traders are "head and shoulders," "cup and saucers," and "rounding bottoms." Other traders believe that prices move in waves and cycles.

It is not our intention here to explore the gamut of technical analysis, but to present a very basic but useful piece of information to the day trader. The important thing to recognize is whether a stock is in a trading range, an uptrend, or a downtrend. Long traders should try to follow stocks that are in uptrends and not consider buying stocks in downtrends. Short traders should look for stocks in downtrends and avoid shorting into stocks that are in strong uptrends. While this strategy of shorting high flyers can be extremely rewarding, it is more frequently extremely painful. A good short trader, who is in the game for the long run, will look to short rallies in stocks that are trending down. In Figure 4-1, point 5 would be a good place to look to short.

What's Happening behind the Scenes

In section A of Figure 4-1 there is fairly equal buying and selling. This generally leads to a sideways move that is very favorable to market makers. The market makers buy on the way down and sell out their inventory on the way up, generally resulting in handsome profits for the astute market makers. Traders tend to find the market choppy as each rally fails and each downtrend is short-lived. Observant traders capitalize by recognizing the range and attempting to profit by buying low and selling high. This works well as long as the traders define what they are willing to risk before entering the trade.

Other traders will be looking for the breakout to try and capitalize on those traders and market makers who are getting squeezed, who are feeling the pressure to cover their shorts as the stock is pushed to a new high. Market makers who previously supplied stock at the old high see new buyers coming in and hope to cover. Traders attempting to profit on the breakout contribute to added demand.

Charts

You do not have to use charts in your trading, but looking at them may give you an understanding of what others, who do use charts, may be thinking. This advice brings to mind a trader who made money for a straight month in STRM (before it was bought out). It made a new high everyday. He bought on every pullback and rode it to higher highs. (See section B, point 2, of Figure 4-1.) Unfortunately, one day the trend changed. The trader found himself buying STRM on pullbacks and not being able to sell it on the rallies—an important signal for a reversal worth considering (section C, point 5, in Figure 4-1). He failed to recognize that the trend had reversed. When the stock bounced, the market makers would sell inventory and the trader had a very difficult time selling the bounces; and when the stock pulled back, it made lower lows. Once the trader realized this, he adjusted his approach and began to make consistent money again. If the trader had looked at charts, he might have recognized earlier that the uptrend had been broken and changed his strategy.

The two important ideas to take from this section are (1) how to identify stocks in trends and (2) how to use this information to place on your system the ones in uptrends so you can recognize them when they begin to move. Doing this will improve your stock selections and increase your chances for success. Charts can prove very useful for developing ideas, identifying trends, and improving the effectiveness of your trading system. The simple concept is to recognize that when a stock fails to make a higher high, the next move is usually a lower low. Understanding this particular pattern should substantially add to your bottom line.

CHAPTER 5

An Insider's Look at the Trading Day

INTERPRETING THE OPENING LIKE A WINNER

Before the opening, traders and investors enter orders. Their decisions are influenced by their current positions and their expectations for the day. These expectations are usually affected by the morning news. Traders generally like to consider several factors: (1) overnight trading in international markets in foreign stocks and in U.S. stocks that trade overseas; (2) economic announcements made by the government regarding unemployment, gross national product (GNP), consumer price index (CPI), produce price index (PPI), etc., which typically come out at 8:30 A.M. Eastern Time; and (3) business news, such as a company's announcements about earnings or future prospects. How the market consensus views this news is generally reflected in the 30-year Treasury bond futures and Standard & Poor's 500 futures that trade all night. **Traders can get a strong indication of how the market in general is going to open from the 30 year bond future and the Standard & Poor's 500 futures.** Higher bond prices mean lower yields, i.e., lower interest rates, which may fuel consumption, which may in turn fuel earnings and, thus, stock prices. Or lower rates just may make stocks more attractive than their lower-yielding fixed-income alternatives. Higher bond prices will typically result in higher S&P futures prices, which will ensure higher stock prices on the opening. (See "The Standard & Poor's 500 Futures" in Chapter 4.)

Individuals can easily get access to all this information in the morning. The Wall Street Journal, the New York Times Business Section, and Investor's Business Daily generally provide a good review of yesterday's markets and some insightful stories that may influence what will happen during the day. Up-to-the-minute news, such as what overseas markets are doing and how bonds and stock futures are responding, is easily available through CNBC on your television or Bloomberg on your radio. These sources offer the information you need in order to determine how the consensus is interpreting what is going on and how the market will open. While all these sources are very useful, we believe that Investor's Business Daily and CNBC are particularly useful for day traders.

Investor's Business Daily

Investor's Business Daily has very important sections for the day trader. The "To the Point" section, with the "Business," "International," "Trends," "General," "Government," and "After-the-Close" subsections, discusses stocks that will generally continue to be in play on that day. The "NYSE Intelligent Tables Let You Invest Smarter" and the adjacent summary section evaluate the relative strength of stocks in play the previous day. Those stocks in the "Greatest % Rise in Volume" column will show movement from the previous day. The "New America" page will discuss new companies that are doing well, and these companies will also usually be in play during the day. If one examines the section "NASDAQ Stocks with Greatest % Rise in Volume" for those that are trading with at least two times normal volume and at least 100,000 shares, one can find stocks that will usually be in play for that day.

Investor's Business Daily includes a variety of other useful features. For example, *Investor's Business Daily* has an "Executive News Summary" that summarizes the key national and international news items of the day on the front page. At the bottom of page 1, the "Investor's Corner" column reviews market conditions. The Monday through Thursday issues devote a full page to "Computers & Technology." This is important for NASDAQ day traders because of the high proportion of high-tech stocks in the NASDAQ.

Investor's Business Daily actually processes its daily stock tables and provides several measurements of stock performance. While these measurements are proprietary to *Investor's Business Daily*, and in themselves may indicate what they are defined to indicate, they are certainly perceived by the investment community to be representative measurements. Therefore, as we discussed before, because stock prices move in response to the trading communities' anticipation of each other's perceptions, these numbers have an impact.

One measurement that is very helpful to day traders is earnings per share (EPS). This lets you compare the earning growth record of any company with that of any other. The rankings are from 1 to 99. An EPS rank of 80 means the company's earning record and growth rate are in the top 20 percent of all publicly owned corporations in America. A 90 EPS rank means the company's earning record and growth rate are in the top 10 percent of all publicly owned corporations in America.

Another important measurement for day traders is the relative price strength rank. This is also measured on a 1–99 scale. Relative price strength measures how a stock has performed relative to the rest of the stock market during the latest 12 months. Stocks with a relative price strength over 80 have exhibited strong performance.

A third measure is the accumulation/distribution rating. This measures the percent change in a stock's daily price and its volume. An A indicates a stock is being bought heavily. An E indicates selling. A strong increase in volume is coupled with increased volatility.

Another measure that also evaluates volume changes is volume percent change. This measure calculates a stock's average daily volume during the last 50 trading days. Each day is compared with this 50-day moving average of volume. If you see a stock with a +800 in the "Volume %" column, it means that there was 8 times more volume than usual. Any volume above +200 is usually good for day trading.

If you are interested in higher-fluctuation stocks, *Investor's Business Daily* gives invaluable information in terms of float size for each stock right near the day's actual volume. Those stocks with a high volume compared with the float, for example less than 10, usually move greater than 1 point during the day. On August 15, 1997, Layne Christensen (LAYN) had a volume of 3.2 million with a float of only 8.5 million. It closed $1\frac{1}{4}$ above its open.

Investor's Business Daily also presents graphs that cover longer periods and have weekly trading volume listed underneath. A graph that shows a stock reaching a new high on high volume is often an indication of a strong stock that will continue to be in play for a couple of days.

CNBC

Stocks noted on "Maria's Check List," broadcast from the floor of the NYSE right before the opening bell are usually immediately in play. The CNBC commentators can also have an influence on the day's performance of stocks. Just by mentioning a stock, guest speakers and commentators can cause it to move immediately. A fast execution can make a trader a quick $\frac{1}{2}$ point or better. CNBC also has a ticker that continuously displays numbers and symbols that help you understand the buying and selling activity of each business day. For example, the upper band of the ticker gives the real-time stock prices and volume data for trades on the New York Stock Exchange from 9:30 A.M. to 4:00 P.M. The lower band displays CNBC's market summary reports along with American Stock Exchange and NASDAQ trades. Amex and NASDAQ stock trades are delayed by 15 minutes. CNBC will also list indexes, averages, and other market indicators. They include the DJIA, the Dow Jones Industrial Average (the Dow); TRAN, the Dow Jones Transportation Average (20 airlines, trucking, and railroad company stocks); UTIL, the Dow Jones Utility Average (15 gas, electric, and power company stocks); and DJCOMP, the Dow Jones 65 Composite Average (average of all stocks in the Dow Jones Industrial, Transportation, and Utility Averages). CNBC also shows the S&P 500. The Standard & Poor's 500 Index is calculated using the stock prices of 500 relatively large companies measured by capitalization. Finally, CNBC lists PREM, an index that indicates the premiums or discounts between the current price of stocks and stock index futures. When a significant premium exists, buy programs are likely to occur. When a significant discount exists, sell programs are likely. As a contract moves toward expiration, the difference between the future and cash price will converge.

CNBC also provides data for the MSH, the Morgan Stanley High-Technology 35 Index, which measures the performance of the electronics-based technology industry. HP, IBM, and MSFT are in this index. In addition, the BKX Philadelphia Stock Exchange/Keefe, Bruyette & Woods Bank Sector Index is composed of stocks representing national money center banks. BancOne, CCI, and Wells Fargo are in this basket of 24 stocks. CRB, the Knight-Ridder Commodity Research Bureau Price Index, tracks 17 commodities. A decline in the CRB indicates commodities prices are falling; this may mean deflation and lower interest rates, possibly leading to higher bond prices and higher stock prices.

XOI, the Amex Oil Index, includes 16 oil stocks. An increase in oil prices leads to increased inflation. XAU, the Gold and Silver Index, comprises seven NYSE and AMEX stocks, i.e., NEM.

The complete ticker guide to CNBC is included in Appendix B.

WHY IT IS IMPORTANT TO BE INFORMED

The big mistake most traders make is to try and interpret a whirlwind of news and information and act on what they think it means. In other words, a trader forms an opinion based on the news. This is likely to be a trader's downfall and lead to some very costly mistakes. The trader will then make a second grave error by determining that in the future he or she is better off not paying attention to any news at all. In one sense the trader is right because the truth is, **the news doesn't actually matter. What matters is what the other traders' positions are (i.e., what they were truly expecting) when the news came out.** A smart trader, whether or not he realizes it, will determine what the other traders' positions are by watching how the markets react to the news. What reading all the papers, watching CNBC and CNN, and listening to Bloomberg will do is to allow you to determine whether the news is good (better than expected) or bad (worse than expected). Don't make the mistake of determining this. Let the commentators tell you. Once you know what everyone thinks should happen, you can now determine what will happen.

It is simple. If a stock (or the market) should go higher and it doesn't, this means that traders already bought the stock in anticipation of better than expected news. If the traders that were interested in the stock already own it and the news doesn't exceed expectations enough to bring in significant new buying, then the traders that bought in anticipation of the good news will not be able to sell the stock at as high a price as they would like. A perceptive trader will easily recognize that a stock is not performing up to par and realize that "the world is long" and sell the stock. This phenomenon explains why stocks sometimes go down on good news and rally on bad news. **If it is supposed to go higher and it doesn't, then it is going lower. The reverse holds just as true: If it is supposed to go lower and it doesn't, then it is going higher.** Read the news, interpret what is supposed to happen, determine the true expectations of the traders (their positions), and you will be pleasantly surprised how easy this is and how easily you will know which way the market or a stock is going to go.

Lord Keynes pointed this out in his classic book, *The General Theory of Unemployment, Interest and Money*:

> Professional investment may be likened to those newspaper competitions in which the competitors have to pick out the six prettiest faces from a hundred photographs, the prize being awarded to the competitor whose choice most nearly corresponds to the average preferences of the competitors as a whole; so that each competitor has to pick, not those faces which he himself finds prettiest, but those which he thinks likeliest to catch the fancy of the other competitors, all of whom are looking at the problem from the same point of view. It is not a case of choosing those which, to the best of one's judgment, are really prettiest, nor even those which average opinion genuinely thinks prettiest. **We have reached the third degree where we devote our intelligences to anticipating what average opinion expects average opinion to be.*** [emphasis added]

THE OPENING FOR A LISTED STOCK: WHAT THE PROFESSIONALS DON'T WANT YOU TO KNOW

Orders are entered based on how people interpret the news (their opinion) and what their positions are (what their expectations were). Specialists take their buy orders and sell orders and arrange them in order from lowest to highest for the buy orders and from highest to lowest for the sell orders. A specialist attempts to find the price where supply and demand meet. Sometimes a specialist will typically have an imbalance of orders to one side or the other. For example, he might have 50,000 to buy market, 10,000 to sell market, 20,000 to sell with a $29^3/_4$ low, and another 50,000 to sell with a 30 low. The specialist has the advantage of knowing where the public buyers and sellers are by what orders are on his limit book. A specialist given the above situation then would consider his position. The specialist could open the stock at any price he wants as long as he fills the market orders and any orders that would be priced better than the opening price.

Given the above example, only the two market orders would be guaranteed to be filled at the open. The specialist could open the stock at any price below $29^3/_4$ as long as he is willing to sell the 40,000-share order imbalance that would occur at a price lower than $29^3/_4$. If the specialist

---

*J. M. Keynes, *The General Theory of Unemployment, Interest and Money*, chap. 12.

wants to sell 40,000 shares, then perhaps he owns a lot of stock (he is long), or perhaps he is short (already has borrowed stock and sold it even though he doesn't own it) and is willing to sell more to prevent the price from going higher. If either of these scenarios is the case, the specialist is likely to open the stock at $29^{11}/_{16}$, the lowest possible increment below $29^3/_4$ where there is additional stock that would have to trade if the stock opened at this price. In this first scenario, the stock opens at $29^{11}/_{16}$, and the "market buy order" for 50,000 buys 10,000 from the "market sell order" and 40,000 from the specialist. The specialist makes the "after-market" $29^1/_2 \times 29^3/_4$, 10,000 by 50,000, hoping to goad the $29^3/_4$ seller into lowering the limit, giving the specialist a chance to buy back some stock for a profit from the trader who missed the sale on the opening.

The second, and most likely, scenario is that the specialist opens the stock at $29^{15}/_{16}$. In this scenario, the specialist gets a little more help from the 20,000 to "go," or sell, with a $29^3/_4$ low. Here, the specialist only has to fill 20, 000 shares, as opposed to 40,000 shares at $29^{11}/_{16}$, and he has the added advantage of always being able to buy back stock from the 30 offer. Keep in mind that the market to sell stock and the stock with the $29^3/_4$ limit all get filled at $29^{15}/_{16}$. Once again, the specialist will likely make an aftermarket that will try and influence the 30 stock to come "off limit" so that he can attempt to buy back stock at a profit. And, as in the first scenario, notice that the specialist opened the stock at the highest possible price given his objective. It would have been foolish of the specialist to open the stock at $29^3/_4$, or any price less than $29^{15}/_{16}$, given the orders he had. Why sell stock at $29^3/_4$ when he could sell just as much at $29^{15}/_{16}$?

The third scenario is for the specialist to open the stock at 30 and not make a sale at all. In this case, the market orders would get filled at 30, the "$29^3/_4$" seller would get filled at 30, and the "30" seller would sell the last 20,000, leaving 30,000 more to sell.

As you may have guessed, the specialist typically has a great opportunity to make money at the open since he sees all the orders and can choose the ideal place to open stock—the price at which he has the best chance to make money.

In the second scenario, the specialist opens the stock at $29^{15}/_{16}$. Then the specialist makes the aftermarket $29^3/_4$ bid for 5,000, 50,000 offered at 30. Say you were offering 2,000 shares at 30. How would you feel? Would you be tempted to hit the $29^3/_4$ bid? Would you consider lowering your offer to $29^{15}/_{16}$ so that you get ahead of the size at "the figure"—"30"? Would it change your opinion if the stock opened up at $1^1/_2$ points? And if one of the other weak hands (speculators) dropped his offer and another hit the $29^3/_4$ bid and the market was now $29^5/_8$ for 5,000 at $29^7/_8$ 25,000, would that sway you to lower the offer? If you consider answering yes to any of these questions, you responded the way most people would have responded. You also responded exactly the way the specialist wanted you to respond. The specialist set up the first potentially profitable trade by opening at the right price and making the right aftermarket. By the way, do you think the 25,000 for sale at $29^7/_8$ is real? Is it the guy at 30 that missed the opening print, or is it a new trader drawn in by the inflated opening hoping to make a sale at this level? Perhaps it's just the specialist trying to make you think the 30 offer came down. Perhaps there never was a 30 offer to begin with, or maybe there really was and it was just canceled. Call the specialist's bluff and stay pat, or fold and hit the bid; only you can make that decision. The specialist seems to hold all the cards in this situation.

As illustrated above, the specialist will attempt to open a stock where he hopes to make money. The opening is perhaps his best opportunity of the day. At the opening the specialist generally has a lot of orders and can easily move the stock to an advantageous price without having to trade stock at each increment. This does not mean that a specialist does not have to maintain continuity in the markets at the opening. The acceptable range the specialist can move a stock on the opening without making prints (trading stock) at each increment is larger than it will be once the trading day begins. A specialist who has a large order imbalance (loosely defined and to a great extent depends on the stock, the news, and the market conditions) may choose to "indicate" the stock. If a specialist has been unable to open a stock by 9:45, then he must indicate the stock. This might occur, for example, when a large sell order comes into the market and the specialist is unable to find a reasonable price (typically within 2 points of last night's close) at which he is willing to supply the liquidity necessary to get the stock opened. The stock closed at 50, the specialist has no buyers, and 500,000 to go. He indicates the stock 43 × 47. This "indication" brings in some buyers and perhaps influences some sellers to cancel. The specialist waits a few minutes and re-indicates the stock 40 × 43. This again brings in buyers and perhaps eliminates some sellers who either cancel or decide to limit how low they are willing to sell. Once the specialist begins to find buyers, he can start to narrow the spread. Perhaps he shows 41 × 42. Once he has indicated the price and has waited 10 minutes to give everyone a chance to digest this "indication," he is then free to open the stock. If he opens the stock at 42, then all orders that were willing to pay higher than 42 must get filled and all orders that were willing to sell lower than 42 must be filled. The specialist is likely to have met the remainder of the imbalance, much the same as was done in the earlier examples; however, the difference is that this time the specialist advertised for help to ensure that the sellers received a fair price.

In this example, any buyers who held out for a lower price may be tempted to bid the stock up, thus giving the specialist a chance to sell some of the inventory he may have accumulated on the opening. As also true in the earlier example, the specialist more than likely opened the stock as low as he could fairly get away with. Once CNBC and Bloomberg let the world know that XYZ is down 7 points on bad news, additional players will certainly be attracted. The specialists open stocks at the place where they believe they can make money. The specialists allow you to participate in that opening. If this is one of the best opportunities for them to make money, then why can't it be one of the best opportunities for you to make money?

Trading like a Specialist Whenever You Can

As a general rule, we feel strongly about buying strength and selling into weakness. However, the opening on listed stocks may be a very good time to make an exception to this rule, especially when a listed stock "gaps" (moves a significant amount). We try to trade with the specialist. Sell a strong opening; buy a weak opening in listed stocks. This is the only time of day we feel comfortable "fading" the market. Before the open, you can place scale-down bids and scale-up offers in several stocks a dollar away from the previous day's close, looking to participate on the opening and make a quick quarter or in some cases more. When entering these orders, you may want to enter them "opening only." This means that the order will be canceled automatically if you do not get filled on the opening. If you are unable to enter the orders "opening only," then you may want to cancel these orders if they are not filled immediately at the opening.

The following is an example of orders you might place before a stock opens. If XYZ closed at 60 yesterday, then you can place a series of orders in the following manner: $59\,^1/_{16}$ bid for 500 XYZ, $58\,^9/_{16}$ bid for 500 XYZ, and $58\,^1/_{16}$ bid for 500 XYZ; also, sell 500 XYZ at $60\,^{15}/_{16}$, sell 500 XYZ at $61\,^7/_{16}$ and sell 500 at $61\,^{15}/_{16}$. Note: The correct way to communicate a bid for a stock is price "for" size. It would be incorrect to say buy 500 shares of XYZ at $59^1/_{16}$. The correct way to offer stock is size "at" price. "For" implies "buy," and "at" implies "sell." This information is important when communicating with a broker or other traders. Even if you are entering your orders electronically, you may choose to communicate with other traders about your strategies and you should know the correct convention for entering an order.

Remember, if you are offering stock at $60^{15}/_{16}$ and it opens at $61^1/_4$, you will get filled at $61^1/_4$, not $60^{15}/_{16}$. Notice in the example above that the orders were entered at the smallest increment beneath or above the obvious number. This is because most people will offer stock at 61, not $60^{15}/_{16}$. When the specialist is trying to derive the opening price, he will typically have more size at the nearest whole number and will frequently open the stock a small fraction away from that whole number. The same fact can help your day trading. As XYZ rallies the specialist, the specialist may let it trade up to $61^7/_{16}$, but not let it trade $61^1/_2$, unless there is enough buying power to trade it higher than $61^1/_2$. This gives the specialist a chance to make a sale "in front" of size or a buy "in front" of size. If the public is more likely to offer at a half, and there is liquidity at a half, the specialist is likely to make small sales at $^1/_{16}$ away from a half, hoping to scalp a small profit as the "half" sellers get frustrated and perhaps hit the specialist's $61^3/_8$ bid. **Think like the specialist; trade with the specialist.** Specialists make money like this, and you can too.

After the Opening

The first 15 minutes after the opening bell tend to be the trickiest time of the day. That is because this is the time when the specialist has the greatest advantage. This is when the specialist knows a lot more than you do. This is when, if you are going to trade, you want to be on the same side as the specialist. Some traders just prefer not to trade at all during this period. Some traders prefer to watch and wait for the "reaction" period.

On most days, whichever way the market, or a stock, opens at 9:30, there will also be a move in the opposite direction between 9:50 and 10:10. If the market opens up, it will typically pull back somewhere during this 20-minute period. We call this move the "reaction." This occurs because after an "up" opening, most of the specialists will be trying to make their stocks look weak in order to get their stocks to trade lower so that they can buy back the stock they just sold on the opening. This period of the day is a critical time. If you have an up opening, then watch for how stocks react as the market pulls back. **Stocks that open strong and do not come in with the market are generally very good candidates to consider buying when the market turns back up.** This is because the traders and the specialist, who "sold" the opening, were unable to get their stocks to pull back and, therefore, were not likely to be able to buy back the stock they sold on the opening. You may also consider bidding for a stock that pulls back once the market seems to have stopped "coming in." But don't buy aggressively until this stock heads upward. Those stocks that trade back above the opening price are likely to go even higher. This is so because it is much more likely that new buying will push a stock to a new high rather than shorts covering their exposed positions. The shorts will be trying to buy on the bid to cover their exposed positions and not be anxious to take a loss unless they are panicking. Once the new buyers push the stock to a higher high, the shorts are more likely to get nervous and push the stock even higher.

This period from 9:50 to 10:10, the reaction period, generally sets the tone for the morning (before 12:00). Pay attention to the reaction and how stocks tend to act during this period. It is likely that two out of three mornings the trend on the opening will continue after the reaction. Pay attention to how much a stock pulls in relative to how much the market pulls in. If a stock or the market goes from an up opening to down, all bets are off. We would likely sell out our longs and consider shorting. On days the market doesn't have much of a reaction, we would look to resumed buying and higher prices. The specialist will demand higher prices if he or she is unable to buy back what he or she has sold.

Consider this example: XYZ opens up at $1^7/_{16}$. You sell a thousand shares on the opening at $61^7/_{16}$. XYZ is strong, and you immediately bid $61^1/_4$ for 500 and $61^1/_{16}$ for 500, hoping that the specialist can bring in some sellers. The stock comes in to 61, you buy back your stock, and you can bet the specialist did too. It is unlikely the specialist would have let it trade at "the figure" if the specialist hadn't had a chance to buy back what he or she needed to buy. Though it was a good trade on the opening, the time and prices at which it traded during the pullback would lead us to not rush to get long this stock. We may become a bit more interested if the stock rallies to new highs.

Consider again the same situation: XYZ opens up $1^7/_{16}$ at $61^7/_{16}$. You make a sale, and it is obvious that the specialist sold the opening too, since it opened at $61^7/_{16}$ instead of $61^1/_2$. The stock comes in $^3/_{16}$ on light volume compared with the opening print. You are unable to buy stock on your

$61^1/_4$ bid. This stock is one that we would look to aggressively buy when it starts to tick up. The specialist and traders were unlikely to have bought back the stock that sold on the opening and are going to demand much higher prices if they are required to sell more. Good traders will take a quick loss on their opening sale and buy stock aggressively as the stock goes on to much higher prices.

NYSE PRINTS, CROSSING, AND TECHNIQUES

Listed securities are primarily traded on the New York Stock Exchange with the exception of a few stocks that are traded only on regional exchanges (e.g., Philadelphia, Boston, Chicago, etc.). All orders are routed via a specialist on one of these exchanges for execution. These peripheral exchanges exist for one reason—to take commission business and order flow from the NYSE. These exchanges had originally intended to compete on the same level as the NYSE by "dual-listing" securities in the hope that customers would trade there if offered some incentive, such as lower execution costs. The NYSE, however, had no intention of giving up this business and still remains the dominant player in listed stocks. Forced to adapt, the peripheral exchanges came up with a creative solution. Rather than having a specialist who was responsible for providing liquidity, they would allow institutions that wanted to take the other side of their customers' orders trade on their exchange. This could not happen on the NYSE because the specialist was able to dominate all order flow on lots of stock less than 25,000 shares. Thus, instead of the NYSE specialist selling stock to a customer, the firm that had the order could choose whether or not it wanted to make a sale, or better yet, pair two of its customers' orders together to consummate a trade. This is what is commonly referred to as a "cross." The specialists on the peripheral exchanges would not enjoy the same order-flow profits as those on the NYSE, but they could charge the institution a fee for doing the trade and that was better than nothing at all. As a result, it is quite common for institutions to use these exchanges to do trades between their customers rather than give the orders to the NYSE.

Crossing

When stock is "crossed," a trade is consummated by a buyer and seller who have agreed to trade at a specified price. This trade may be done without the participation of the specialist or orders that are placed on the specialist's "book" of orders on the NYSE. For stock to be crossed between the buyer and seller, the amount of stock must be 25,000 shares or more. If the order is less than 25,000 shares, the broker will ask the specialist for permission to cross the stock in the special-ist's market. At this point the specialist must decide whether or not the cross is in the best interest of the orders on the book. The specialist may allow the stock to trade between two outside parties because he may have a long or short position in the stock and not want to add to or cover this existing position. The reason that traders choose to cross stock rather than simply give the specialist the order is that they are able to charge commissions to both the buyer and seller at the same time. If the specialist or a trader in the stock's crowd does not want the stock to be crossed, he may then block the transaction under NYSE rules.

INSTITUTIONAL TRADING

To better understand the ideology behind listed trading and crossing, let us first examine the process of an institutional trade. The first stage of the trade actually comes in the form of research. Then, analysts crunch their numbers, salespeople take out fund traders and ply them with wine and steak, and by hook or crook, an order is placed with the institution. Instead of a firm simply going into the marketplace and buying the stock, the firm's desk of institutional traders (or sales traders as they are sometimes referred to) will "shop" the order. In essence, they will call other accounts that may be long the stock and see if they want to make a sale.

"Hey, Benny, it's Flanny over at Neuberger. Remember that call in Xerox I gave you 2 months ago—yeah—well the stock is up $13 since then. I know you bought 75,000 through me—and only you know how much more you bought through Goldman. How about lightening the load a little up here? I got a buyer of 150,000 in my pocket, and the guy is not exactly 'smart money' if you know what I mean."

Thus, the salesperson knows that these accounts already own the stock as he was probably the one who told them to purchase shares at some point in the past. If the fund wants to make a sale of 25,000 shares or more, the sales trader calls his order room and tells them to cross the stock at the specified price and bills both the buyer and seller a commis-sion, usually $0.06 per share.

If the fund does not want to make a sale, the trader may call one of his "fast-money" accounts. These may be hedge funds or day-trading accounts that specialize in putting on these prints. For instance, if the market in XRX is $67\frac{1}{2} \times 67\frac{3}{4}$, size 2,000 × 50,000, the fast money might want to make a sale on the offer. He may do this because he has heard of another seller in the market, because he may think the market is selling off, or for a myriad of other reasons. He also knows that his risk is somewhat limited as he can always go into the marketplace and purchase up to 50,000 shares at $67\frac{3}{4}$. Usually, the sales trader will not tell a fast-money account the size of his institution's order for fear that the trader might "front-run" the order. Front running is the practice of buying stock in front of a known order in the marketplace. In this instance, if the trader reveals his institutional buy order for 150,000 shares to fast-money accounts, these accounts might go into the marketplace, purchase the 50,000 shares for sale at $67\frac{3}{4}$, and attempt to sell them higher, probably to the same buyer. Obviously, this would make the real buyer extremely unhappy as he is paying up for stocks he could own at a lower price. On the other hand, if a sales trader has one of his fast-money accounts sell 25,000 XRX on the offer and then goes into the marketplace, buys the 50,000 shares at $67\frac{3}{4}$, and then runs the stock up another $1 filling the remainder of the order, his fast-money account won't trade with him anymore. Thus, the sales trader must be careful enough not to burn his big accounts, yet savvy enough to get buyers and sellers together to generate two-sided commissions.

"Locating" the Print

Because the NYSE requires prints of 25,000 shares or more in order to cross stock, traders may elect to cross stock on other exchanges for lots smaller than 25,000. When looking at the prints, it is important to note where the stock is trading. If all the prints in a stock are on the NYSE and then you see 10,000 shares trade in Boston, you may ascertain that there are other buyers and sellers in the marketplace besides the size that the NYSE specialist is displaying. It is also important to note on what side of the market the stock is trading, as fast money or hedge funds will usually take the other side of institutional orders. For example, for the aforementioned market in XRX, $67\frac{1}{2} \times 67\frac{3}{4}$, if 15,000 shares trade on the offer in Boston, it can be inferred that an institution is buying stock and a trading firm is selling, or taking the other side. These peripheral exchanges desire to cross these shares, as it increases their volume and billing potential. It is also important to note that the NYSE specialist does not like it when stock is crossed in his market. The specialist does not get to bill anyone for these shares, but most importantly, the specialist loses order flow that he could potentially profit from. If there is a huge sell order in the specialist's crowd, the specialist would obviously like to sell a portion of a buy order if it was traded in his or her market.

Many traders who are in the business of trading on this type of order flow are most interested in "cleanup" orders. These orders are supposed to represent the end of much larger orders that may have had an effect on the way the stock was trading. For example, if there were a large sell order in a stock (e.g., 3 million shares in a stock that normally trades 5 million shares per day) and the order is almost finished, then buyers might be interested in purchasing a large block of stock in anticipation of a "pop" or lift in stock once the seller has been cleaned up. Thus a fast-money account might buy 100,000 shares of the last 500,000 traded. This account is obviously aware that 400,000 other shares were traded and does not know the game plan of these other traders. Will they attempt to sell the stock up a quarter for a quick profit? Are they longer-term players? How long is long term? A day? A week?

Some traders simply hope to break even on print trading. The more volume they do with an institutional desk, the more valuable customers they become. As valued accounts, they will be allocated greater shares of stock on new IPOs, which would be impossible to obtain anywhere else. These IPOs tend to get priced at a discount to where the underwriter values them, and as a result, these stocks tend to open higher. This is essentially a free ride for valued accounts, as they usually sell, or "flip," these shares for a quick and sometimes substantial profit. Other firms may trade with certain institutions in return for soft dollars. For example, a hedge fund may place an order with another firm, and instead of receiving commissions, it receives free quote services or some other form of compensation.

Bullets

Another type of cross is used to print, or put up, "married" stock. Otherwise known as a "bullet," this cross is used in conjunction with the purchase or sale of options which gives the trader the ability to sell stocks on minus ticks. For example, a trader might buy stock and sell calls with another trader, which gives him the net effect of having offsetting profit and loss as the stock moves up or down. As the stock goes up, the trader makes money on the stock he is long but loses the same amount on the calls he is short, and vice versa when the stock goes down. However, because the trader actually holds long stock in his account, he has the ability to sell stocks short on minus ticks if he chooses. He may want this ability because he feels the market is going to sell off or because he thinks or knows that there is a seller in the marketplace. A listed trader could be made aware of this situation when he sees the same size printing first on the offer and then on the bid. The first print is the married stock, and the second is the trader actually "hitting the bid" or selling the stock in the marketplace. Thus one could assume that there is word of a seller in the market or that a trader is simply speculating on a decline in the stock and is going short. Incidentally, the reason these prints are called "bullets" is that they are used to literally sell down, or "kill," a stock.

Go-Along Orders

Another situation in which prints could be important is with a "go-along" order. Go-along orders specify that whenever a buyer or seller trades stock, another trader wishes to purchase or sell the same amount. For example, if there is a pattern of two identical prints one after another at the same price in a stock, there is probably a trader who wishes to participate in the volume being bought or sold in that stock. An example would be 3,400 shares trading on the offer immediately followed by another 3,400 shares. It might be prudent to be on the side of the go-along order as buyer or seller has been identified.

Analyzing the Tape

Now that you are aware of a few of the "behind-the-scene" reasons for prints in stocks, let us examine how analyzing these prints may benefit an astute tape reader. When looking at the prints and crosses in listed securities, it is common to see stocks "trading toward size." This phenomenon makes stocks look like they are weak when they are strong and vice versa. For the same XRX market as before, the stock appears to have a much greater sell interest than buy interest. However, no respectable trader is ever going to advertise his intentions to purchase the stock or, for that matter, make a stock look strong by bidding for large quantities. Thus, just because a market is 2,000 × 50,000 is by no means an indication that there are no buyers in a stock. It would not be uncommon for this stock to start printing sales on the bid in lots greater than 2,000 shares. For instance, a trader might see 500 shares trade on the bid, and the size of the bid is reduced by 500 shares to 1,500. Then, 5,000 shares might trade on the bid, and the size and the price of the bid remain the same. Next, 7,400 shares trade on the bid, with a similar effect on the bid size and price. Lastly, 37,600 shares trade on the bid, and the new market reads $67^{1}/_{2} \times 67^{7}/_{8}$, 10,000 × 3500. In this situation, the seller was offering stock at a higher price, $67^{3}/_{4}$, and was trading with customers or the specialist on the first two prints. The last and largest print was a buyer "taking out" or "cleaning up" the seller. This stock is probably going up as a seller has left the market for now, and the stock is said to have traded toward size—that is, it is about to move in the direction where the previous market ($67^{1}/_{2} \times 67^{3}/_{4}$, 2,000 × 50,000) showed the greatest size, or volume.

Large Prints

Large prints also could be an indication of the beginning of a big order. Mutual funds frequently will give the same order, such as a buy of 50,000 shares, to multiple firms. The firm that comes back to the fund with the best execution price will then get an order to buy 3 million shares over the next few days. Thus, although prints or crosses typically symbolize the cleanup of a buyer or seller which might be a reversal point in the stock, they can also be a prelude to a much larger order that may drive the stock in the same direction as the cross (i.e., stock crossing on the offer could signify a buy order, and stock trading on the bid would be a sell). Sometimes you can gauge the strength or weakness of these stocks by analyzing their size and price after the print as well as the next few trades. If the market, as above in XRX, changes to $67^{1}/_{2} \times 67^{7}/_{8}$, 10,000 × 3,500, and then 4,000 shares trade at $67^{7}/_{8}$ and the new market reads $67^{3}/_{4} \times 68$, 3,000 × 2,500, it could be inferred that a seller has in fact been cleaned up and the buyers of the seller's stock are not immediate sellers. On the other hand, if the 37,600 shares trade and the new market is $67^{1}/_{2} \times 67^{7}/_{8}$, 10,000 × 3,500, and the next prints are 4,000 at $67^{5}/_{8}$, 12,300 again at $67^{5}/_{8}$, and then 5,000 at $67^{1}/_{2}$, it can be inferred that the buyers of the 37,600-share print that traded at $67^{1}/_{2}$ are looking to make a small profit on the stock or that there are more sellers in the market. This could force the stock lower as the buyers of the $67^{1}/_{2}$ stock will be forced to sell out their position.

Although it is difficult to gauge when buyers and sellers are entering the market, analyzing the prints in stocks can be helpful in deciphering institutional order flow and, subsequently, stock movement. Remember that traders must protect their customers in order to retain their commission business but must also generate as much business as they can with their accounts. Also, be aware that specialists in certain stocks will have different techniques and styles for making stocks look strong or weak. One specialist might show large size for sale on the offer and never show the entire size of the bid when he knows there is a buyer in the crowd. Another specialist might constantly add and subtract stock size from the bid or offer to make it appear that stock is trading when, in fact, there are no prints of buys or sales on the tape. Identifying these patterns via prints can prove extremely valuable.

A good feature to have on your quote machine is a list of the last three prints next to the size and price of the stock. This will help you quickly access the latest activity in the stock. Furthermore, you should have access to all the daily prints in the stock as well as the quoted market size and price at the time of the print. This will allow you to essentially "research" the tape and look for large prints and where and when they printed.

Predicting Order Flow from Prints

When entering a trade based on prints, the day trader must be aware of the possible outcomes. When traders see these large crosses on the tape, they should be aware that it could be a cleanup print and a sign of reversal in the direction of a stock. Otherwise, it may be a signal that the stock is about to move in the direction of the print. Although no one can know all the order flow, institutional sales traders and specialists really have a handle on the true order flow in their stocks. Remember that funds may not want to tip their full hands to these salespeople as they do not want the stocks moving on them. As a trading desk tries to find someone to take the other side of a fund order, the salesperson's other customers might attempt to front-run the order. In essence, trading in this manner becomes a poker game between the funds, the salesperson's firm, and that firm's other customers. The salesperson must maintain the delicate balance by giving customers good fills, but also generate commissions as this is the salesperson's livelihood. An institution that receives a fast execution at a good price will usually give the same salesperson its first call on the next big order. Examining prints can prove a valuable means toward gauging the strength and weakness of stocks as well as alerting the trader to possible movements based on order flow.

THE TRADING DAY ON THE NASDAQ

The Opening

Unlike listed stocks, orders are not centralized in the NASDAQ market. Instead, there are several different market makers representing different customers trying to influence the opening. Unlike the specialist who knows most every order and holds all the cards, market makers are more like poker players cautiously trying to figure out who really has what. Market makers start to influence the market before the opening. They can bid or offer stock on NASDAQ level 2 without having to honor their markets until 9:30. MASH (Mayer Schweitzer, represents Charles Schwab), which may have a customer who would like to buy some stock, starts to bid up a stock at 9:20. MLCO (Merrill Lynch), which also has a buyer, may bid it higher. MLCO and MASH are trying to feel out the market and see how the other market makers are reacting to their bids.

Typically during this time of day, a lot of markets are crossed, or bid above the offer and offered below the bid. This may also be apparent on ECNs such as Instinet. For example, the bid in a stock may be 1 point higher than those who are offering to sell stock because the firms on the offer have not adjusted their quotes yet. The stock may also be "bid up" on Instinet while other market makers are offering lower on level 2. These situations will normally correct themselves before the opening as market makers adjust their markets. If the market makers did not, traders would quickly force them to change their markets by taking advantage of the arbitrage opportunity at hand. For example, the trader might be able to sell stock at 100 to a firm that was bidding and buy it back at 99 from 10 firms that had the stock for sale. The firm that just bought stock at 100 would obviously not want to buy additional stock at this level as it could just as easily purchase it at 99 from other firms or day traders.

This opening is even trickier than an opening run by a specialist because here no one really knows what all the orders are. In listed stocks you could key off from what you think the Specialist is doing, but in NASDAQ the opening is more of a feeling-out period. In some cases, this is the easiest time for a market maker who has sizable orders. Just as the player who is dealt a full house can confidently bury his opponents, the market maker with the real orders can easily take advantage of the aggressive speculator (a weak hand). The first 15 minutes in NASDAQ tend to be a good time to absorb what is happening. If you are tempted to trade, we recommend that you are selective and agile. The market makers have the biggest advantage at this time of day, and it is not so easy for you to tell right away which market makers truly have the orders. During this period, you may attempt to identify which market makers really have orders and note how stocks react during the up moves and pullbacks.

What the Market Makers Hope You Don't Understand

Until recently, NASDAQ market makers were only required to display a bid or an offer. They were not required to display the quantity they were willing to buy or sell. If you have access to detailed level 2 quotes, you will be able to see which market makers are actually bidding and which market makers are actually offering. You will also be able to see the quantity that they are willing to buy and sell. This information can be extremely informative to the perceptive trader.

Let's look at how the market makers move their markets independent of the size that they display. Market makers are generally required to make two-sided quotes. In other words, they have to indicate a price they are willing to pay for a stock and a price they are willing to sell a stock. While, in some markets, market makers are expected to be on both the inside bid and ask, on NASDAQ it is generally accepted for a market maker to be on one side of the current market. If the current market is $50 \times 50^1/_4$, it is typical for a market maker to be 50 bid at $50^3/_4$. Keep in mind the $50^3/_4$ offer is irrelevant for the moment since there is stock offered at $50^1/_4$. Suppose the market maker who is bidding 50 buys stock. What information could be derived from how he quotes his aftermarket?

Market Makers Buying Stock

Scenario 1: The market maker buys on the bid and does not change his quote. The market is $49^7/_8 \times 50$. The market maker pays $49^7/_8$ for the stock and refreshes.

Interpretation: The market maker is a buyer of stock and believes that there are other market makers that are interested buyers. In this case the market maker is unlikely to change his market.

Scenario 2: The market maker buys on the bid and lowers his bid one level. The market is $49^7/_8 \times 50$. The market maker buys at $49^7/_8$ and lowers his bid to $49^3/_4$.
Interpretation: The market maker is a buyer of stock but is hoping to buy additional stock at a better price. He is testing the waters to see what will happen if he does not prevent the stock from coming in. He is most likely buying stock for his own account, but may be trying to get a better price for a "not-held" or "scale-down" customer order. A not-held order is one in which the customer will not hold the broker to the order. He enters this type of order to give the broker the opportunity to use his discretion for a better price. A scale-down customer order is one in which a customer enters a series of orders to buy stock at each level down. Buy 1,000 IBM every $^1/_4$ from 102 down to 101 is an example of a scale order.

Scenario 3: The market makers pays $49^7/_8$ for stock and moves from the bid to the ask. The market is at $49^7/_8 \times 50$. The market maker pays $49^7/_8$ and then offers to sell at 50.
Interpretation: The market maker bought stock and doesn't want it. This market maker is not a buyer or would like to lead you to believe that he is not a buyer.

Scenario 4: The market maker pays $49^7/_8$ for stock and moves to one level above the offer. The market is $49^7/_8 \times 50$. The market maker pays $49^7/_8$ and then offers to sell at $50^1/_8$.
Interpretation: The market maker does not have a real interest either way for the moment. The market maker is participating in the market, but his only real interest is to fulfill his market-maker responsibility. In this case, he bought some stock on the bid, and if it goes up a couple of levels, he sells it. If it comes in a few more levels, he may buy a little more.

Market Makers Selling Stock

Now let's look at the other side. A market maker is on the offer and makes a sale. How may he react?

Scenario 1: The market maker remains on the offer. The market is at $49^{7}/_{8} \times 50$. The market maker offers to sell at 50 and refreshes.
Interpretation: This indicates that he has sold some stock and is willing to sell some more. The market maker is a seller and clearly is not a buyer at this level.

Scenario 2: The market maker sells stock and moves one level above the offer. The market is $49^{7}/_{8} \times 50$. The market maker sells at 50 and then offers to sell at $50^{1}/_{8}$.
Interpretation: The market maker is a seller and is trying to get a better price. He is testing the waters to see what will happen if he does not prevent the stock from going higher. He is likely to believe that there are no real sellers in the stock and that he can get a better price for his stock. He is probably trying to sell stock for his own account.

Scenario 3: The market maker goes from the "ask to the bid." The market is $49^{7}/_{8} \times 50$. The market maker sells stock at 50 and then tries to buy back stock at $49^{7}/_{8}$.
Interpretation: The market maker sold stock and would like to buy it back quickly.

Scenario 4: The market maker sells stock on the offer and moves to one level beneath the bid. The market is $49^{7}/_{8} \times 50$. The market maker sells stock at 50 and then moves to the bid to buy at $49^{3}/_{4}$.
Interpretation: This is an indication that the market maker has no real interest either way and is participating in the market in an effort to fulfill his market-maker responsibility. He buys a little stock a few levels down, and he sells a little stock every few levels up. The market maker is taking a small risk in an effort to make the spread or what is referred to as "scalping."

Other Possibilities

Scenario 1: The market maker is repeatedly the "high bid." The market is $49^{3}/_{4} \times 50$. The market maker bids $49^{7}/_{8}$, thereby becoming the high bid.
Interpretation: The market maker would like to push the price of the stock higher. He is likely to be holding a buy order for a customer and would be happy to buy stock for sale on his bid, but he is not likely to unless there is a large seller in the stock. The market maker is attempting to push

the stock to a price where he is willing to facilitate his customer's order. This means that if no one sells him the stock as he pushes the price higher, at some level he is likely to provide the liquidity to fill his customer's order by taking stock from his inventory or by shorting the stock to his buyer and clean up the order.

Scenario 2: The market maker repeatedly is the "low offer." The market is $49^7/_8 \times 50^1/_8$. The market maker offers to sell at 50.

Interpretation: In this case, the market maker is attempting to push the stock lower. The market maker is likely to be holding a customer's sell order and is indicating to everyone that he would like to sell stock. Traders who are not real buyers are likely to move out of the way and let the seller sell the stock down. If the market maker eventually has to facilitate his customer's order, then he is faced with a dilemma. He would like to buy the stock at the lowest possible price, but he would also like to impress his customer by filling the order at a price that will satisfy his customer. The market maker faces more risk with a larger order and an illiquid stock, and, therefore, he will give himself much more leeway in filling an order.

UNDERSTANDING THE MARKET MAKERS

A quote on a stock tells you the best bid (the best price that will be paid) and the best offer (the lowest price at which someone is willing to make a sale). This is currently referred to as the "inside market" for NASDAQ stocks or "the market" for listed stocks. Market makers also display the quantity that they are willing to buy or sell at the quoted price. When specialists or market makers display a quote, they are free to display a bid or offer for whatever size they want as long as they honor the quote that they display. **Market makers can and will intentionally display an inaccurate quote to try and influence buyers and sellers.**

The catch is, they run the risk of getting caught. It is similar to the poker player who raises the limit when he really has nothing. The poker player may try and bluff players who may have better cards at the risk of a player with a stronger hand staying in. A market maker may display an offer when he really has buyers in an attempt to draw in sellers at the risk of having to make a sale. Detailed NASDAQ quotes (level 2) show a trader the actual market makers that are on the bid and the offer as well as the minimum size they are willing to honor at this price. Listed quotes are much simpler because there is only one real market maker, i.e., the specialist.

INTERPRETING ECNS AND ISLAND FILLS

As described in previous chapters, ECNs, such as Island, are a non-mandatory execution systems where orders will only be filled if another party chooses to trade at that price. Market makers may elect to purchase or sell the stock at the specified price, if they so chose. A trader can get access to this information through advanced order entry terminals such as Watcher, which will tell you who is buying or selling. Watcher offers FYI (For Your Information), which informs the trader whenever a market maker or trader executes a transaction using NASDAQ's preference system. There is a great deal of information that can be deduced by the day trader while individually trading on Island and being aware of other ECN fills. Most importantly, interpreting executions on Island can aid the day trader in identifying market makers who might have orders to buy or sell certain stocks. By identifying "players" in these stocks, the day trader who is savvy and alert should find tremendous opportunity for easy profits.

When trading on Island, any one of four basic scenarios might aid the day trader in identifying or ruling out market makers as potential buyers or sellers of particular stocks. The following scenarios, along with the implied reasoning behind a market maker or trader initiating these trades, are by no means general rules or definite signals that pinpoint the identity of true buyers or sellers in particular stocks. However, the following scenarios are generally indicative of market situations that may help identify real buyers and sellers.

Scenario 1: The day trader sells stock at or near the offer to a market maker who is not currently advertising his intentions to buy or sell stock. For example, the market in stock ABCD is:

$$48\tfrac{1}{2} \quad \times \quad 49$$

TSCO	MSCO
SALB	GSCO
FBCO	BEST

and Joe sells 1,000 shares of ABCD at 49 to SHWD on Island. Since SHWD is not advertising his intention as a buyer or seller—he is not on the list of market makers within the current quote—it is inferred that SHWD either is covering a short position or is a real buyer. SHWD might be short only 1,000 shares from being SOESed at $48\tfrac{3}{4}$, or he might be short 100,000 shares from a previous position. To determine this, the astute day trader must be cognizant of SHWD's prior movements in ABCD to make a deduction about SHWD's intent. Was he on the offer at $48^3/_4$? Was he listed on the bid previously? Did he stop the stock from going down before? If SHWD was indeed on the offer at $48^3/_4$, he is most likely covering a 1,000 shares short which he does not want to keep in his position inventory. However, if the day trader noticed SHWD previously bidding on several occasions, or SHWD was the last market maker left on the bid as ABCD came down, it might be inferred that SHWD is indeed a buyer of stock. In this case, if SHWD went high bid at $48^3/_4$, ABCD would probably be a good buy at 49.

Scenario 2: The day trader sells stock to a market maker who is currently on the bid. For example, the market in stock ABCD is:

$$48^1/_2 \quad \times \quad 49$$

MLCO	GSCO
SHWD	MSCO
TSCO	SNDV

and day trader Jane sells 1,000 shares of ABCD at $48^{15}/_{16}$ to TSCO on Island a teenie ($^1/_{16}$) below the offer. Since TSCO is currently among the market makers bidding for stock at $48^1/_2$ and is also actively buying stock near the offer, it can be inferred that TSCO is a real buyer of ABCD stock and TSCO can pay higher than his current bid. This inference might be confirmed by seeing that other day traders, through FYI, are also selling stock to TSCO at or near the offer. At this point, ABCD is likely a buy. If TSCO creates a new high bid at $48^3/_4$, then ABCD is probably going to go higher and the stock is most certainly a good buy at 49. If the market maker buys a teenie off the offer and is also on the bid, then the market maker is a real buyer.

Scenario 3: The day trader sells stock to a market maker who is on the offer. The trader sells to a market maker who is also acting as a seller. For example, the market in ABCD is:

$$48^1/_2 \quad \times \quad 49$$

GSCO	BARD
NEUB	SALB
MSCO	SBSH

and day trader Joe sells ABCD at 49 to BARD. This scenario is most common after a stock has just come up through several levels. The most common explanation is that BARD has just been SOESed at 49, where he is now short 1,000 shares. Instead of trying to purchase the stock back at a lower price—and there could be a number of different reasons why he isn't doing this (e.g., the market is going up, he is executing a large customer order in another stock which requires all of his attention, he knows of a real buyer, etc.)—he elects to repurchase the stock at the same price to close his short. Another explanation for this occurrence might be that BARD is falsely advertising his intentions as a seller when he is actually a buyer. By masking his true intentions and subsequently holding the stock down, BARD might be purchasing stock from a customer, buying stock on Instinet, or getting long using Island. Once again it is the job of the astute day trader to piece together clues from BARD's previous actions in the stock in order to deduce his real intentions.

Scenario 4: The day trader sells stock on the offer to another Island customer. For example, the market in ABCD is:

$$48^{1}/_{2} \quad \times \quad 49$$

GSCO	TSCO
MLCO	MSCO
SALB	HRZG

and day trader Joe sells stock to either BWAY or DATK, a firm that uses Island. The reasoning behind these executions is usually one of three possibilities. The first is simply that another trader thought that the stock was going to go higher. The second is that the trader needs to cover a short. The third is that another trader was not really paying attention, saw some movement on his screen, and made a rash decision.

Whatever the reasoning behind an Island execution, it is in the day trader's best interest to make logical deductions regarding the actions of both market makers and other day traders. Identifying real buyers and sellers in stocks is certainly the best means of profiting while trading. Obviously, it is not always an easy task to discover the intentions of market makers, as they have become adept at masking their true agendas. They will often do things that you will not understand, such as buying stock on the offer and immediately selling it on the bid. Maybe they made a mistake.

Two of the greatest tools that day traders can utilize in their quest for this information are cooperation and, most importantly, communication with other day traders. This is obviously made easier by keeping a close eye on FYI, but by announcing your trades, or if you are in a trading room with others willing to do the same, it will also help decipher the actions of market makers. By comparing and analyzing each other's Island, day traders might be able to uncover true buyers and sellers in their respective stocks. This knowledge is usually followed by profitable trades, which are of obvious benefit to all those sagacious enough to capitalize on the opportunities created by cooperation and communication.

MARKET MAKERS AND THE TREND

NASDAQ market makers representing customer orders are likely to provide liquidity to keep their customers happy. Those that do not will probably lose customers to other firms more likely to take risk. Market makers who provide the most liquidity tend to attract the most customer orders and thus bill the most commissions. Those who attract the most orders tend to do so by selling to customers who want to buy and buying from customers who want to sell. It is the market maker's job to take this risk. And those who do are rewarded with both commission dollars and order flow. The commission dollars' value is clear and measurable. The order flow's value is much more difficult to measure. The more order flow that market makers attract, the more spreads that they can earn, the more liquidity that they can have, and the more informed that they are of the true supply and demand in the stock. This information can be extremely valuable to market makers. It can give them the edge to know when they are really beat and need to change their position.

Let's look closely at an example of how an institutional order may work for a NASDAQ stock. The following scenario will explain the dynamics of the different buy and sell orders that over time generate the "upward trend, pullback, upward trend" price versus time chart you examined before in Figure 4-1.

Uptrend Dynamics

The upward trend starts when a large mutual fund decides to accumulate a position in ABCD. The fund calls its favorite broker at Merrill Lynch, Ted, with a buy order for 50,000 shares of ABCD. Ted calls the Merrill Lynch market maker, Joe, in ABCD to see what's around.

Joe says, "The market is a $50^1/_4$ to $50^1/_2$. I'm currently on the offer, but I have no real interest either way."

Ted informs his market maker he has a size buyer who would like to buy 50,000 shares. Joe, who is long 30,000 ABCD, replies, "I can sell 15,000 at $^1/_2$, 15,000 at $^3/_4$, and the balance at the figure (51)."

Ted says, "Do the best you can."

Joe at Merrill Lynch (MLCO) "puts on 15,000 shares at $50^1/_2$."

This means that MLCO handles both sides of the transaction. Ted's customer buys the stock, and MLCO as a market maker, sells it. He reports the transaction to NASDAQ, which disseminates the information, or "puts it on the tape (the ticker tape)." This information is reported in what is known as "time and sales." NASDAQ makes public the price, the size, and the time of the transaction. After the trade is made (the print), MLCO goes off the offer and bids $50^3/_8$ for stock. MLCO goes high bid in an attempt to force the stock higher. A new high bid is a market maker's way of saying, " I need to buy stock, and even if I do not need to buy stock, I want you to think that I do." This action allows Joe to use SOES traders to move stock to a price where he is willing to provide liquidity. SOES traders, sensing that MLCO is a buyer, then SOES the market makers on the offer. In this case Smith Barney (SBSH), Morgan Stanley (MSCO), and Goldman Sachs (GSCO) lift their offers. This indicates to Merrill and you, the trader, that there are no real sellers at the $50^1/_2$ level. The new market is $50^3/_8$ to $50^3/_4$. Merrill Lynch "puts on" 15,000 at $50^3/_4$. Once again MLCO sells, the customer buys. Following the same pattern, MLCO goes "high bid" again, hoping to push the stock higher. The market makers on the offer once again lift. The new market is now $50^1/_2$ to $50^7/_8$. MLCO goes high bid, the $^7/_8$ offers lift, and with the stock now $50^3/_4$ to 51 Merrill Lynch prints 20,000 at 51 to complete the order.

MLCO reports back to the customer, "You paid $50^1/_2$ for 15,000, you paid $50^3/_4$ for 15,000, and you paid 51 for 20,000."

This movement represents the first move up in the trend that is about to develop. Before we go forward, it is important to note certain points. MLCO who was the aggressive bidder in most cases, will not be able to buy a lot of stock. MLCO would like to buy stock on its bid because this would result in a better price for its customer and less risk for him, as he does not have to take a position in the stock. In many cases MLCO is not fortunate enough to buy stock when he is bidding. MLCO bids the stock up in an effort to force the price to a high enough level that he is willing to take the risk of shorting the customer the stock. MLCO who was just long 30,000, is now short 20,000. MLCO was able to use the SOES traders to help him to move the market.

After the customer's order is filled, MLCO who is now short, switches from the bid to the offer. This is MLCO's way of saying, "I'm done buying for now." SOES traders who bought stock because they believed MLCO was a buyer recognize this and frequently get shaken out. As the weak hands, they sell out their longs since the reason they bought the stock appears to no longer exist. SOES traders hit out the $50^3/_4$ bid and drive the stock back down. At this point, the chart of price versus time (Figure 4-1) shows the pullback.

Pullback Dynamics

As the stock comes back in, MLCO tries to buy back some of the stock it sold. MLCO bids $50^1/_2$. Weak traders sell the stock on their market sell orders at a half, while smart day traders, recognizing that MLCO is back on the bid, enter bids. MLCO manages to buy a few thousands shares, as does the astute trader. A few minutes later, the fund calls back with 50,000 more to buy. This time MLCO, who is now short, offers him 10,000 at $50^3/_4$, 10,000 at 51, 10,000 at $51^1/_4$, and the balance (20,000) at $51^1/_2$. Having gotten the order, MLCO begins to bid ABCD up, putting on prints at the prices he offered the stock at. MLCO trades 10,000 shares of stock at $50^3/_4$, 51, and $51^1/_4$. MLCO bids 51, hoping to move the price up to $51^1/_2$ where he is willing to fill his order. This time SBSH (Smith Barney) decides to stay at $51^1/_4$. MLCO now has a choice. It can call Smith Barney and see if the Smith Barney trader will sell him stock at this price. Or MLCO can sell the stock at $51^1/_4$ to his customer. MLCO cannot trade the stock at $51^1/_2$ with SBSH at $51^1/_4$. MLCO bids $51^1/_8$ in attempt to get the SBSH trader to lift his offer. SBSH fills a couple of SOES orders drawn in by MLCO's high bid, but does not lift. MLCO, already short, calls the SBSH trader on the phone to see what he is willing to sell. SBSH sells MLCO, who is representing a customer, 20,000 at $51^1/_4$. MLCO having bought what it needed, moves from bid to ask, making the market 51 bid at $51^1/_4$ offer. Once again SOES traders panic out and bring the stock in for MLCO. MLCO this time lets it come in to $50^3/_4$ before he bids. Once again, astute traders and MLCO buy a few thousand as scared traders panic out. This scenario is typical of how an institutional order works. Now take a closer look and see how you can make this work for you.

Restarting the Uptrend

At this point the price versus time day chart for ABCD, previously discussed, shows the upward trend resuming.

Summary: You are following ABCD and have watched MLCO bid it up and recognize MLCO as the buyer. The SBSH trader, having been the only seller at $51^{1}/_{4}$, has indicated he is a seller at the right price.

Now you want to examine the dynamics of ABCD's price movement and how to decipher the causal relationship of its movement to the market maker's movements. You have to ask and get answers to certain questions to unravel the logic behind ABCD's price movements. Put yourself in the market maker's position. Think like a market maker and analyze the consequences.

First, as MLCO bids up ABCD, ask yourself the following questions: How did the market makers react to MLCO's bid? How quickly do they leave the offer, where do they move to, and who is the last to leave at each level? How many levels does the stock move up during each move? Is there stock on ECNs such as Island? As the stock moves higher, what happens to this stock? Does the stock pull back after each move up, or does it hold? How does the buyer (MLCO) react on the pullbacks? How is the stock performing compared with the rest of the market? This is what you need to know how to interpret in order to be a winning trader. The explanations and examples in this book should allow you to interpret this type of information.

Market makers who "lift" are not real sellers; market makers who "stay" are willing to sell some stock. The more levels a stock moves, the larger the imbalance of orders or the less liquidity available. Size offered on Island frequently indicates that momentum players are in from lower levels. If it doesn't trade (if you have a system such as Watcher you can use FYI to tell you which market makers are buying the stock), the stock is likely be tired and not likely to go much higher for now. If it gets gobbled up, the stock is freer to move higher, as this indicates that real buyers are aggressively taking the day trader's stock. If the stock doesn't pull back, this indicates that MLCO was not able to bring the stock in and is likely to be short. An aggressive trader may consider buying stock on the offer. If the stock does not pull back, then watch what it does on the next move up. If it makes a higher high, then it is likely that the buyers are back. If it can't make a higher high, then it is likely that the move was a result of shorts covering. In the absence of new buying, as is the case in this scenario, it may be time to consider getting out of a long.

THE MARKET-MAKER GAME

"Playing market maker" is a momentum-based technique that will work in almost any equity market to some degree but has been highly efficient and most effective in the NASDAQ stocks. The foundation lies in the premise that stocks will not continue to trade in one direction on a short-term basis, but rather trade to saturation points where there will be low-risk opportunities to enter and exit trades. For example, a stock may trade up $^3/_4$ of a point as buyers enter the market and slowly stop going up as traders look to take profits or a seller appears to take advantage of higher prices. At this point, where the buyers have momentarily subsided and sellers have entered the market, the stock is said to have reached a point of saturation. The same phenomenon is evident as stocks sell off as well. The reason that this technique has proved more valuable to NASDAQ day traders is that they can access the marketplace with lightning speed and efficiency, which allows them to exit a losing trade quickly while taking advantage of winning trades.

The primary goal of the market-maker game is to buy strong stocks on dips and short weak stocks on upward spikes. This is more easily achieved in NASDAQ stocks than in listed securities. The reason is that NASDAQ traders can watch the speed at which market makers move their prices and also watch the individual movements of the market makers themselves, and this can aid the traders in locating or predicting saturation points. By contrast, listed securities will show the size and price of the market, but it is harder to tell when a buyer or seller might "take a stand" and stop the momentum in a stock. When trading on an advanced order entry terminal, such as Watcher, the trader can easily see when market makers refresh their quotes, buy stock on SelectNet or Island, or refuse to move from a price level. These factors, coupled with relative strength, the trend, etc., can define prices where low-risk high-percentage trades can be entered.

Although the same buy-dips–sell-rallies theory can be applied to listed trading, it is important to realize that information provided on level 2 is a much greater asset than simply reading a size and price market displayed by the NYSE specialist. Furthermore, although the market-maker game requires buying on pullbacks and selling rallies, it is by no means an attempt to pick tops or bottoms in stocks. Rather, the opportunity exists when the stock has reached its point of saturation (or the spot where the momentum in the stock has momentarily subsided) and the trader is unable to buy stock on the bid or sell it on the offer and then uses SOES or a market order as a guaranteed means of execution to purchase or sell the stock as it turns around and momentum begins to build in the opposite direction. When trading listed securities, it may be hard to obtain fills at these points simply because the specialist has yet to update his market, or worse, he is purposely showing a market that may or may not represent the true buy and sell interest in the stock. The specialist also enjoys a 2-minute window on DOT orders where he may "miss" an incoming order and thus the trader misses the opportunity to make his trade.

On NASDAQ, by contrast, if a market maker is advertising to buy or sell at a certain price, there will always be the opportunity to trade with him via online access. You simply need to be fast and alert to capitalize on opportunity. Most importantly, to trade successfully in this manner you must know exactly where the stock has just traded and in which direction you may expect it to move next. The good news is that if you implement the procedures explained in the following paragraphs, you should be able to capitalize on the thousands of opportunities that exist every trading day. Before you examine the actual sequence of a trade and the possible situations that will exist as a result of how you make an execution, it's a good idea to refresh your memory regarding methods of buying and selling stocks.

The Two Ways to Buy and Sell

There are two primary ways to buy a stock. Either you buy the stock at the offer price, or you attempt to purchase it at any price under the offer, including, but not limited to, the bid, using a limit order.

There are two ways to sell stock. You sell the stock either at the bid price or at any price above the bid, including, but not limited to, the offer, using a limit order. As is the case with both buying and selling, either you are initiating the action, or someone else is initiating a trade against you. By contrast, when you buy stock on the offer or sell stock at the bid, you are initiating action against another party, be it a market maker or another trader. The other party has already determined the price at which he wishes to make a trade (this can be referred to as a limit order or could be the actual bid or offer price as is the case with a market maker), and you are reacting, or initiating action against this price. When you buy stock on the bid or any price under the offer or sell stock on the offer or any price above the bid, another trader or market maker is electing to trade with you. You have already entered a limit order, and another party has come and "hit" your bid or "taken" your offer. The most important thing to remember is that when you initiate action, it is in anticipation of the stock continuing on the path of momentum on the side of the market on which you are trading. If you buy stock on the offer, then it is in anticipation of price appreciation and vice versa on the sell side. Traders initiate in this manner when they open a trade or when they are forced to cover an existing position.

On the other hand, when you are buying stock under the offer or selling over the bid, another trader knows or thinks that the stock is going in that direction. The other trader is initiating action against you. This other trader could be someone who is covering a position that has gone against him and he is being forced to "pay the spread," or the trader could be an institutional trader who simply has an order to buy or sell the stock. When you buy or sell stock in this manner, you are usually covering a trade that is going in your favor or opening a position with the anticipation that the current momentum in the stock is close to a saturation point and the stock is about to reverse direction. Remember, no traders are ever going to sell you stock if they think or know it is going up, and no traders are ever going to buy stock when they think or know it's going down. The only exception is if they made a mistake, which is very rare, or if they panicked. It is still a rational market in that the players are not altruists. **They're not there to give away their money**. These distinctions become extremely important as you become more involved with the market-maker game, since the manner in which you enter your trade will determine not only your risk but your potential profit as well.

Importance of Levels

Another important concept that is vital to understanding the market-maker game is the physical mannerisms that stocks exhibit. By now, you are aware that market makers are required to make a two-sided market; i.e., if there is some price at which market markers are willing to purchase a stock, then there must also be a reasonable price at which they are willing to make a sale. Furthermore, these prices, or levels, are inherently different for each issue. Liquid stocks trading on heavy volume will usually tend to have tighter spreads ($\frac{1}{16}$, $\frac{1}{8}$, and $\frac{1}{4}$), whereas less liquid issues will have wider spreads ($\frac{1}{4}$, $\frac{3}{8}$, $\frac{1}{2}$, or wider). If the market in a stock is $50\frac{1}{2} \times 50\frac{3}{4}$ and the subsequent offers by the market makers above the current offer are

$50^7/_8$, then 51, then $51^1/_8$, then $51^1/_4$, and so on, the stock is said to have levels that trade in eighths. These levels represent the difference in price from one offer to the next higher offer or one bid to the next lower bid. Levels do not represent the spread in the stock, which in this case was $^1/_4$ when the stock was $50^1/_2 \times 50^3/_4$. This is an important distinction as **you are primarily concerned with how the stock is behaving or reacting when it is moving, not when it is sitting still.**

Stocks that are less liquid will usually trade with a greater variance between levels. For example, the price in the stock may still be $50^1/_2 \times 50^3/_4$, but the next higher offer by a market maker is 51, then $51^1/_4$, then $51^1/_2$, and so on. A two-level move in this stock, which can be defined as the stock starting at the original spread price of $50^1/_2 \times 50^3/_4$ and then trading up past the $50^3/_4$ offer, past 51 (the first new level), to $51^1/_4$ (the second level), is equivalent to a four-level move in the aforementioned scenario with $^1/_8$-wide levels. Thus, the offer price in each stock moved up $^1/_2$ point, but there was a four-level move in the first and a two-level move in the second. **This distinction is extremely important, as the market-maker game requires intense concentration on how many levels the stock is moving, not how much the price has moved.**

Learning the Levels

Levels play an important role in any form of any trading as they are a general measure that may allow the trader to predict where a stock will trade to. Each stock will behave differently on any given day, but if you pay close attention, you will begin to get a good feel for the **average** number of levels, then, that a stock moves when it is in motion. We could not give you a list of stocks and say that these three will move up an average of six levels and these three will only move four. What we can tell you is that on any given day stocks will exhibit mannerisms that can be loosely categorized as a pattern. One day DELL might be particularly strong and move six or so levels every time it makes a run. The next day DELL might not be as active and only move three levels, and INTC is moving around a lot more.

The only way you will be able to determine these levels is by studying the movements, observing the market makers, and watching the levels like a hawk. This may seem a tedious task, but the best day traders will always be able to tell you exactly where a stock has just been, how many levels it has moved, and what direction they anticipate it will move in next. **This requires extreme concentration and discipline.** (When we first got involved in this business, a very savvy trader, who was one of the founding members of modern-day trading, told us, "If you concentrate 100 percent of the time, you will be 100 percent effective. If you concentrate 95 percent of the time, you will be 90 percent effective. If you are concentrating 90 percent of the time, go home." These were some of the greatest words of wisdom we have ever heard!)

Buying on Dips—Using Limit Orders and Momentum

The most important factor in playing the market-maker game successfully is timing the levels and knowing where to bid for your stock. When you begin to play the game, you will essentially be attempting to use Island or an ECN to open trades. In doing this you will attempt to open long positions by purchasing stock on the bid or open short positions by selling stock on the offer. As mentioned above, this process will prove challenging as no traders are going to sell you stock on the bid unless they think it is going down. Therefore you must attempt to make these trades at points where if you do buy stock on the bid, you will only incur a limited amount of risk. These areas are the aforementioned saturation points where momentum slows, sellers are starting to dry up, and/or buyers have stopped fleeing the market and may actually take a stand by buying more than 1,000 shares. The trader will be made aware of this by the number of shares that the market makers are displaying to buy as well as by the market makers' refreshing their current bids.

When you attempt to buy stock on the bid, you will obviously need to be careful as you do not want to buy stock and have it continue to go down. Some day traders will liken this experience to standing in front of a bus or catching a falling safe. The best way to avoid this scenario is simply to be aware of exactly how much the stock has come in from the last saturation point, which will usually be higher. Because you have been studying the stock and have a pretty good feel for the number of levels it is moving on that particular day, you have picked a point where you think the stock should trade to.

The Initial Move

For example, if DELL is strong and is trading up approximately $3/_4$ of a point, or six levels (DELL trades in $1/_8$-wide levels) on every run, and only pulls in three levels, you should be able to gauge a price where DELL will sell off to after reaching its upward saturation point. So DELL starts moving up from the price of 120 and trades up to $120^3/_4$. As this occurs, you will be able to gauge the rate or speed at which market makers leave the offer and place their name on the bid. The first level of market makers on the offer will usually lift very quickly, as they do not desire to sell more than one SOES lot to day traders. The next level will also lift very quickly, and you may even notice that there are 1,000 or 2,000 shares for sale on the Island. These offers will disappear quickly, as they will be bought by other day traders or the market makers. The third level, $120^3/_8$, may not disappear as quickly as the second, but may still exhibit strong upward momentum. Again there may be a few thousand shares for sale on the Island, offered by day traders who have bought the stock lower and are looking for a quick profit. This stock will trade, or the potential sellers will cancel their pending orders if they feel that they may make a higher sale.

During the fourth and fifth levels there will be a noticeable slowdown in the momentum. There will also be more shares for sale on the Island as all those who purchased stock at lower levels will be looking to take profits. Remember that the greater number of levels that a stock goes up, the more day traders have bought it in anticipation of a continued rise. Therefore there will be that many more traders who will be looking to make sales at the offer, or who eventually will be forced to sell stock on the bid. As the momentum really begins to grind to a halt at the final level, $120^3/_4$, there will usually be a great number of traders trying to make sales on the offer. Some stock may even trade there.

Reaching a Saturation Point

The market makers who were scrambling to cover stock that they were selling at lower levels to day traders on SOES are not as anxious to cover their shorts as they were before. They know that there is a great deal of stock for sale, and they may be able to purchase stock at a lower price as day traders now scramble to get out of their longs. Day traders who bought the stock at very low levels usually have the mentality that they just want to make a sale at any price to lock in their profit. Traders who "paid up" in the stock, or bought it late in the rally, are simply trying to get out at a price where they won't lose money. For example, after the stock makes its run, the market is likely to be $120^5/_8 \times 120^3/_4$. There will undoubtedly be a good number of market makers on the offer and most likely only a few on the bid. Furthermore, there will also be a decent number of shares for sale on Island or SelectNet. Once sellers on the offer at $120^3/_4$ realize that the buying in the stock has dried up, they begin to offer their stock at lower prices to try and entice buyers into the market. Thus, if there are 9,000 shares for sale on Island at $120^3/_4$, then one trader will undoubtedly offer his stock lower, at $120^{11}/_{16}$, to try and get a sale off. Once in a while that trader may get lucky and make a sale to another trader. If the trader makes a sale to a market maker, it usually means that the stock will continue to go higher regardless of how much is for sale in the marketplace. The only reason a market maker would make this purchase is if he knew or thought the stock was going higher. He can plainly see the 9,000 shares for sale at $120^3/_4$ but is buying stock because he has a buy order or he knows another market maker has a buy order. If another firm calls the market maker and bids him for 200,000 shares, that market maker will be anxious to cover any short positions and would like to get long. Therefore he may purchase the stock at $120^{11}/_{16}$ because he knows that if he does not buy the stock now, he may not be able to cover until a much higher price. All the stock offered at $120^3/_4$ could be gone in a second if the real buyer chooses to pay that price or as other market makers scramble to cover their stock for the same reason.

Don't Give Away the Potential in Your Trade

Smart day traders will cancel their offers when they see this activity and force the buyer to pay higher prices as well as force the market makers to cover their shorts up a few levels. This is one of the most important aspects of successful day trading. *When a stock you are long in, has reached a saturation point, do not leave your offers in for very long (a few seconds at the most)—you are only making the stock look weaker. Do not offer the stock at lower prices—you are only making the stock look weaker. If a market maker buys the stock from you at this level, he is not doing it for his health or just for laughs. He knows the stock is going higher. By making the stock look weaker, you are simply advertising to the entire trading community that the buying has subsided. You are forcing the stock down on yourself. Cancel your offer and wait. If the stock starts to go down, hit the bid (sell the stock)—or wait. That is what you were going to have to do anyway. If you do make a sale to a market maker, the stock is going higher and you could have gotten a better price. By offering stock in this manner, you are giving away the upside potential in your trade. If the stock starts to go down and you sell it, that is what you would have had to do anyway. If the stock restarts momentum on the upside, you are going to sell it at a higher price!* Once again, this is one of the most important aspects of successful day trading.

Most of the time, however, by offering stock at a lower price, this trader is simply advertising to both fellow traders and market makers that there are no more buyers in the market. Once other traders see this, they offer stock at an even lower price, hoping to make a sale. When no one buys the stock and the trader leaves the offer for everyone to see, it reconfirms to other traders and market makers that the buying in the stock has subsided for the moment. These other traders are now preparing to sell the stock on the bid, using SOES, at the first sign of weakness. Remember that there may be a great number of day traders long the stock as they have bought it from various market makers for several levels. At the same time, the market makers are realizing the day traders are long the stock and are unable to make sales. They have shorted the stock on the run up and are eager to purchase it back, but obviously desire to do so at a lower price if possible. As they witness day traders lowering their limit orders in attempts to make sales, they may even pull their name off the current bid or even the bids at the next subsequent prices. Then one market maker will go low offer at $120^5/_8$ in an attempt to panic day traders out of their longs. Once this market maker lowers the market, one or two day traders usually sell their stock on the bid, which forces these market makers to leave the bid and place their names on the offer. This sign of weakness is all it takes to begin an avalanche of sell orders. These sales occur much in the same manner as when the stock was bought up in the first place. The initial bids disappear very quickly, as a great number of day traders are trying to get out, and the subsequent bids at various levels will disappear until the momentum begins to slow. Again, there will be traders on the Island who are bidding for stock on the bid as the stock trades lower. These traders are either buying dips or covering short positions that were initiated higher. This process continues until the market-maker momentum slows and the stock has once again traded to a saturation point.

Starting the Game—When Do I Bid for Stock?

It is during this down leg or sell-off in the stock when the market-maker game begins. During this move the trader must try and ascertain the reason for the sell-off in the stock. What was the catalyst that made day traders sell their longs? Had the stock reached a saturation point that was indicative of the average number of levels that the stock had been trading that day? Is there a sell-off in the S&P futures which is affecting the stock's behavior? Is there a particular market maker who stopped the momentum last time who is stopping it again? Who went low offer? Who left the bid? Is there news in the stock or any other stocks which might affect its run?

If the trader feels that this is just a normal release of pressure from the buy side, as is usually the case with the first two questions, the trader may wish to attempt to buy the stock on this pullback in anticipation of the buyer or buyers reentering the market. If the trader feels that a certain market maker may have an "ax" (or sell order) because the market maker keeps refreshing and is always the last to leave or hold the offer, the trader may feel it wise to trade another stock or wait for a better situation than this one.

The market-maker game begins by placing bids in at prices where the trader thinks that the momentum may grind to a halt. If DELL is coming in only a few levels every time before it makes a run up, then the trader should attempt to make purchases on these dips. The trader will actually want to put in bids that are at lower levels than the current price and then cancel them if the stock is coming down too fast. For example, as DELL trades up to $120^5/_8 \times 120^3/_4$, the trader may want to place bids in at $120^1/_4$ or $120^1/_8$ in anticipation of SOES sellers driving the price down as they sell out their longs. As the stock begins to come in, the trader can gauge the rate of momentum and cancel his bid if he feels that the stock is coming in too fast. Thus if the stock is now $120^3/_8 \times 120^1/_2$ and is still coming in fast, then the trader has the option to cancel the bid before it reaches his level. He may now wish to place another bid at a lower level, 120. Again there is the option to cancel if the trader desires. It may not be prudent to keep placing bids if the stock begins to trade lower than its initial price. Remember that if a stock begins to make lower highs or lower lows, it may be a sign of a reversal of the uptrend or the start of a downtrend. The benefit of putting in these bids is that even if the trader is wrong about where he put in the bid, he can always cancel. Furthermore, because the trader has money at risk, he is much more apt to pay very close attention to the mannerisms and levels of the stock.

Buying on the Bid as a Market Maker—
Who Sold You the Stock?

If the stock comes down to the level where the bid is and it appears to be slowing down, then the trader will want to leave his bid in an attempt to purchase the stock. If the trader buys the stock from another trader, then using the Island system or another ECN is usually a good sign. The trader on the other side is usually panicking out of a long position that he has had from the run up in the stock and is trying to get out. This other trader bought the stock up too many levels and too close to its saturation point. He does not want to let a little loss turn into a big one and is selling the stock at $120^{1}/_{4}$ because he bought it at $120^{1}/_{2}$.

The other way that the trader may purchase stock on the bid is to have a market maker sell him the stock. If this occurs, the trader must immediately decipher the market maker's standing in at the current quote. If the market maker is listed on the offer and even creating new low offers, beware! As you learned when interpreting FYIs (if you have a system such as Watcher which alerts you), this seller may be categorized as aggressive. He is advertising to make sales at higher prices at the same time he is going into the marketplace and selling stock at lower levels. Remember that other day traders who may be long the stock will also see this information and now sell out any long positions that they may have held from before. If you purchase stock on the bid from a market maker who is listed as a seller, then it is usually best to exit the trade immediately using SOES. You are essentially buying stock from one market maker at $120^{1}/_{4}$ and selling it to another market maker at $120^{1}/_{4}$. Because you have placed your bid at a level where a good deal of the downward momentum has subsided, you should have ample time to exit the trade. Most other day traders have exited their longs at the previous levels, and the only ones left are those who chose to hold the stock through this dip in anticipation of greater price appreciation on the next leg up. Because most other traders have already sold their stocks and the momentum has slowed, you should be able to sell your stock at the same level as you bought it. If not, you should definitely be able to sell it one level lower.

On the other hand, a market maker who sells the trader stock on the bid may also be listed as a buyer at that level. For example, MLCO may sell stock to the day trader even though MLCO's name is listed on the $120^{1}/_{4}$ bid. Most of the time, this market maker has just bought the stock on SOES from another day trader. He is simply selling the stock out at the same price that he purchased it for any number of reasons. Maybe he is handling a huge order in some other stock and does not want to be bothered with additional stocks to watch. Market makers will do this to limit their risk when they are involved in other segments of the market. No trader would want to purchase this stock, forget about the position, and find out it had gone against him $1 or $2 before he figured it out. Usually a clerk will assist the market maker in filling orders and monitoring positions on that trader's list. A conversation on the trading desk may sound something like this:

> *Clerk:* "Dave, we just got hit at a quarter in DELL. You're long two on the way down." This means that the firm just bought DELL on the bid at $120\frac{1}{4}$ and is currently long this 1,000 shares plus another 1,000 that was bought on this pullback at a higher level.
>
> *Market maker:* "How's it look?" The trader wants to know if there are any big bids or offers in DELL which might affect the current market.
>
> *Clerk:* "$\frac{1}{4}$ bid for one only and nothing below until 9 and $\frac{3}{4}$." This means that there is a $120\frac{1}{4}$ bid for 1,000 shares, which might be from a day trader, and there are no other bids on and ECNs until $119\frac{3}{4}$.
>
> *Market maker:* "Bang it out. I don't like it here. The market is selling off a bit anyway."
>
> or
>
> *Market maker:* "Hit that bid. I've got no feel for this thing."
>
> or
>
> *Market maker:* "Just sell it out. I haven't been paying attention."
>
> Some other replies might be:
>
> *Market maker:* "Can't you see I'm working this huge order in INTC you moron! Take care of it." In this case the clerk might just sell the stock out at the same price it was purchased for fear of losing money.
>
> or
>
> *Market maker:* "I don't care what you do with that Mickey Mouse SOES stock."

Translation: "I trade much bigger size than that—you take care of it."

or

Market maker: "Can't you see I'm eating?"

Regardless of the specific instance, there can be any number of factors that will make a market maker hit a bid when he has just bought SOES stock there. Remember that most of the time the market maker will either sell the stock because he does not want to watch it or because he has something else to do, which is a lot of the time. As this market maker is not a real seller of the stock, he is just getting out of a newly established position. It may be an advantageous level for the day trader to enter a trade.

The other reason a market maker may sell stock at this price is because he knows the stock is going lower. A seller of 300,000 shares just called him on the phone, and the trader is getting out of his position or even going short. Maybe he has been watching the stock very closely and does feel that it will continue to go down, or maybe he just got a sell order on his desk. Whatever the case, you must try and decipher this market maker's movements after he makes the sale. If he remains on the bid, then chances are that he was selling the stock for no real reason other than he does not want it in his position list. However, if that market maker goes low offer immediately after selling the stock, it may be a signal that the stock is indeed heading lower for a more real reason, such as a seller entering the market. The day trader should probably sell out his long at that time as other market makers and day traders will undoubtedly decipher this information in a similar fashion, sending the stock lower.

USING A MARKET MAKER TO LOCATE A LEVEL

Another way to discern which levels may be good places to put in bids is by watching the market-maker movement. If the MSCO market maker is the one who forced the stock up in the first place by going high bid and was buying stock on the offer, then it is safe to assume that MSCO has some type of order in the stock. Therefore, if you are looking for a good level to put in a bid and the MSCO market maker has his name on the bid, there is a good chance that the MSCO market maker could refresh his bid once he has bought stock. Because you ascertained that he was a player on the way up, you will want to see how he reacts on the way back down. If he refreshes in an attempt to buy more stock than he is required, you know that MSCO probably still has an order to buy the stock. An even better sign is when you see FYIs that are reporting that MSCO is buying stocks via preferences. Then, you can be almost certain that MSCO market maker has bought stock from SOES traders and is buying more stock, not because he is obligated to, but because he wants to. On the other hand, if the MSCO market maker drops his bid right away as do the other market makers, you will probably want to look for him at lower levels to see if he has further interest in the stock or could be done with the order. If the MSCO market maker has placed his bid at the next level and then again at one level below that, it is possible that he is still accumulating stock but attempting to get better prices for his customer. If MSCO is nowhere to be found, then the trader may want to reevaluate.

If MSCO stays on the bid, even though the momentum looks as if the stock is going down, MSCO may hold the stock up until it begins its next run to the upside. This is an opportune moment to buy stock on the bid, as other day traders will most likely be panicking out of their longs. As soon as other traders recognize that MSCO is a buyer, they will stop trying to sell their stock, while other traders will be preparing to buy the stock in anticipation of another upward move. Because you have identified MSCO as a player, you may be able to buy stock from another trader who was not paying attention or did not recognize this pivot point where the momentum reverses to the upside.

Using Prices to Find Levels

Yet another way to gauge when to put in bids and offers, in addition to momentum, is by comparing the price of this run to the previous one. If the stock appears to have support or resistance levels that exhibit the characteristics of higher highs and higher lows, you should be able to pick spots where the stock should pull in to. For example, if you notice that DELL runs up to $120^3/_4$ and then comes in to $120^1/_4$, you now have a baseline to gauge the next move. If on the next upward run the stock trades up to 121 (which is higher than the previous high of $120^3/_4$), then you would hope that the stock would sell off in a similar manner as it did during the first run. In this case the stock may sell down to $120^1/_2$ or $120^5/_8$ (both are higher lows that the previous low of $102^1/_4$). If the day trader notices this pattern, it would probably be wise to attempt to purchase the stock on the next pullback if it continues to make higher highs and higher lows. The continuation of these higher lows represents a pivot point where selling momentum stops and the momentum reverses to where the upside buyers enter the market. If this pattern is broken and the stock sells off to a lower low or fails to make a higher high, then it is time to take a step back and reevaluate the momentum in the stock, as this could be the sign of a reversal.

The 20–1 Rule

When putting in bids in an attempt to buy stock on the bid, it is important to remember that as in all limit orders, you only want to show your intention to buy the stock for a couple of seconds and then cancel the bid. If you leave the bid in for a long period, then you are showing other day traders that the momentum has stopped. They will never sell stock to you once they realize that the selling has subsided, because the stock may turn around and they may get a better price. If the stock begins to go down again, then they will sell it on the bid at the same price using SOES, which is what they were going to do in the first place. Furthermore, if the stock is sitting still and the trader is bidding and a market maker sells the stock, the stock is probably going down as discussed earlier. *When you attempt to buy stock on the bid (and "attempt" is the key word), you may only actually make a purchase one out of twenty times. The trader wants to make that "sweet" buy, where the momentum is coming to a stop and a careless or panicking trader or an indifferent market maker is selling you the stock. Furthermore, by constantly putting in these bids, you will also get a really good feel for how the stock is trading and how many levels it is moving until it reaches a saturation point.*

What to Do When You Buy on the Bid

When you succeed at making this purchase, you have several options. First of all, do not immediately offer to sell the stock out. You will only make the stock look weaker. Instead, simply wait. If the stock continues to go down, you must decide how many levels you are willing to risk. The mentality is that the stock has just come in several levels and the momentum has slowed, so how much farther will the stock go down? To quantify how much you may be willing to let the trade go against you, you must also ascertain how much you will profit if the stock stops and begins to go back up. Remember that if this is a pivot point in the momentum, there will be a great number of day traders attempting to buy the stock on the offer as it begins to go back up. This is why you do not want to immediately offer to sell the stock once you have bought it. Once the stock resumes up, you should be able to make a sale up at least one or two levels to a market maker or another trader.If you work hard to make a good buy at these levels, then do not just give your stock away. Remember how many levels the stock went up on the last run, gauge the speed of the momentum, and place your offer at a level where you should get "taken," or make a sale, on the offer. Whenever you are using a momentum strategy, you should remember the old saying, **"Get out when you can, not when you have to."** You will make more money in the long run selling your longs on the offer on the way up instead of waiting for the momentum and selling stock on the bid using SOES to get out. Buying stock in this manner will produce some of your most profitable trades as you are buying stock on the bid and selling it on the offer. You are not paying spreads to the market maker, but rather acting as a market maker yourself and capturing the spread to make a profit.

USING YOUR INFORMATION
AND BUYING WITH SOES

Far more profitable, however, are trades that stem from information created by the 19 in 20 times that you are unable to purchase stock on the bid. As the stock comes in and you are engaged in the process of putting in bids and canceling them, you are actually feeling out the market as well as concentrating on the exact number of levels that a stock has just moved and the direction it has come from. No one in his right mind would ever enter an order to buy a falling stock without knowing where it had just been or how fast it was falling. The market-maker game forces you, the trader, to concentrate on both of these aspects, and that is the ultimate reason why it succeeds.

Day traders will make more money buying strong stocks on the offer using SOES than buying weak stocks on the bid without SOES. They are purchasing from market makers who do not want to make sales, and they are selling the stock as it moves up to market makers who are covering their shorts or to other day traders who are looking to get in. If the trader can buy stock at or around saturation points, then he will have the greatest opportunity to make money. No trader will ever be able to buy stock at the bottom and sell it at the top all the time, or even 50 percent of the time for that matter. If, however, the trader can locate pivots that occur at points of saturation, then the trader will be able to participate in the bulk of the move. This allows the day trader to profit even if he is unable to buy stock at the bottom or sell at the top. The day trader only needs to capture the smallest margin in between to be successful.

Because the market-maker game forces you to be cognizant of these potential pivot points, you will have the greatest opportunity to make successful trades. If you have put in your bids as the stock has sold off, you must once again ascertain the reasons for the decline in the stock. Was it just blowing off a little steam, or are there other factors (a sell-off in the S&P futures) that made it come in? When the momentum in the stock has halted, be ready to make your buy using SOES. When you are unable to purchase the stock on the bid, this is a sign that most of the day traders have sold out and the market makers have stopped selling. Here you must formulate a game plan. Do you risk paying the spread, or buying stock on the offer, when it begins to go up again.

Remember that a good number of other alert traders will be looking for this exact spot and will also be attempting to buy the stock as market makers come off the ask or on to the bid. These traders should help to push the stock up on the first sign of strength because they are buying on SOES. This fact in itself reduces the risk of buying the stock on the offer, as you should be able to sell the stock to another trader or market maker during this initial buying spree if the momentum on the upside does not seem to be significant enough to carry the stock higher.

Getting Out with the Momentum

When the day trader enters a position using SOES, the momentum at this point should be the most violent and fastest-moving section of the leg up. The big question at this point is, "When, or how, do I get out?" In response, the best traders always "get out when they can, not when they have to." Remember that when you are selling on the offer, into the momentum on the upside, you will have a much greater chance of getting a trade off than if you wait for the momentum to slow or die. *Do not wait for the stock to pile up for sale on the offer before you attempt to get out, because chances are you will not make a sale.*

Looking at it from the other side of the coin, if you were a buyer in the stock, would you wait until the momentum in a stock has stopped and there are volumes of stock for sale? The answer is obviously no. So if you think that you will be able to make a sale at this point, ask yourself, "Who is going to buy it?" Or, "Would I be buying the stock up this many levels?" As explained earlier, when selling on the offer rather than selling on the bid with SOES, the stock does not have to move as many levels. You will obviously have a much better chance of making your sale in this manner and, over time, will also be much more profitable.

Some traders feel that they should wait until the momentum in the stock has stopped—let it go up as much as it can to the next saturation point and then sell the stock on the bid. What these traders do not realize is that every time that the stock does go up a few levels, the smart traders are selling stock on the offer and netting profits. Meanwhile, the greedy traders looking for the big move are constantly buying stock on the offer and either selling the stock back out on the bid when they get faked out or, more likely, selling the stock at a lower price. The smart traders will realize that they can always buy a strong stock again. Many traders have difficulty with this concept. The strong traders also realize that it is all right to purchase a stock at higher price than they just sold it if it is going even higher. Hitting singles day in and day out will produce a winning method. Swinging for the fences will result in a lot of strikeouts. *It is much easier to make four quarters than make a dollar in a single trade.*

THE RISK OF BUYING ON THE OFFER– LOSING THE SPREAD

As a day trader, you must realize that when you decide to buy stock on the offer at these saturation points, you are actually incurring some risk. If the stock does not go up from these levels, there are now a number of traders who are long the stock and must sell if the momentum pivots and starts down. The market makers will realize this and attempt to bring the stock down to even lower levels in order to profit from the pain and misery of the day traders who just bought the stock. Here arises one of the greatest dilemmas in day trading. You have bought stock at a level where you thought you were safe. The momentum halted and you were unable to buy stock on the bid only a few minutes or even seconds ago. Now the stock is starting to go down again, and you must make a decision. To sell or not to sell. If you do not sell, there is the risk that the other traders who are long will sell the stock down to a level where you will incur a substantial loss. "I was begging to buy this stock 30 seconds ago, and there wasn't a seller in sight" is the common mentality. "How could they possibly be doing this?" "This is insane!" "What the heck is going on here?" "I can't believe I let this thing go so far against me" are some other common sentiments. These traders will be forced to sell the stock on the bid using SOES at a level below where they initially bought it or even lower. The dilemma arises when you finally sell out your stock right as the stock reaches another turning point. The stock immediately turns around and goes not only up through the original purchase point but up to the levels where you had initially intended to make a sale after you bought the stock. There is nothing more frustrating than locking in this loss and watching what you knew was a good trade to begin with finally come to fruition. On the other side of the coin, if you are not disciplined and do not sell out your long, the stock will undoubtedly continue lower and you will incur an even greater loss.

TAKE SMALL LOSSES—
DON'T PRAY FOR A REBOUND

The whole problem with this dilemma is that it is like an addictive drug. Every time traders hold a long position as it goes down and then end up making a profit on the trade, they have renewed their faith in God, modern man, and all the other powers that be. They were right! They knew they were right! Unfortunately this method of thinking is the force that provides traders with that one glimmering ray of hope as they hold the positions that they know they should be closing. The best day traders we have seen in the business usually take the first initial small loss in this situation. If they are the least bit wrong, then they are gone. Because they are used to taking many small losses, they will never get married to a losing position and will live to "fight another day." It is not unusual for some of the best in the business to enter a trade at a potential saturation point and sell it out several times before they capitalize on the real move in the stock.

SUMMING IT UP

Buying on offers and selling on higher offers is the most productive form of day trading. Opportunities are frequent, and the trades seem to feel so right. They are quick and efficient, and there is no need or cause to second-guess what you are doing. In sum, you were right! The mentality of successful trading seems to require no mentality at all. You thought something was going up, you bought it, it went up, and you sold it.

The most important things to recognize and reinforce in your trading are the factors that made you buy the stock in the first place. Why was the stock going up? How did you pick this spot to enter the trade? How did you recognize the pivot and capitalize on a reverse in momentum? All these questions can be answered with information provided by playing the market-maker game. It tells you where the momentum is stopping, it gets you physically involved, and it puts you in position to enter at a high percentage zone. These zones occur at the beginning of the pivot where momentum should be strongest.

Remember, buying on one offer and selling on a higher one is never a bad trade—even if the stock goes higher. With time, diligence, and practice, getting out of trades will become easier. The important part is when to get in. The market-maker game will provide you with these points. The greatest part of the game is once you learn it, you won't need it anymore. You will be able to recognize these situations and feel out the levels with a greater sense of efficiency without the need to place in numerous bids and offers. Instead, you will graduate to a level where you will only put in a few bids, and if you can't buy stock on the bid, you know you should buy stock on the offer as it turns up. This is where day trading really becomes fun and the trades seem to roll off your fingers. As in any other game, sport, or competition, you have to practice and to want to succeed more than the next guy. A day trader's most valuable asset is concentration. Focusing on the market-maker game has been the secret to many highly profitable day traders' successes.

In summary, find the pivot point, attempt to gain the spread by buying on the bid, and, if not, consider SOESing on the offer. Once you own it, get out when you can (while it is moving up), not when you have to (once it saturates and begins to pull back).

SURFING THE MARKET MAKERS' WAVES

Market makers have both ethical and somewhat shady ways to generate trading profits. The following are excellent examples of both the actions and the mentality of market makers. When reviewing these procedures, it is of paramount importance to be cognizant of what the "other guy" is thinking. The market maker is attempting to profit at the day trader's expense.

The Bulldozer Effect

The simplest manner in which market makers generate profits is to "move" the stock to a desired level and "put on a print" to clean up the order. Once this order is out of the way, market makers will attempt to cover at a favorable price. These traders have tremendous amounts of capital at their disposal, which they will use to run, or "tank," a stock in order to shake out other traders. These moves are commonly referred to as "short squeezes." They occur when traders push the prices of stocks high enough to make short traders cover their positions. These moves are brief and violent. However, recognizing the "bulldozer effect" at or near its genesis can produce a windfall gain for the astute day trader. A characteristic pattern of this bulldozer effect is observing a single firm buying large quantities of stock on the offer—by getting it from other traders in the office or by preferencing the Island which shows on FYI—while simultaneously going high bid. In summary, by pushing the price of the stock up, some of the shorts are forced to cover. This creates a chain reaction of other shorts trying to cover, which further accelerates the price upward.

Arbitrage

Another method used by market makers is arbitrage, or the existence of a simultaneous price difference between the different trading systems available on NASDAQ.

For example, the trader has just received an order from his customer to buy 10,000 shares of ABCD. If the market in ABCD is currently $48^1/_4 \times 48^3/_4$ and 5,000 shares are for sale on Instinet at $48^1/_2$ (Instinet is not required to display non-market-maker bids and offers on level 2), then the trader will put his name on the list of sellers at $48^3/_4$. He will tell his customer that he has just bought ABCD at $48^3/_4$, and simultaneously he will buy the Instinet stock that was offered at $48^1/_2$. The trader has a net profit of $^1/_4$ point on 5,000 shares, or $1,250, but is still short 5,000 shares in his proprietary account. He will either take his name off the list of sellers, while advertising to buy the stock, or wait to buy the stock back at a better price. The rationale behind this method is that even if ABCD does continue higher, the trader will have ample time to cover his short at the break-even point of 49. If ABCD moves down, however, the market maker stands to reap a significant profit.

In summary, if you are a market maker, buying at a lower price on Instinet for your proprietary account while selling to your customer at a higher price at the market price guarantees you an arbitrage profit.

Holding the Stock Down by Pushing the Spring Down

Somewhat similar to the aforementioned situation, market makers will often advertise as sellers when they are actually buyers. By holding the stock down while purchasing stock via other means and then lifting their offer following with a high bid, market makers can create a momentum that benefits their positions. A telltale sign of this practice is the market maker buying stock on an ECN such as Island, while he is actually advertised as the lowest offer in the current quote. However, the astute day trader must differentiate between one of two possibilities. Either the firm in question is simply covering a position it acquired by just fulfilling its responsibility as a market maker, or it is really establishing a position. Recognizing the difference requires extreme concentration and practice. Specific market makers have different styles of trading. They frequently repeat their styles of trading in certain stocks where these behaviors are recognizable.Concentration and focus over time will allow you to recognize these patterns.

Upside or Downside Overlaps

Upside or downside overlaps are another tool that market makers use to advertise or even mask their intentions. This situation occurs when the market in stock ABCD is $48^{1}/_{2} \times 49$ and the market maker advertises a 49 bid or even a $49^{1}/_{4}$ bid. These actions usually create a buying frenzy by day traders which subsequently pushes the stock higher. Contrary to popular opinion, this phenomenon is not an accident or a bad bid. To initiate this bid, the market maker must actually reprogram his quote machine, which is normally equipped with a fail-safe to prevent this exact situation. The market maker's intentions are either (1) to bull the stock higher so he can make a sale or (2) simply to advertise his intentions to possible sellers that he has a massive buy order. Some online trading systems will alert day traders to these situations. Upside and downside overlaps usually perpetuate violent market actions, which can prove either extremely lucrative or very costly—be careful!

ADDITIONAL TRADING TIPS

Timing

Different times of day and different types of markets should affect how you exit, or close, a position. In a trending market, you may try to let your profits run. In a sideways market, you may find making one level more realistic. Midday, most of the time, is relatively trendless. This is a good time to be more selective and not look for major moves. The biggest moves tend to happen at the opening and at the close. Traders can select some good stocks to trade during the "reaction" time period (typically between 9:50 and 10:10) and may like to sit in them as long as they keep going their way. Strong stocks will make a series of higher highs and higher lows. As long as this pattern is in place, you may want to stay with your position. If this pattern is broken, then you may not want to stick around. This pattern is created by market makers demanding a higher price each time new buying comes in and attempting to influence stocks back down during periods of weakness to buy back inventory or cover shorts.

The Ticker

Many systems will offer a ticker. Proper use should substantially improve the results of your trading. Some traders find chart patterns useful, while others follow stocks in the news. Assume that you have gotten a hot tip, or that you follow a certain research letter. The beauty of the ticker is that it doesn't matter what your criteria are. They can be technicals, fundamentals, news related—you name it. Just load the ticker up with stocks that may become movers, i.e., stocks that may provide opportunity. Let the ticker monitor the stocks you choose and alert you to movement in these stocks.

The best traders may find 30 or more potential stocks that meet their criteria each day. They use their ticker to tell them when the stocks they selected are moving. They use electronic executions to get instantaneous executions and use limit orders to get out before the upside momentum halts. Sometimes they make tidy profits in just seconds. Other times they stick with strong stocks for hours. It is best to constantly rotate to the stocks that are moving. By using their ticker effectively and constantly moving into the movers and getting out before the move ends, traders are able to amplify their buying power. It is not uncommon for top SOES traders to trade 30 to 40 times their capital during the course of the trading day without ever exceeding Regulation T (Regulation T restricts a public customer from trading more than two times his capital at any one time). An efficient trader will only tie up capital in stocks that are moving. This allows you to tie up cash only in the stocks that not only meet your criteria, but also are moving. **Proper use of your ticker coupled with electronic access and agile trading allows you to amplify your buying power many times by rotating your money out of stocks that are not moving and putting your money into stocks that are moving.**

EXITING POSITIONS

Always ask yourself how much you are willing to risk when you enter a trade. Always have a reason when you enter a trade. If that reason continues to exist and you haven't exceeded what you decided was an acceptable level of risk, then stick with your position. Exiting trades can be more difficult than entering trades.

Things to keep in mind: Do not expect to sell at the top. If you can consistently do this (no one can), then you will not have to trade for very long. **A profitable trade is a good trade.** Do not fret over selling a stock that goes up $2 more after you sold it. This will happen sometimes. You will tend to remember those times it went up, rather than the times that it went down $2 after you sold. If you are selling stocks that continue a lot higher after you sold, this is a good sign because it shows you are able to pick strong stocks. In time, you will learn when to let stocks run and when to take the quick profit. In time you will have the confidence to go back into a strong stock at a higher level than you last sold it. As your skills of interpreting the market improve, you will be more likely to make larger gains in the future.

By the way, there is nothing wrong with buying a stock that you sold earlier at a higher price than you sold it at and then selling it at even a higher price. If a stock is not in motion, there is little reason to trade it! As an online day trader, your edge is to trade stocks in motion, because you have the ability to get an execution when most traders cannot, especially when you are using SOES. If you choose to trade stocks not in motion, then you are generally trading at a disadvantage because you are giving up the spread. The exception to this rule is if you feel confident that there are real buyers in the stock and you choose to be the catalyst. Instead of waiting for someone else, you can ignite the movement by buying or selling the stock.

What should you do if you buy a stock in motion and it stops? You will generally improve your results by waiting for the motion to resume before exiting the position. If the stock is not moving and you get filled on a limit order, then the chances are very good that the stock is going to move in that direction. If the next move is back down, then you can hit the bid, which is what you would have done anyway. There is little harm done waiting, and you have left yourself an opportunity to profit. By the way, if the motion does resume higher, then do not just sell it on the offer, where you were originally hoping to sell it. You will, generally, be able to sell it up at least one more level in this situation. **Try and sell stock when others will want to buy it. And buy stock when others might have a reason to sell it. Good traders buy on the offer and sell on a higher offer. Learn to sell into strength.**

THE VWAP

Most of market maker firms' biggest customers are large pension funds, hedge funds, or large institutions whose commission dollars are an integral part of revenue and profits at these market-maker houses. Further, the actual traders are paid on the revenue they generate from these customers. Thus, keeping the customer happy is what keeps Bear Stearns on Park Avenue and a Porsche in the driveway of the trader. To do this, traders must provide their customers with better executions than their competitors would—i.e., better prices.

Furthermore, most institutional traders will explain the need "to beat the VWAP" (pronounced vee-wop) on large customers' orders. VWAP stands for value-weighted average price and connotes the average price at which the greatest volume of stock was traded on that day. Traders don't want to call their customers at the end of the day and explain why their buy order in ABCD was executed at an average price of 49.75 while the VWAP in ABCD on that day was 48.625. This is one of the reasons for abnormal fluctuations in prices of stocks. Traders who have to beat the VWAP will often run or kill a stock at the end of the day in order to make themselves look good in the eyes of their customers.

CONCENTRATION, FOCUS, AND DISCIPLINE

The aforementioned situations represent some of the myriad situations encountered by the day trader on a regular basis. Obviously, the best way to make money is to recognize who the respective buyers and sellers are in each stock and use that information to capitalize on trading opportunities as they arise. Every second of every trading day there are new opportunities, events, and catalysts that have excellent potential for profit. Trading for a living is not an easy profession, but it can be extremely rewarding.

The best way to sharpen your skills is to **concentrate, focus,** and **discipline** your efforts in a productive manner. These attributes will allow you to discern and even decipher the movements and ideology of market makers in their quest of the aforementioned goals. Understanding how and why market makers make their profit will allow you to make a profit. Surfing the market makers' wave is better than drowning in their wake.

CHAPTER 6

The Truth about Technical Analysis and Random Markets

The Talented Coin Syndrome. You set out to find a talented coin—one that likes to come up heads rather than tails. You start with fifty coins, toss them all and then discard all the ones that come up tails. You then toss the remaining coins and once again discard the ones that come up tails. You repeat the process until you are left with one or two coins which have always come up heads. All the evidence suggests that these particular coins prefer to come up heads. They have never failed in the past—why should they fail in the future? They are sure things!'

William Gallarher, Winner Take All

TECHNICAL ANALYSIS AND TRADING

There are countless books dedicated to technical analysis. This is what we think is most important. The truth about technical analysis is that both the traders and the academics are wrong. Neither of them understand why technical analysis may work. The truth is that good traders will make technical analysis work, and bad traders will not. Good traders will make more money, and bad traders will lose more money using technical analysis.

Some traders can make money being right as little as 25 percent of the time, or perhaps even less. They do this by making a great deal of money when they are right and only losing a little when they are wrong. Some traders are right 75 percent of the time, or even more, and still lose money. They do this by losing more money when they are wrong than they make when they are right. **Winners admit when they are wrong, and even more importantly they react when they are wrong.** Losers hope when they are wrong. Losers tend to quote fundamentals or research and forget the real reason they entered a position—a quick trading profit. They are like gamblers who double-down or play a martingale strategy. They say things like, "If only MU rallies, I will never try and pick a bottom again." Or they justify their decisions by saying, "It was just trading at 200; it's cheap at 120" (PRST for you newcomers, DEC for those of you who are veterans), as they watch the stock plunge another 50 or perhaps 100 points. Things that are cheap get cheaper. Any trader who can't take a loss might as well be an investor.

Winners, and even losers, will use technical analysis to help them to identify entry points. Whether these entry points are good or bad is far less important than what the trader does, and how he reacts to what happens after he enters a position. A winner will ask himself, "How much am I willing to risk?" A winner will actually stick to this amount if things do not work out. A loser will ask himself, "How much money can I make?" If and when this amount is attained, he will reconsider what he originally was willing to be satisfied with, believing he can make more. When things eventually turn, he is reluctant to make only a half a point in a position when he should have and could have made a full point. Before long, a loser turns his winners into losers.

Being on the wrong side of a trade or the market can become a very vicious cycle. If you are on the wrong side, it is very difficult to get on the right side. For example, a typical troubled trader decides he likes a stock so he buys it. It starts to go against him, he does not want lose again, so he offers it out. It starts to go lower, so he tries to hit the bid, but it trades ahead and the bid becomes the offer. He hopes to get lucky and sell it on the offer, so as not to incur a large loss. The market seems to be going out strong, and he feels that he has a good chance to get out at the offer. At the last second, he contemplates hitting the bid but decides it's already down $2 from the high and it will probably bounce in the morning. The next morning bad economic numbers are released. The trader determines that if it only opens down a little, then he will take his loss. The stock opens down sharply. The trader knows that he has let this go way too far against him. He rationalizes that if everyone loved it at 50, then it must be really great at 45. He considers buying more, thinking that he can get his money back if the stock only rallies a couple of points. Several points lower, having broken every rule he has ever learned, he sells out. Sure enough, as soon as he sells, the stock turns. The trader ends up selling the stock just when he really should have been buying it. But if he just sold it at 42, then how can he justify paying 43? The next thing you know, the stock is trading 45. The trader now realizes he was right all along and buys the stock at 45, only to watch it go lower, and repeats the same pattern that took place starting with not wanting to lose again. Following rules could have made all the difference here.

Start with not taking home losers, limiting losses, and never averaging down. Do not think about at what price you bought the stock (unless to limit your losses). This will cloud your thinking and has nothing to do with where the stock is going next. Do not get married to a stock. Do not return to a game you keep losing. Go on to the next opportunity; there will be another one in a second or two. Being obsessed with a losing position will surely affect your ability to find other winning situations. Be disciplined and have the conviction to stick to your rules.

We used to think that the key to profitable trading was to get on the right side, and perhaps there is some truth to this. To get on the right side, we relied heavily on technical analysis. Many traders get caught in this trap. They spend years trying every method searching for the philosopher's stone, always looking for a way to consistently pick the right entry point. But we are certain that the real key is to know when you are on the wrong side and to get off it. In order to determine when you are on the wrong side, the best tools you can use are rules and discipline. Discipline is nothing more than the conviction to stick to your rules. Rules take time to develop. Technical analysis can be used to determine entry and, equally important, exit points. The key is to use it for two purposes: (1) to generate ideas and (2) to determine lines in the sand (your entry and exit points). Seat-of-the-pants traders need discipline. In other words, those who trade by how they feel at the moment are affected by many other factors than just what the market is telling them. Technical work can help them eliminate other factors that affect their trading. A little science helps them to use their art more effectively and tempers the emotions.

You missed your train; it's raining; it's sunny; your significant other broke up with you; your kids kept you up; the bills are piling up; or you have lots of cash to spare—these can all be factors that have a major effect on how you react to what you see on the screen. If you use a little science to take the emotion out of your decisions, and combine this with a few rules that make you more disciplined, then your chances of being successful are greatly improved.

A good trader will make money with a poor system, and a bad trader will lose money, even with a great system. Having had the opportunity to meet and work with hundreds of traders, we have tested this hypothesis. We found that giving losers a good system does not make them winners. And if we give great traders a poor system, they will still come out winners. We will not discuss good systems. However, discussing a random system will help us make the point we really want to make. It will help us to explain the truth about technical analysis.

A control example is a system without any underlying logic, such as a random system. The random system can be as simple as flipping a coin to decide how to instruct a trader. If we flipped a coin and got heads, we would tell the trader to buy; and if we got tails, we would tell the trader to sell. Now we do not inform the trader that this is what we are doing. In fact, we tell the trader that we have developed a sophisticated model that we believe can forecast direction. He does not know how we are making our decisions. He only knows that there is a signal, a buy or sell signal depending upon what we tell him (which in turn depends on whether we get heads or tails on the coin flip). However, we have given him an entry point. When and how he chooses to exit this position is the biggest factor in determining if he will be successful in the long run. The point is that technical analysis can give traders a reason to enter a trade. What traders do after that is up to the trading rules they follow and whether or not they stick to them. These rules, and traders' self-discipline, are more important than the entry point.

The truth about technical analysis is that technical analysis can help traders determine when to trade and when not to trade. Technical analysis is widely followed. Therefore, even if the theory is nonsense, sometimes the theory will become a self-fulfilling prophecy. Markets are constantly changing, and the system that works now may not work tomorrow. In other words, it is easy to generate buy signals that work in a screaming bull market. However, in choppy markets the exit points can become more important than the entry point. Also, systems that worked well in previously bull markets may never work in bear markets.

Technical analysis can be a very useful tool to generate ideas and to help one develop discipline, if used properly. Markets change, but good trading rules do not. Disciplined traders with lots of ideas tend to make money and appear to use technical analysis successfully. Without technical analysis and the ideas it generates, these traders would be less successful.

Trading rules and ideas are sprinkled throughout this book. Winning ideas include **easing in and out of positions, not taking home losers, and not picking bottoms.** Many traders will benefit from these ideas. Many additional rules can be found or learned from reading *Reminiscences of a Stock Operator* by Edwin Lefevre. There are many good trading books that can help you to discover trading rules, and we recommend that you read as many as possible. It is always best to learn from others as much as possible before risking your own money. But the best rules that you will develop will come from keeping a diary of your own trading. Write down what you do when you trade well, and what you do when you trade poorly. In time, you will recognize what works and what does not work, and it will be up to you to have the conviction to follow these rules.

Use technical analysis. Take advantage of your ticker to only play the stocks in motion. Develop the discipline to follow the rules you make. Technical analysis is a useful tool; and combined with good rules, discipline, and perhaps proper trading tools, it will help increase profits.

As Lefevre wrote in *Reminiscences:* "There is what I call the behaviors of a stock, actions that enable you to judge whether or not it is going to proceed in accordance with the precedents that your observation has noted. If a stock doesn't act right, then don't touch it: because, being unable to tell precisely what is wrong, you cannot tell which way it is going. No diagnosis, no prognosis. No prognosis, no profit."*

CAN YOU MAKE MONEY IN A RANDOM STOCK MARKET?

In 1900, J. Bachelier published a paper in the *Annales Scientifiques de L'Ecole Normale Supérieure* demonstrating that the Bourse, the French stock market, was random. So it seems that the stock market is perceived and understood as random and efficient by the academics and the professionals. How is it, then, that when traders make money consistently, they feel there is some underlying order and that the market cannot be random?

This paradox of perception is resolvable. We will explain the definitions of "random" and then present one of many "random" models of

---

*Edwin Lefevre, *Reminiscences of a Stock Operator,* John Wiley & Sons, New York, 1923.

traders that allows day traders to evaluate their (1) stock picks, (2) entrance points, (3) exit points, (4) the market itself, and (5) the amount of money they should be making if they were "randomly" addressing the previous four points. We will also demonstrate that very consistent money can be made in a "random" stock market.

The model of the toss of a coin is "random" in the specific sense that each toss is independent of the previous toss and the coin has no memory. There is no correlation between tosses. This simple coin model is sometimes called a binary distribution. The chance of finding a run of two heads in a row is $\frac{1}{2} \times \frac{1}{2}$, or 1 chance in 4. The chance of finding a run of, say, five heads in a row is $\frac{1}{2} \times \frac{1}{2} \times \frac{1}{2} \times \frac{1}{2} \times \frac{1}{2}$, or 1 chance in 32. If one plots all the probabilities of all the combinations of chances of getting only heads, and heads and tails, and then only tails, one gets a binary distribution. How can you make money in a random stock market if there is no order? The answer to the question comes from reformulating the definition of "random" to determine which set of constraints or rules or patterns, when "randomly" combined, generates the model that best fits the data. The question for analyzing the stock market becomes: Which set of rules or patterns, when randomly combined, generates a model of the stock market that allows predicting, for example, the number of advancing stocks versus declining stocks for a day or the amount of money per share you should make in a random bull market?

We have run a set of experiments buying and selling about 20 different stocks a day in 100-lot shares in strong uptrending markets where advance-to-decline ratios were 2.5 to 1 and in strong downtrending markets (the day the Japanese prime minister, Hashimoto, casually remarked he might buy gold instead of U.S. Treasury notes) where the ratio of advancing-to-declining stocks was $\frac{1}{2}$ to 1. In this bull market this ratio spread of $\frac{1}{2}$ to 1 all the way to 2.5 to 1 for advancers versus decliners seems to cover the greater majority (over 80 percent) of the days observed. On the Hashimoto day, 0 cents per share was made; on the 2.5-to-1 day 50 cents per share or .50 dollar was made.

What do these ratios mean to each other? How are they related to earnings per share? Is earnings per share a fair measure? Can we set up a random model that relates these variables to each other? Yes we can, and we have.

Imagine that your ability to pick stocks is such that on the average you pick two gainers for each loser. At this point in the discussion, the picking strategy is your own. An optimum strategy will be discussed later.

Imagine that you put in stops on the downside of $\frac{1}{2}$ and you put in sell orders on the upside of $\frac{1}{4}$. That is, every time your stock goes up $\frac{1}{4}$ point, you take your profit. If your stock goes against you, then you get out at $\frac{1}{2}$ point. This is a very conservative strategy. It also fits in with the normal psychology of taking your profits when you can. One would think that with a good picking strategy of two gainers for each loser, one would make a lot of money.

However, if the stock market is random, then this strategy will not make any money. You can only break even. This can be calculated theoretically, and these theoretical results have been confirmed experimentally. In this raging bull market we traded over 10,000 shares of stock in 100-share lots on strong bull days when we picked advancers to decliners in the ratio of 2 to 1 and when the market overall had advancers to decliners in the ratio of 2 to 1. This predicted and experimentally confirmed profit and loss statement (P&L) of zero using this strategy tells us we now have a random model that relates pick strategy, entrance and exit points, and profit per share. From this random position we can now change and identify the various variables to test which will give us a positive P&L per share, and we can actually create a graph that relates the market ratio or pick strategy ratio to price per share. Needless to say, if your pick ratio is better than the overall market, you will make more money; but even if your pick strategy is a random pick of a bull market, you will still have a positive P&L per share.

Let us go back to the random model given above. We will explain why the expected P&L is zero. Suppose you pick three different stocks. If your pick ratio is 2 to 1 (which is considered an excellent pick ratio), then two of these stocks will go up and one will go down. Now your profit taking on the upside is $\frac{1}{4}$ on the upside and get out at $\frac{1}{2}$ on the downside you will make $(\frac{2}{1}$ times $\frac{1}{4})$ $\frac{1}{2}$ on the upside for the two trades overall. On the downside you will have one stock losing $\frac{1}{2}$ point. Therefore, the total profit for the day will be $\frac{1}{2}$, and the total loss for the day will be $\frac{1}{2}$. Thus, the overall P&L will be zero, even though your pick ratio is 2 to 1, winners to losers.

An examination of *Investor's Business Daily*'s "60 NYSE Stocks with Greatest % Rise in Volume" over several months shows that the average price change for up stocks is about $1\frac{1}{8}$ and the average price change for down stocks is about \$1. This is true for days that on the average have a 1.2 advancers-to-decliners ratio. This is the average ratio for this bull market. On days when the ratio is 2 to 1 or greater, the average price change for up stocks is about $1.5, while the downside stays about the same.

Therefore, given a random distribution for the number of stocks that are up about a dollar on a day, we can multiply by one standard distribution (67 percent) and find that the majority of stocks will hit somewhere between $\frac{5}{8}$ and $\frac{3}{4}$ of a point. Thus, for most strong up stocks in this bull market, we expect to see them gain at least $\frac{5}{8}$ of a point. Needless to say, they will on the average also go down $\frac{5}{8}$ of a point. Therefore, we now can see that in a good 2-to-1 market of up versus down, we can gain $\frac{10}{8}$ and lose $\frac{5}{8}$. On the average this is a gain of $\frac{5}{8}$ of a point per 3 shares, or 21.0 cents per share (if you subtract commission of 4 cents per share = 17 cents per share). However, 2-to-1 days occur, on average, in this bull market about once a week. The average ratio, as we said before, is about 1.2 to 1. This changes the average daily take to $\frac{6}{8} - \frac{5}{8}$ which is a profit of $\frac{1}{8}$ for 2.2 stocks or 6 cents per share (if you subtract commission of 4 cents per share = 2 cents per share profit). This is close to not making any money, though for 1 million shares it is a profit of $20,000.

How can you increase the daily take? Can you increase the average price increase in the stock picked? No. Can you increase the ratio of up stocks to down stocks to improve the 1.2 to 1 average daily ratio. Yes, but this requires external information that is available on the relative strength of the stocks picked versus the average, i.e., the S&P 500 and at least four other criteria (which we will discuss in general, and some of which are discussed in this book previously). However, even with powerful rules to pick strong stocks, you might move the pick ratio from 1.2 to 2, but usually not much more. The reason for this is that you don't know the direction of the market when it opens and you have to effectively probe the market as it moves in its general trend, usually doing as well as the trend and sometimes better. Can you decrease the average price loss in the stock picked? Yes, this is the one area in which you can manipulate the numbers to your advantage. You can cut your losses at less than the average. However, if you cut your losses too dramatically, then you also don't give a stock a chance to fluctuate, especially if it is a strong stock. Interestingly, this is the converse of the normal psychology of trading, but it is very clearly presented as the professional way to trade in *Reminiscences of a Stock Operator*. The normal psychology is to grab and keep a profit in a strong stock going up and to wait and hope for a weak stock to turn around when it is going down. The formula-rules presented here suggest that you can define an upside profit, but the money will be made by limiting the downside loss.

For instance, if we use the example of a 1.2 up-to-down ratio, and we take an upside profit of $^5/_8$ which will cover the majority of strong stocks and we limit our downside to $^3/_8$, we calculate that our profit per share is $^5/_8$ times 1.2 minus $^3/_8$ divided by 2.2 shares, which is 17 cents a share (minus 4 cents = 13 cents a share net profit). This is starting to look like real money. And this is on your average day.

One can argue that limiting the downside to $^3/_8$ is too tight, but we found it doesn't change the gainers-to-losers ratio too much. We have tested several upside profit-taking points against several downside exit points, and we have developed a general rule that seems to work in most markets—markets that vary from Hashimoto days to roaring bull markets.

Taking a $^3/_8$ exit point on the downside allows you, on the average, a 0 dollar profit at an 0.51 ratio of gainers to losers, $^1/_8$ of a dollar at 1/1 ratio, $^3/_{16}$ of a dollar at 1.2/1 ratio, $^2/_8$ of a dollar at 1.5/1 ratio, $^3/_8$ of a dollar at 2/1 ratio, $^4/_8$ of a dollar at 2.5/1 ratio, $^5/_8$ of a dollar at 3/1 ratio days, and $^6/_8$ of a dollar at 4/1 ratio days. The frequency of days having the various ratios follows a skewed distribution with a peak mean at 1.2/1 ratio, and tails at 0.5/1 and 3/1 ratio days. That is, most market days have a 1/1-to-2/1 ratio of advancers to decliners. These numbers were generated from our more recent bull market. However, as the market changes one can develop a shorting strategy that can give us a 1/1-to-2/1 ratio of winners to losers and this will be equivalent to the 1/1-to-2/1 ratio of advancers to decliners.

Therefore, when we are talking about good days, i.e., about once a week, where the ratio is 2/1 and the downside exit point is $^3/_8$ and you can take an upside of $^6/_8$, you are talking about $^{12}/_8$ minus $^3/_8$, or $^9/_8$ for each 3 shares, or $^3/_8$ of a dollar per share, or 38 cents a share. For a million shares this is $375,000. In actuality, this is a bit conservative, because on 2/1 days, the upside average can be $^7/_8$. This would give $^{14}/_8$ minus $^3/_8$ for each 3 shares, or 46 cents per share. This is getting close to half a million dollars profit for each million shares. To calculate the percentage yearly return we need to know the amount of capital needed to trade a million shares. In this market, a million shares cost about $100 million. Therefore, $^1/_2$ a million profit on $100 million per day is 0.5/100 return per day. This is equal to $^1/_2$ of a percent per day. However, not every trading day gives a return of 50 cents per share. On the average these 2-to-1 days show up 1 in five days. So we multiply $\frac{1}{2}\%$ per day times 300 trading days per year divided by 5 which comes out to 30% return per year, with relatively little risk.

We have added another strategy to this model, which allows us to find those stocks that do not pull back more than $\frac{3}{8}$ on their upward momentum, and continue to move at least 3 points. This allows a Fibonacci amplification of at least eightfold. For example, let us say MMM was at a new high and we bought 100 shares, at 103. As it moves up to $103\frac{3}{8}$, we buy another 100 shares. As it moves up to $103\frac{3}{4}$, we buy 200 shares, and so on. The Fibonacci series increases as the sum of the previous two in the series; i.e. 1, 1, 2, 3, 5, 8, 13, etc. Depending on how far the series continues, we will sell in a Fibonacci manner after $\frac{3}{4}$–1-point gain on each purchase. The return on this strategy is on the order of 0.75 cents per share. However, one needs to probe the momentum of at least 15 to 20 stocks, before one finds such a stock. This ratio seems to hold in 0.5/1 markets as well as 2/1 markets. In the better bull markets, one can usually find two such amplifications. The above two strategies can be combined. They are complementary. In addition, one can develop a shorting strategy as long as one develops a set of rules that give at least a 2/1-win pick ratio.

CHAPTER 7

How Can I Get Involved?

TRADING SYSTEMS

Online trading systems are currently experiencing explosive growth. This phenomenon is a result of technological advancements that have made it possible to provide a secure, affordable order entry system directly to the public. A rapidly growing number of brokerage firms are now offering online trading systems that compete on price and service. These systems make it possible for people to get accurate real-time market data and fast executions from almost anywhere. As a result of these services, traders now have access to information and executions that until recently were available only to professionals. Equally important, traders are now able to execute trades far cheaper than at any other time in history. Technology, low commissions, and a raging bull market have fueled the explosive growth of online trading.

Today's technology allows the user to send and receive massive amounts of data necessary for price quotes, technical and fundamental analysis, and up-to-the-minute news and market information through both conventional phone lines and the Internet. The result is a growing number of investors and traders who expect more services for less money, with many investors putting aside their traditional broker/customer relationships. Customers are finding the allure of entering their own orders through online services more appealing than relying on a broker. These systems are substantially cheaper, faster, and, in many cases, a better resource of information. As a result, online trading is quickly becoming the wave of the future for the brokerage industry.

Perhaps the most underestimated appeal of these systems, and the silent engine to their growth, is that *Online systems have leveled the playing field for the customer. Professional traders have long maintained an insurmountable advantage in cost, speed of execution, and real-time information. Electronic systems have closed a gaping hole and have made day trading a realistic profession for the non-exchange member. These systems enable the trader to use the strategies outlined in this book from anywhere. These systems give the trader a realistic chance to succeed in what is perhaps the most exciting, dynamic, and potentially rewarding career possible.*

As we write, many of these systems are evolving. We originally intended to give specific details and ratings of a variety of systems to meet a variety of trading needs. This approach proved pointless. Rapid changes in these systems made any evaluation obsolete. As a result, we have decided to present you with a framework of what to look for when considering an online trading system and a brief look at two systems we think should be worth considering.

There are two basic types of online access available to the trading public. First, there are the myriad of services available through the Internet. These systems are accessible via the Internet through some of the biggest names in the brokerage business (such as Dean Witter Discover's Lombard system, Waterhouse Securities' E*Trade, Ameritrade's Accutrade, and Quick & Reilly's QuikWay, to mention just a few). Second, there are online trading systems that link the customer directly to the clearinghouse through phone and modem or through dedicated lines. The firms that offer the online systems usually specialize in this type of trading and are generally not household names. They are well known by the upper echelon of savvy day traders who demand the fastest access to the markets. A few of the market leaders are Broadway Trading LLC, which offers Watcher; All-Tech Investments, which offers Attain; and Block Trading, which offers Cybertrader. Because these systems are directly linked to accounts via dedicated phone lines, the speed, efficiency, reliability, and security of entering orders is much greater than that which current technology can offer through the Internet. Both methods have advantages and disadvantages, and many of the factors you may want to evaluate are relevant to both:

EXECUTION: ORDER ROUTING

Perhaps one of the least understood factors in these systems is how they route the customers' orders. There are several ways that firms can route your orders—directly to the marketplace, to a firm trading desk, or to a regional exchange where a firm or entity actually pays your brokerage firm for the privilege of taking the other side of your orders.

In most cases, it is to the traders' advantage to have direct access to the marketplace. Most of the online dedicated phone systems route their orders directly to the exchange. This means that New York Stock Exchange orders will be sent directly to the New York Stock Exchange, American Stock Exchange orders will be sent directly to the American Stock Exchange, and NASDAQ orders will be sent directly to NASDAQ. Direct access to the markets gives traders fair access to the true market, where price is actually established, where they are most likely to receive a fair execution, and where there is also the opportunity to potentially receive a better price. Many professionals would not permit their orders to be routed any other way.

Many of the Internet services route their orders to their trading desk or to a third party. In both cases a trader or market maker frequently takes the other side of the order. These firms, just as specialists or market makers do, hope that they are able to attract enough order flow, so that they are able to prosper from making the spread on each transaction. Some firms actually pay other firms for the privilege of filling their customers' orders. This controversial practice is called "payment for order flow." Firms that route their customers' orders in this fashion receive commissions on both sides of the trade. Firms that pay for "the flow" attempt to profit from making spreads or by trading. These firms have the advantage of "leaning against the real market." They can always go to the real market if they need to cover a position. And generally they can guarantee the quoted market to firms that are willing to pay for orders. They are usually willing to take on most customers (other brokerage firms) on a trial basis hoping to attract retail business or orders that they believe they will have a high probability of profiting from. These firms will shy away from traders who make consistent money and will generally not provide guaranteed executions to any firm that seems to have more than the normal percentage of "smart money" accounts. It is widely perceived that orders routed to the third market (not to the main exchange) and NASDAQ orders that are not sent directly to NASDAQ are less likely to get a fair execution. Let's take a closer look at how this may work.

Suppose a customer wants to buy 500 GE when the market on the NYSE is 85 × 85$^1/_8$ (2000 × 5000). His brokerage firm routes the order to a regional exchange such as Boston or Cincinnati, where another firm, which is willing to pay for the privilege of filling the order, takes the other side of the transaction. The firm willing to take the risk of selling the stock to the customer hopes to buy the stock back at a lower price. However, if the stock appears to be moving up, then the firm may buy the stock back on the NYSE to avoid a loss. If the stock starts to go down, the firm will have the opportunity to cover its sale for a profit.

Most firms that engage in "either side of payment to order flow" are not fast to admit it. A phone call to several of the Internet providers above did not provide much insight. When asked how their orders were routed, most firms left us on hold or gave us the runaround until we gave up. **How, when, and where your order was executed should be indicated on your trade confirms,** but may or may not be easy to determine. Listed traders who have access to time and sales can do a neat experiment to quickly figure out how their orders are being routed. A good way to tell is to enter an order to buy an odd lot such as 137 shares. All transactions must be reported to the consolidated tape. A quick check of time and sales will tell you what exchange your order traded on.

NASDAQ traders can try a different experiment. NASDAQ trades take place only on NASDAQ regardless of who fills the order. What's important here is to assure that your firm is properly following the new order handling rules. These rules ensure that your order is either executed or represented in the market. Here's the test: Pick a stock that is at least a quarter of a point wide. Enter an order to buy or sell 100 shares or more (this rule doesn't pertain to less than 100 shares) in the middle of the market. According to the rules a firm must either fill that order or post it to NASDAQ. Limit orders can be represented either by a market maker or on an ECN such as Island, where they are shown on all level 2 screens and provide limit order protection for the customer. If your firm follows the rules, then you will get filled at your price before the stock trades at a worse price. See how long it takes to get an execution, or see your order become part of the quote (difficult to determine without level 2). Anything more than a few seconds and the firm is likely to be taking advantage of your order (the firm will fill only if it believes it is to its advantage). Some traders like to have a third party guaranteeing the other side of their orders because they feel that these firms will be forced to give them an execution that they might not be able to get in the real marketplace. On the other hand, many traders feel that orders that are not directly routed are only being executed when market conditions are favorable to the third-party firm and are conveniently being missed when the market conditions favor the customer. **Essentially, the customer is buying stock when he does not want it, and is unable to buy it when he really wants it.** Each system is different, but only systems that give you direct access to DOT, SOES, and ECNs ensure that the order is being fairly represented in the marketplace.

While brokerage firms that do not route their orders directly to the market generally can charge a lower commission, the money saved in commission may not be worth the extra savings if the executions are not as good.

QUOTE

Another significant difference between online systems and dedicated systems is the quote that each provides. NASDAQ provides several levels of quotes which disseminate varying levels of information to the user. Internet systems generally provide the user with a level 1 quote. Level 1 quotes display the inside bid and offer prices as well as the number of market makers willing to buy and sell at those prices. For example, a typical level 1 quote might read: INTC $128^1/_4 \times 128^3/_8$. This quote provides you with the basic information necessary to see where the stock is trading.

A level 1 quote is fundamentally inadequate for gauging real market-maker interest in the stock. First of all, it doesn't tell you who is bidding or offering stock. You would have no way of knowing if you were attempting to sell stock to GSCO (a big fish) or NITE (a small fish). Second, you have no way of knowing how much stock each market maker is advertising to buy or sell. There can be one market maker on the bid willing to buy 10,000 shares and one market maker on the offer willing to sell 100 shares. A trader looking at the level 1 quote will not be able to determine which market makers are willing to buy and which are willing to sell.

Fortunately, NASDAQ has another quote option that shows not only the number of market makers on the bid and offer, but also the amount they are advertising to buy or sell, as well as the actual name of the market maker. This level 2 quote is accessible on most online trading systems and is an invaluable tool for gauging the strength and size of stocks as well as finding out who the key players are. The same quote on a level 2 screen might read:

INTC 10 128¼   GSCO   ×   1 128⅜ MSCO
                                1 128⅜ SALB
                                1 128⅜ MLCO
                                1 128⅜ PRUS

A major reason that most Internet systems do not offer this service is primarily due to cost. NASDAQ charges each user a fee to view these quotes, and most online systems do not want to incur this additional expense. A second reason (the one they don't want you to know) is that level 1 makes it easier for market makers to trade around, or "game," customer orders. If you cannot see who is on the bid or offer and the size, then there is no way to tell if your order is being represented properly in the marketplace. Market makers may be able to profit from your order flow by executing orders when market conditions are favorable to them. Therefore, active day traders will want access to a level 2 quote to ensure that they are getting the most complete market information available. Trading with a level 1 quote definitely puts the trader at a disadvantage as the trader is unaware of the size or the players in the marketplace, which may influence a stock's direction.

OTHER CONSIDERATIONS

If you made it through the first two criteria and still have not narrowed the field, here are some additional things to consider:

1. How important are fast executions? As with order routing, active day traders need to be able to get to stock *fast!* This obviously gives them the greatest opportunity to capitalize on short-term price fluctuations. Others may feel that fast execution is important, but they are not relying on it to make money. Furthermore, it is valuable to know whether or not you have done a trade, and slow execution time can be very detrimental to the trader's P&L, as well as the trader's psyche. If you do not have confidence that you will be able to easily and efficiently enter and exit positions, it can become mentally damaging to your ego. This holds especially true when attempting to exit losing positions.

2. Is the system reliable? This is one of the most critical aspects to weigh when choosing a trading system. There is nothing worse than being in positions and having your access to the market cut off. As with any other type of disaster, these problems usually never occur when the market is inactive but rather (as uncontested proof that Murphy's law truly exists) when Alan Greenspan is explaining to Congress that the market has reached a state of "irrational exuberance" and "unbridled euphoria" and your positions are the most bullish they have been in weeks. (It is rumored that if you listen very carefully, you can actually hear the crackling sound of your money being burned at a such a high rate, with such intensity, that it could power a small city.)

As a general rule, online systems will be more stable than an Internet connection. If you plan to be on all day, you might want to pay the extra money for a dedicated connection. This will pay for itself many times over, as it deters these nasty little mishaps. If you are able to get through to the brokerage firm's customer service department, ask a few questions. How long has the system been in use? (A year is a long time.) How many customers trade on the system? How much volume is transacted daily through your system? How often does the system go down? (If the firm says never, it is lying—even NASDAQ and DOT have gone down occasionally.) Ask the representative how long he has been with the firm. And also inquire about alternative ways to do a transaction if the system is having problems. Keep in mind that if you had trouble getting through now, it is not likely you will be able to get through when hundreds of calls hit the switchboard when a problem arises. Reliability is extremely important. Don't overlook this issue.

3. Is the system easy to use? When evaluating a system, it is important to be aware of the actual physical mechanics that will be necessary to execute trades as well as monitor your account and positions. Some systems make you toggle back and forth between pages to perform different functions. The best systems display all relevant and necessary information on one page. This page should serve as a window to your account and also provide execution capabilities. There is obviously no benefit in placing the order on one page, checking to see if it was executed on another, and looking at current positions on a third. If you do choose one of these systems because you rely on its charting capabilities or you get free news on it, make sure that the time it takes to toggle between pages is minimal, as it will aid you in getting fast executions.

Another aspect to consider regarding ease of use is whether or not you want to use a system that relies on a mouse, keyboard, or combination of both. Make sure that the keyboard functions are logically mapped out so you do not have to think too much when making a trade. You should be focusing on the trade rather than worrying about whether or not you are pushing the right buttons or if you double-clicked with the right key on the mouse instead of the left. You also want orders to be entered with a single keystroke rather than having to type out the full instructions. This is time-consuming, and unless you are really prepared, it will undoubtedly result in missed opportunities. How easy is it to enter orders? How easy is it to cancel orders? How easy is it to determine where you stand?

4. Is the system safe? You will want to make sure that the only possible person with access to your account is you! Ask the company if there have been any instances of hackers who broke into the system. (One could just picture the joy on a hacker's face as he sees how much Intel he could short in a screaming bull market before anyone finds out.) Make sure there are ample passwords, phone numbers, or access codes that will ensure your safety and peace of mind.

5. What services does it offer? This will be one of the greatest factors when determining which system to use. Ask yourself what is most important to your trading and see which system best fits your needs. There will probably be some tradeoffs. If you want the fastest speed, then you may have to give up charting, as this requires vast memory and slows the system down. If news is important, then you may end up paying an expensive monthly fee. Some systems are designed strictly for trading NASDAQ stocks, while others will let you trade anything from pork bellies to illiquid Japanese bonds. We found that systems designed to do a lot tended not to do any one thing all too well. On the other hand, systems that were designed to just trade one market tended to serve their purpose well.

When evaluating Internet and Online systems, you must also decide what features or services are most important to you. News, charts, technical analysis, and market summaries are some features of interest. Systems that provide an abundance of these features may demand a greater commission in return for these services. Many traders are satisfied with the news available through CNBC. Anything more informative is likely to be costly and perhaps not worth the added expense. Market summaries are important and can be used to help determine relative strength and the overall trend. Information such as the change in key indexes could prove useful, but it is available on CNBC. Charting packages and technical analysis are nice if they don't lead you to overanalyze each trade. Many good traders review this information outside of the market hours; others won't make a trade without reviewing it first.

6. How much does it cost? All people like to feel as if they are saving money or getting a good deal. The real question here is, Are you really saving money if you trade with a super-low-cost provider? The answer lies somewhere between the old adages "You get what you pay for" and "Less is more." While it is true that some of the fastest systems may cost a little more than others, the benefits of getting to stock fast far outweigh the extra cost of the trade. We would much rather pay $0.02 per share (or $20 per thousand) and be able to get executions when we want than $0.01 (or $10 per thousand), using a system that did not provide direct access to the market. On the other hand, if you are extremely active and you can save a couple of bucks by using a comparable system that may not have quite as many features, then you might be better off. Other things to consider are whether the firm is billing you by the share or by the trade. You will have to crunch the numbers and look at your average trade size to see which is better for you. The good news is that with increasing competition for customer accounts, the recent price trend has been on a downslide and some services will even let you trade for $10 a trade or cheaper. If they charge per ticket, ask them how they define a ticket. A market order could get filled at more than one price or in NASDAQ by more than one market maker. Some firms may consider this trade more than one ticket. If they charge per share, ask them if there is a minimum charge per trade. Ask if there is a charge for canceling an order. Also, ask if there are any additional charges, such as monthly fees or a minimum number of trades, before reaching a conclusion on this issue.

   7.   What types of hardware and software are needed? Some systems require that you have a computer equipped with the latest chips and expanded memory, while others may see your computer as a "dummy" terminal that simply sends your keyboard messages to a "real" computer that does the processing at another location. Most Internet trading systems are designed for use with regular computers and do not require a turbocharger to handle the workload. You will also want to check the baud rate of your connection. Remember that speed is a critical aspect for profitable trading. Fast high-quality modems and big high-resolution monitors are generally necessities with most systems.

   You will also want to check if the firm charges you for use or installation of software. Most systems are free, and you should negotiate if you choose a system that intends to charge you.

   8.   Do I need to be on it all day, or am I just going to use it periodically? Remember that with any system, you will be tying up a phone line. Do not rely on one line to service your personal phone needs as well as provide you with trading access. It might even be smart to have two lines with different carriers. If AT&T goes down, it is comforting to know that you can plug in the MCI line to get out of your positions. Is the service going to be a local call or long distance? If you find a system that requires a long distance call, past experiences dictate that you pay a little extra money for a quality line from a reputable company. Other services may be cheaper, but the quality may not be as good. This could cause costly delays in your data feed or, worse, result in missing data. You will also get better response time from customer support staff if you have a problem.

9. How is the customer service? You do not want to be unsure of a trade and not be able to speak to a representative who can quickly and efficiently give you the status of your account. You may want to call and see how quickly you can get a competent individual to answer a few questions before you open your account. Ask a few questions about the system. Considering testing the representative's knowledge. Ask questions like, "Can I enter a GTC (good to cancel order)?" See if the representative knows what you are talking about. Try a question about shorting, or perhaps ask how long the representative has been with the firm. Incompetent assistance can be more frustrating than not getting through at all. The rapid growth of these systems has left many firms with few truly competent people.

10. Are the portfolio management tools good? A good system will include features that will make your job easier. A system should track your trades, your P&L, and your positions. Does the system dynamically update your account? Does it keep track of your open orders, open positions, and available buying power? Is this information readily available? Will you always know where you stand?

11. What about interest and margin? Many traders overlook this. Ask if you will receive interest on your credit balances and what they will charge you on your debit balances.

Perhaps the most important thing to take from this is that you need to choose the system that is right for you! Only you can ultimately determine this. You will find that there are many tradeoffs, and none of the systems will be perfect. You should ask yourself a few questions before making your final choice. How much money can I afford to risk? How often do I plan to trade? What is the typical size lot I plan to trade? What markets do I plan to trade? Answering these questions should help you choose the right system. Internet systems are more than adequate for the part-time trader or investor who does up to 10 trades in a day. Generally speaking, several Internet access systems provide acceptable access to the listed markets. Here a second or so may not be critical. Internet systems generally offer a broader scope of markets, with some offering access to mutual funds and options in addition to the basics. Internet systems can be inexpensive, efficient ways to access the markets. Traders can open an account with as little as $3,000 and trade small lots. Many of the strategies recommended in this book can be used through these systems. Only a few offer access to level 2, SOES, and ECNs.

Online systems generally require higher balances, with many requiring at least $50,000. These systems provide a significant edge when trading the NASDAQ market. Generally, the better ones will offer access to level 2 quotes, as well as to SOES and ECNs. Reliability is a critical factor with these systems. These systems are generally designed for traders who want to trade 1,000 shares or more at a time and demand the fastest possible executions. These systems are generally more expensive since they require that you connect over the phone lines or use a direct connection. Attain and Watcher can be used from anywhere. Watcher will work through a regular phone line. The best of these systems can provide the trader with an edge in the market and can be well worth the added expense for active traders (10,000 or more shares traded a day). If you are interested in doing this for a living, then you will probably want to consider an online system.

The bottom line is each trader must decide which system is best suited to his or her individual needs.

WATCHER AND DATEK ONLINE

This book is written for serious day traders. It provides proven strategies for successful day trading that can be used by all traders. And it also provides an innovative approach to successful day trading that can best be used with specific order entry systems that we, the authors, believe are the cutting edge in technology. This section is written to introduce you to the trading systems that we believe will provide you with an edge. These are the systems that we use, and you should be aware of the advantages they offer.

Serious day traders must have reliable access to information and the markets. They must be able to get fast, accurate executions. They need to be able to know the status of their positions, their orders, and the stocks they are considering trading. Day traders need information and liquidity.

Datek Online and Watcher offer these features coupled with what we believe are superior executions. These superior executions are based on how these systems route their customer orders.

Datek Online offers fast, accurate, inexpensive executions for both listed and NASDAQ stocks over the Internet. Most firms route their listed orders directly to the floor of the exchange, where they have the opportunity for price improvement. Other firms route their orders to what is referred to as the third market, where they are in some cases guaranteed a fill at the best advertised price. Datek Online attempts to take advantage of both.

TRADE LIKE A NASDAQ MARKET MAKER

Both Datek Online and Watcher have direct links to Island and allow customer to quickly and easily take advantage of the power of entering orders on Island. This allows traders to actually participate in the NASDAQ market. Orders entered into Island that are not immediately executed become part of what is equivalent to NASDAQ's limit order book. Thus, these orders will have what is referred to as limit order protection, which means that stock cannot trade at a worse price without this order being filled. Island orders are part of the market. Traders with the ability to enter orders on Island have the ability to determine price.

Watcher and Datek Online also take advantage of what is called Island divergence. In simple terms this means that all orders entered on Island will attempt to match with other orders entered on Island before being sent through other means of execution. Island divergence frequently results in pairing of customer orders and instantaneous unrestricted executions.

This section is written to give a brief insight into two systems that we feel confident in recommending. While it is true that the technology is certain to change, we believe that these systems are the leaders. They are the cutting edge and are continually being updated to be the cutting edge. Both systems route their orders extremely efficiently and provide fast executions. Both systems are extremely reliable, and one of the two should generally appeal to everyone. As you will find with all these systems, there are certain tradeoffs. But we hope that this section will help you to spend more time trading and less time worrying about what system is best for you.

THE AVERAGE TRADER

For the average investor or day trader, we recommend Datek Online. We have found this system to be an inexpensive, reliable, and efficient method of accessing the markets via the Internet. Datek Online offers trading in both NASDAQ and listed securities. Orders are routed in the most efficient manner possible and are frequently paired with other customers' orders. Datek Online offers many of the tools necessary to implement the strategies outlined in this book. One major drawback is that at this time, Datek has not incorporated level 2 quotes into its service. We anticipate they will introduce this service in the fututre. This system provides everything one needs to get started trading both listed and NASDAQ stocks. Once level 2 is introduced, this system will provide all the tools necessary to apply the more advanced strategies featured in this book. Many of the features mentioned, including charts and portfolio management tools, are more than adequate here. This system should appeal to those who must have the flexibility to trade listed and NASDAQ as well as the flexibility to enter orders for various amounts. For speed and reliability this system will be difficult to beat.

POWER OF WATCHER

This section on Watcher is intended for those of you who plan to take day trading a little more seriously and for those of you who are considering trading for a living. This section is written to introduce you to the online trading system that we believe will give you a special advantage. This book has provided proven strategies for successful day trading—strategies that can be used by all traders and many that can be used with all systems. However, traders who want to maximize their ability to apply what is taught in this book should consider trading on Watcher. Watcher is specifically designed to trade NASDAQ stocks. Watcher does not as of yet offer access to anything other than NASDAQ. Rather than offer the gamut of services, Watcher focuses on dominating a market where it actually offers a trader an edge.

Watcher is the most powerful tool available to NASDAQ day traders today. It is geared toward customers who trade frequently during a typical day and primarily trade lots of 1,000 shares or more at a time. Watcher provides vital trading information, instantaneous quotes, powerful tickers, and the fastest executions available anywhere. It is not uncommon for Watcher traders to do several hundred trades a day.

Watcher dynamically updates your trading statistics, essentially eliminating many of the tedious tasks, such as ticket stamping and tracking positions, that take time away from making money. It tracks your profits and losses, number of transactions, exposure, and amount of capital you are using. Furthermore, it allows you to review all transactions that you have entered into during the day. It also calculates your average profit on each transaction on a cumulative basis or on an individual stock basis. Watcher allows you to review your profits by stock or by transaction on a daily or monthly basis.

Watcher tracks market-maker movement in four locations, which a trader can view simultaneously. It allows you to focus on inside market changes for all stocks, market-maker movement in stocks you select to follow more closely, the quote window in stocks you are considering executing an order in, and the position window for stocks in which you currently hold a position. Watcher also alerts traders to institutional buying and selling via the FYI (For Your Information) feature. Because of the enormous volume on Watcher, FYI has become an invaluable method of deciphering market-maker order flow. Watcher uses colors and arrows in a format that allows you to easily process an enormous amount of information, enabling you to maximize trading opportunities. Furthermore, it informs you of big gainers and losers, locked markets, news, and indexes (including the Dow Jones, the S&P cash and futures, and the NASDAQ composite).

In addition to keeping you abreast of all of the above-mentioned information and statistics, Watcher provides you with the most powerful execution system available. The system is designed for speed and efficiency and allows orders to be entered directly by the trader with a simple keystroke. Watcher also allows you to easily enter market orders and limit orders and to access Island.

The Island is a unique execution system that eliminates many of the limitations of SOES. The Island is a virtual trading market with its own trading characteristics. It has no size restrictions or time restrictions. The Island can be used by both the professional and the nonprofessional trader. Furthermore, it provides virtually instantaneous executions at frequently improved prices. The Island is growing everyday and has the potential to be the future of electronic day trading.

Watcher is a proven system that currently dominates SOES and Island executions. It is constantly being enhanced, upgraded, and kept on the cutting edge. It eliminates the need for registered order entry personnel and creates a paperless system of tracking transactions, which saves time. No other system provides the information, the executions, and the results that it does. The authors believe that if you are trading NASDAQ stocks on any other system, then you are trading at a severe disadvantage.

See Appendix A for the Watcher guide.

CHAPTER 8

A Trader's Philosophy

DEVELOPING YOUR OWN PHILOSOPHY

The market is nothing more than a vehicle for making and losing money. Some traders think that because they are long or short a thousand shares, it will change the course of events that are about to unfold. Assume responsibility for your own actions. An individual who looks to lay blame elsewhere will never grow. Consider keeping a diary. Make notes of things you do when you trade well and things you do when you trade poorly. Study the reasons for your successes and failures. Develop your own trading philosophies. Make your good ideas habits. Eliminate your bad habits from your trading. Review your bad habits when you are doing well. This will help you to avoid slumps. Review your good habits when you are doing poorly. This will help you to return to your winning ways faster.

Part of trading is losing. You must be able to accept this. If you find yourself down, then how you got there is no longer relevant. Don't dwell on it. The longer you do, the longer you will remain stuck there. Don't wallow in your own self-created misery. You have choices. Make the changes that will be to your benefit and not to your detriment. Take action!

Listen and observe what is going on around you. Use this information to help you make your own decisions and learn as much as possible from others' mistakes, as well as their successes. Find someone who is getting the results that you want and learn everything that you can from that person. This approach will work much more effectively than trying to reinvent the wheel. However, while it is important to absorb as much as you can from all available sources, it is equally important to **think independently.** Remember, it is your money you will be risking, and an approach that is appropriate for one investor might be totally inappropriate for another.

Be disciplined, patient, and selective. There will be countless opportunities to make money during the course of the day. Sometimes the hardest thing to do is to sit in front of the screen and just do nothing. Wait until you recognize the opportunities that exist. You should be able to identify the reason for entering into every trade. Do not trade just to trade. Remember, you can only make money if another investor or trader, who would prefer to be the one to make the money, does not. Keep in mind that even if all the right reasons exist to enter a trade, this does not assure you of making money. Trading is not an exact science, and nothing will work all the time. On certain days taking quick profits works best; on others letting profits run works best. But limiting losses works best on all days.

CHOOSING STOCKS TO WATCH

- Remember that a good way to get started is to trade stocks under $55, $1/4$ of point wide or less. This will help you to minimize risk while you are learning.
- Look for stocks that move frequently. The average daily range should be at least five times the spread between the bid and the offer.
- Keep in mind that the most obvious stocks to trade are also the most competitive.
- Use a ticker to help you to anticipate motion.

INCREASING YOUR CHANCES FOR SUCCESS

- Take note of the time of day. Be selective in the middle of the day.
- Use limit orders. Don't give up the spread twice.
- Know where the motion started.

- Buy up stocks. Sell down stocks.
- Do not trade stocks you consistently lose money in.
- Be aware of underlying trends.

HELPFUL HINTS

- Stocks move in the path of least resistance. If it is hard to buy, it is going higher. If it is hard to sell, it is going lower.
- If the stock is supposed to go higher and it doesn't, it is going lower.
- Only play stocks in motion. This is where your edge is. Any other attempts to play this game will start with a disadvantage.
- Identify the catalyst that triggers any other short-term traders' actions. This will help you to anticipate and react more effectively. Try to be the catalyst instead of waiting for one.
- There is nothing harder than trying to pick tops and bottoms. Strong stocks are strong for reasons, and weak stocks are weak for reasons. Buy up stocks; and sell down stocks!
- Watch industry and market leaders for clues to determine strength and weakness of market.
- Be aggressive in trending markets. Be selective in markets that lack a trend.
- Play market maker, use limit orders to open, and make spreads work for you.
- Try to establish who the real buyers and sellers are in a given situation.
- Get out when you can, not when you have to.

HABITS OF A SUCCESSFUL TRADER

1. Take a position only when you perceive that you have an edge.
2. Acts frequently on initial instincts.
3. If you find yourself hoping or wishing, get out and go on to the next trade.
4. Think independently!

5. Don't get married to a stock or a position. Don't try and win a game you keep losing. Recognize that every second of every minute there is another opportunity to make money.

6. When losing money with a position, take the loss by the end of the day.

7. Don't let an eighth get in your way.

8. Assume responsibility for your actions.

9. Play smaller when things are going bad.

10. Study reasons for your success and your failure.

11. Discipline! Discipline! Discipline! Discipline! Discipline!

A WINNING PHILOSOPHY

As a trader, you must understand the product, the players, and the market. You should also understand related products and related markets. But, most of all, you must understand yourself and your actions. You must make your own decisions and not be swayed by others. It is your opinion that counts. It is your money that you will lose. If you do not have an opinion or are not sure, then you should sit and wait. There will be plenty of other opportunities. As a trader, you must recognize when you are wrong. However, just recognizing your mistakes is not enough. You must also admit being wrong by taking some action. When you react, you are no longer wrong, and you can then attempt to get back on track. If you take no action, then you are just left hoping. This is a sure sign that you should have acted. However, when a bad trade is made, not all is necessarily lost. You can learn from your mistakes. In addition, as a smart trader, you can learn from other people's mistakes.

Ignorance, greed, fear, and hope could be your worst enemies. You must look at the big picture. When you have what you want, take it and run. Don't wait for the market to take the money back. You must now watch out. You're most vulnerable to getting caught up with your success. As a trader, you must realize that nobody wins all the time. However, if you win more than you lose, then you are ahead.

Perhaps, no trading philosophy would be complete without suggesting that you buy low and sell high. After all, nobody ever made money doing anything else. But you must recognize that buying at the

bottom and selling at the top is a rare feat. If your opinion has changed, whether winning or losing, then it is never too soon for you to act.

Most of the chapters in this book are derived directly from our personal experiences as well as insight inferred from teaching others. Online traders hail from a myriad of diverse backgrounds, and prior experience is not necessary.

Our goal here is not to tell you that our methods, combined with these systems, are the only means to day trading success. Rather, our aim here is to provide you with the knowledge, techniques, and discipline that are used by an elite rank of day traders who consistently yield the highest returns in the business. We cannot tell you exactly when to push the buttons, but we can show you the situations when pushing the buttons works to your advantage. A great number of day traders who have studied and applied these ideas have become phenomenally wealthy during the past few years. We can only hope that you too will enjoy the great success that these individuals already have enjoyed.

Trading for a living for many of you is likely to be completely different from any other previous career or job you may have had. For others, trading your own money or using an online system may be a completely new experience. Keep in mind that it takes time to learn a new field. Trading is certainly not an exception. Even if you study this book carefully, it will still take time to consistently apply these techniques with favorable results. Think of the first time you took a tennis, golf, or even piano lesson. Once you were taught the skills, it took practice and repetition to learn to apply them. The same goes for many of the approaches you will learn about trading from this book or any other reference. Trading for a living is an extremely challenging endeavor. It constantly changes, yet in many ways stays the same. If you are successful at trading, then you can potentially make more money than you ever dreamed of making.

However, to be a good trader, you have to be a good loser. A big part of trading is losing. Everyone makes winning trades. It's those who do not lose as often or as much who come out ahead. We have presented you with strategies and systems that we use firsthand and have taught hundreds of others to use successfully. It's up to you to be disciplined enough to take advantage of the framework we have presented.

When starting, limit the risks you take. Start with the following conservative strategy. Pick 10 to 15 stocks you would like to follow, which are between $5 and $55. Make sure that the bid/ask spread is a quarter of a dollar wide or less. An exception to this rule can be made if you are applying the market-maker technique described earlier in this book, where you are trying to use the spread to your advantage. Look for stocks that move frequently; the average daily range should be at least five times the bid/ask spread. If you are not sure of the range, either get to know the stock better or consider looking at a historical chart to determine if the stock fits these criteria. Charts can be found through numerous inexpensive online services and/or from daily chart books. Stay away from the hot stocks of the week and the most well-known names. You do not need to compete with the smartest market makers and countless day traders from day 1. Choose stocks the average person never heard of and make sure that there are at least three or four market makers on each side of the market. That will give you more of an edge. Once you are satisfied with the results you are getting, you may consider some of the more competitive or risky situations. However, do not take on more risk until you have profited from stock transactions that fit within this framework. If you cannot make money at the $5 table, do not sit at the $100 table!

Many new traders are so anxious to get started that they frequently push the wrong keys or buy the wrong stocks. Take your time learning the system you use. If you do make a mistake, it is usually best to take a small loss and just continue. Do not let a mistake turn into a big loser. Whether you bought a stock by mistake or not, one helpful rule is to concentrate on where it's going next. Do not worry about where you bought it, unless you're limiting your losses. This is a very common mistake traders make. They bought ABCD at 50 so they do not want to sell it at $49\frac{1}{2}$. The next thing you know, it is trading at $47\frac{1}{2}$.

Stocks move in the path of least resistance. If it is hard to sell, then it is going lower. If a stock is hard to buy, then it is going higher. If a stock is supposed to go higher and it doesn't, then it is going lower. Do not fight the tape. This is a losing play for the individual day trader.

Do not buy down stocks and do not short up stocks. Stocks that are down are down for a good reason. Cheap stocks get cheaper. Stocks that are up are up for a good reason. Stocks that are high go higher. Yes, buying down stocks and shorting up stocks will work sometimes, but your chances are better staying with the trend and not fighting it. It is true that market makers by definition do sell into strength and buy into weakness. If you acted as a market maker and did this with thousands of stocks, earned commissions for doing it, had the spread working for you, and had the capital to weather the storms, then you would make money doing this, too. Otherwise, you have no shot!

Good trading generally entails getting smaller when things are going bad and getting bigger when things are going well. A sure sign of a losing trader is one who is generating margin calls on days he or she is losing money. If you buy a stock and things are going your way, then consider buying other stocks. Perhaps your timing and general read of the overall market is right today. However, if stocks you are trading are not moving in your direction, then do not add to your positions. Look to get smaller. In general, you need to make as much money as possible when the opportunity is there and lose as little as possible when the opportunity is limited. There will always be other opportunities. Remember, trending markets and stocks have more potential than sideways or choppy markets for non-market makers.

Limit your losses. Only you can determine what is right for you, but whatever you decide, make sure you stick to it. Many traders limit themselves to one or two levels, at the most. This means that in a stock that is a quarter of a dollar wide, they do not let themselves lose more than half a point. While this might not seem like much, any more can add up quickly. Remember that you are a trader and not an investor. Set a limit on what you are willing to lose per trade and also per day, and make sure you stop at this point. Another good stop point is likely to be the point at which you find yourself hoping or wishing. This is a good sign to get out. Do not let yourself get married to a position. Recognize that every second of every minute of the trading day there is another opportunity. There is no reason to insist on being there when a stock in which you have taken a beating turns. Do not let one bad day or a bad position ruin a week or month or even a year of hard work. We have seen this happen. Perhaps the most important rule we ever learned from trading is never to take home a losing position. Sure stocks come back sometimes, but in the long run this rule is a must: **Do not take home losers.**

Take home winners. Winners are generally good to take home, and in the long run this will prove profitable. In fact, some traders build a whole career around taking home other people's winners. They do this by buying stocks in the last hour that are up on the day, that are trading on good volume, and that go out strong. This strategy tends to work because the market makers in these stocks usually are forced to go home short. With this in mind, any buying pressure at all the next morning will generally push the stocks higher, while selling pressure can be absorbed by the market makers covering their shorts. *A few words of caution here:* Overnight trades equal higher risk and therefore higher returns. Be respectful of earnings releases, expected news, or the potential for unexpected news. *Barron's* lists some of the upcoming earnings. Also, companies will generally tell you their earnings release date if you care to call them. In addition, be careful with options and futures expirations. They can cause unusual moves that tend to reverse the following morning. Expirations and their effects are generally scheduled for the third Friday of the month, but sometimes positions can be unwound earlier.

SUMMARY

In this book, we described why this is the best time in history to day trade, presented proven strategies for trading both listed and NASDAQ stocks, offered a framework to interpret the intentions of the players in the market, demonstrated how to gauge the overall strength of the market, and discussed the most advanced technology available. The strategies presented can be used to some extent with any system, but are best suited for online trading. All work extremely well in the right situations, and they can all work poorly in the wrong situations. They will all help you to gain an understanding of how stocks move and how market makers and specialists react to different situations.

The market-maker strategy will teach you the timing necessary to get fills using limit orders. Furthermore, the market-maker strategy substantially increases your profits by cutting down the amount of times you give up the spread in both entering and exiting trades. While we emphasize using the market-maker strategy to trade NASDAQ stocks, the concepts can be applied, using limit orders to gain the spread and market orders (instead of SOES) when you must have the execution, to trading almost any market.

In addition to these strategies, you should have gained an understanding of how to anticipate and gauge the strength of the market, the industry groups, and the individual stocks. Look for clues to deciphering what the market makers' and the specialists' intentions really are at that particular moment. In addition, please heed the "don'ts" of trading emphasized in this book. While there is no guarantee that you will profit if you follow all the "dos" in this book, we can assure you that in the long run you will lose a lot less money if we can get you to follow the "don'ts." We cannot emphasize enough how many individuals have failed and will fail at this, because either they did not limit their losses, they doubled down on a loser, or they insisted on picking bottoms. Please give extra attention to these ideas.

You have been reading a comprehensive book providing you with an approach used successfully by hundreds of traders. You must now learn how to apply this material. Keep in mind that no approach will work all the time. An approach that works more than 50 percent of the time can be extremely profitable. Our experience shows that it generally takes 3 months to a year for most traders to effectively and profitably apply these strategies consistently. This is not a get-rich-quick scheme. This book is designed to provide you with the information you need to develop the skills necessary to be a successful trader. Study this book and follow the approach. You have an opportunity to learn a great deal by learning from other people's mistakes. Do not take this for granted! Making mistakes in the beginning will be the most likely reason for your failures. Lack of concentration will be the second most likely reason. Follow your rules, limit your losses, stay informed, and **GOOD LUCK!**

If you would like to learn more about Online day trading or any of the techniques or technologies described in this book the authors offer a supplemental video and a week long course on day trading. More information can be attained from Broadway Consulting Group in New York City at (212) 378-4000 or at our web site at www.electronicdaytrader.com.

Epilogue
We believe that the basic engine that drives any market is liquidity, and for markets to be liquid they must offer fair pricing for all who choose to participate. Markets need market makers who, for the privilege of being able to earn the spread off customer orders and for the privilege of being able to trade with professional margin rates, must provide continuity and liquidity in these markets. We believe that the more liquidity, the more investors, traders, and speculators will be attracted to their markets. We believe that the more players in the market, the more volume. Increased volume leads to smaller spreads since higher-volume businesses can work on lower margins. Higher volume and tighter spreads lead to fair pricing and thus greater liquidity in the markets. The more liquidity they can provide, the less risk there is to the various players in the market. The increased liquidity and low risk are two of the

three essential factors (the third one being return) which draw investors to a market. The more investors in a market, the more capital that can be raised to help our companies grow and improve the quality of life for all of us.

Day traders and electronic access are critical to the growth of our markets. These facts will become evermore important in the global markets of the twenty-first century. These facts assure that online trading is just in its beginning stages. The New York Stock Exchange will continue to exist as a result of its unmatched efforts to provide fair pricing. But the NYSE will increasingly depend on technology and will have to adapt as the markets evolve. NASDAQ was fortunate enough to have the SEC point it in the right direction. The NASD must recognize that new rules, while painful to its members in the short run, will become the building blocks of its future markets, just as May Day played a painful but beneficial role in the recent past. The markets of the next hundred years will be featuring billions of shares trading hourly from everywhere in the world. This future would not be possible without electronic day traders.

Electronic systems have leveled the playing field for the customer. Today's technology affords customers lightning executions, nominal commissions, and access to information that was previously only available to professional traders, eliminating the once insurmountable advantages of exchange members. Electronic systems filled a vast void and have made day trading a realistic profession for those who are up to the challenge. The systems outlined in this book enable traders to use sophisticated day trading strategies from anywhere. Electronic systems give the trader a realistic chance to succeed in what is perhaps the most exciting, dynamic, and potentially rewarding career possible.

A Guide to Watcher

The Watcher Guide is included in the book for a general understanding of how the system works. Please keep in mind that the Watcher is constantly being upgraded and enhanced to reflect changes in market dynamics. Therefore, this guide can never be complete or completely accurate.

Watcher is designed to buy or sell 1,000 shares at a time on NASDAQ's Small Order Entry System (SOES) or through ECNs (Island, ISLD; Instinet, INCA; Bloomberg, BTRD; Teranova, TNTO). It also tracks any positions you might have, keeps you abreast of stocks that you choose to watch, and provides you access to detailed level 2 quotes (displays which market makers are bidding and offering).

The Watcher screen is divided into three areas: the bottom, middle, and top. The bottom area consists of three quote windows. The middle area provides messages on trades that you might be doing, or on market activity in stocks that you already have a position in. The top area allows you to view a variety of pages, providing you information about your positions, market movement, your transactions, your account, and news. Watcher also has two red status bars, one containing information about the market and the other summarizing your trading.

GETTING A QUOTE

To get a quote on a stock, simply type the four- or five-letter stock symbol and press <Enter>. The quote will appear in the quote window that is highlighted by a yellow border. The quote shows:

- Inside bid and ask prices
- Number of shares bid for or offered at the current inside market
- Stock's tier level (the maximum number of shares per SOES order)
- Net change from yesterday's close based on the mean of the bid and the ask
- Today's high and low prices

The quote areas show you the market makers who have the best bid and ask prices. Those with the best bid prices are listed on the left, and those with the best ask prices are listed on the right. Market makers who are on the inside bid and ask are listed in blue. A * appears next to the market maker who most recently updated his or her quote. An example of a quote area:

GEKA ↑ 99 × $99^1/_2$ (16 × 9)
L96 H $99^1/_2 - ^1/_2$ SM5
1NQMS   99   9TSCO $99^1/_2$
10COWN*   99   10GSCO   100
5PIPR   99   2HRZG   100

The above quote area shows a quote for a stock symbol GEKA. The up arrow indicates that the last bid tick was an uptick. The bid tick is important for short selling, which we will cover later. It shows that the inside market is 99 × $99^1/_2$ and that there are three market makers on the bid (NQMS for 100 shares, COWN for 1,000 shares, and PIPR for 500 shares), each willing to pay 99 for stock. One market maker (TSCO) is willing to sell 900 shares at the ask—$99^1/_2$. COWN most recently updated its quote. This stock is an SM5 stock, which means we could, at most, buy or sell 500 shares per order on SOES. The average of the bid and the ask is $^1/_2$ lower than the average of the bid and ask at yesterday's close.

You can watch three different stocks at the same time in the quote areas; however, only one window is the active window. This active windows is highlighted by the yellow border. Pressing <Tab> or <Shift><Tab> will switch your active quote window. *All order entry is done on the stock in your active quote window, so make sure you have selected the right window before trying to enter an order.*

To get a quote on a different stock in the same quote window, just type the stock symbol and press <Enter>.

ENTERING ORDERS

All order entry is done by holding down the <Shift> key and pressing a letter key, depending on the type of order you want to do. *An entry message describing the order will appear in the middle area of the Watcher screen.* An order will always be entered on the stock in your active quote area. *Do not use the shift keys unless you are trying to enter an order.*

NOW Orders

There are three different types of orders: NOW, SOES, and Island divergence. In each type, the trader is attempting to pay the offer or sell at the bid. Therefore, a NOW buy order will attempt to purchase stock at the best available offer, and a NOW sell order will attempt to sell stock at the best bid. These orders are routed to SOES for execution against a market maker or to Island. If there is stock bid or offered on Island which is the same price as the current inside market or better, a NOW order will attempt to buy or sell the stock from Island **first.** If someone traded the stock on Island before you, or the order was canceled, you will receive an "Island Limit Away" message. If there is no stock on Island, your order will be automatically routed to SOES.

SOES Orders

SOES is NASDAQ's Small Order Execution System. On SOES you, the customer, always buy stock on the offer from a market maker or sell stock at the bid to a market maker. SOES orders are executed by NASDAQ on a first-come, first-served basis. Market makers can have one order executed against them automatically every 20 seconds that they remain on the inside market. Market makers are only obligated to honor their market for the amount of shares they display in their quotes.

Since SOES orders are executed automatically, they are a very powerful tool for getting executions that otherwise might be impossible to achieve by conventional methods (i.e., phone trades).

The maximum number of shares that can be executed in a single SOES order is determined by NASDAQ on a stock-by-stock basis. Stocks break out into three SOES "tiers": 200 shares, 500 shares, and 1,000 shares. For your reference, these are shown in the quote area as SM2, SM5, and SM10.

SOES provides very fast order entry for sales at the inside bid price and for buys on the inside ask price. SOES orders are entered immediately after you press the appropriate key.

WARNING: **Since SOES orders are entered immediately, please** *make sure that the stock you want to trade is highlighted in the quote window at the bottom of the screen.*

Regular SOES orders will either be executed or timed out after 10 seconds after 9:35 A.M. Before 9:35 A.M., a SOES order will not be timed out for 30 seconds. Under normal circumstances, you will get either a "U R Out" message, indicating that the order could not be executed, or an execution confirmation message in the middle area.

SOES Outcomes

While SOES is the most powerful tool available to anyone to get executions on the NASDAQ stock market, *not all SOES orders entered get executed.* The total number of SOES executions available depends on how many market makers are on the inside price and how many shares they choose to display on that market. If there are four market makers on the inside ask price, each displaying 1,000 shares, then there is the potential for four immediate buy executions through SOES. If you are one of the first four orders in the system, you will get an immediate execution against one of the market makers at the inside ask price. After each market maker has executed an order, he is given 20 seconds to update his market before another SOES order can be executed against her.

After you enter your SOES order, it is presented to NASDAQ. If your order is executed, you will see a message in your middle window telling you that you have opened or closed a position. Your positions on your F1 page will also be automatically updated.

Once your order times out (10 seconds for normal orders), Watcher will send NASDAQ a message to cancel it. Usually NASDAQ will acknowledge the cancel and you will see a "you are out" message ("U R Out") in the middle window. This means that your order was canceled and can no longer be executed. You are free to reenter the order if you still want to do the trade.

It is also possible to get a "Too Late" message, which means that our cancel message reached NASDAQ after the order was already executed, hence too late to cancel. You should receive your execution soon.

Finally, you may see a "No Find" message. This message almost always occurs at the opening or when NASDAQ is having computer problems. The literal meaning is that NASDAQ was not able to find your order to cancel it; it is lost somewhere in the computer system. There is no way to know what the final outcome of the order will be except to sit back and wait. We will automatically continue to try to cancel your order periodically until you get back either an execution or a "U R Out." This is the reason that we enter all SOES orders before 9:35 A.M. with extended time-outs.

Monster or Market Orders

Monster orders used to take advantage of a loophole in the SOES system that gave orders priority based on price. As of January 20, 1997, marketable SOES orders are executed strictly on a first-come, first-served basis. **The monster key now functions as a market order.** The order is entered instantly and routed similarly to other NOW orders. These orders have a better chance of execution because they can be executed at a worse price if the market moves. You can get an execution at any price, but not worse than the quoted market at the time the order is executed. **Market orders never time out but will be canceled if the only entity on the inside market is an ECN (such as INCA, TNTO, BTRD, and in some cases the Island).**

Island Divergence

As previously explained, if there is an Island bid or offer at or better than the current inside market, your NOW order will be routed to the Island for execution before it is routed to SOES. This allows a trader entering a position to trade without the restrictions of SOES and adds a tremendous amount of liquidity for the Watcher customer exiting a position. Instead of having another Watcher customer buy stock from a market maker and then the market maker deciding whether or not he wants to buy stock from you, the buy order is routed directly to Island for execution. This essentially takes liquidity away from the market makers and places it in the hands of Island and Watcher customers.

Note: NOW or market orders diverted to Island can be executed by either SOES or the Island. This means that if you enter a NOW order to buy 1,000 shares and 300 are offered on the Island, you will get filled on 300 and the balance of the order will be diverted to SOES. Orders that go to SOES may be filled until the order is canceled. So it is possible to send a SOES order (in this case a market order) and buy 300 shares, and then 5 seconds later buy 200 shares, and then 30 seconds later buy another 500 shares. It is also possible to send an additional order to buy stock from the Island while the SOES order is still in the system. Any pending order will be reflected on the F6 page where you can see the status of the order or cancel it.

DEFAULTS

Now that you are aware of the manner in which your orders will be executed, let us examine the default quantities (or number of shares) that Watcher will enter for you.

One Lot

This order enters exactly one round lot. The number of shares in a lot varies by stock and can be either 200, 500, or 1,000 shares. The size of a lot is displayed in the quote window for each stock. *Example:* In an SM10 stock, a lot is 1,000 shares.

Closeouts

These orders enter enough shares to close out your position in the stock. *Note:* When using a limit order or a non-SOES order, you will be able to enter a closeout order for any number of shares you currently have opened. However, if using SOES and your position is greater than the SOES tier level, you will only be able to buy/sell the maximum number of shares allowable through SOES. Thus, if you are long 157 shares of a stock and you wish to exit this position, you will want to enter a closeout order.

ACTIVE QUOTE SHIFT KEYS

Orders are entered when pressing the shift key and:

Shift B—NOW buy one lot	Shift S—NOW sell one lot
Shift H—Market buy one lot	Shift E—Market sell one lot
Shift N—NOW buy closeout	Shift D—NOW sell closeout
Shift J—Market buy closeout	Shift R—Market sell closeout

LIMIT ORDERS

As with NOW orders, there are three different types of limit orders. Limit orders may be entered on Watcher directly to the Island, on SelectNet, or through preferencing. Unlike NOW orders, limit orders are not automatic executions. This means that if you enter a limit order, you will only get executed if another party chooses to fill your order. However, limit orders can be a very useful tool because it gives you the opportunity to trade stock at prices anywhere within the inside market price, and potentially gain the spread as opposed to paying it. For example, entering a limit order may allow you to sell a stock at the offer as opposed to selling it at the bid. Limit orders can be displayed to all market makers, to Island customers, and in many cases to all those with level 2 screens.

When you place a limit order, text will appear on the top line of the Watcher screen. Review the order before you press <Enter>. If you make a mistake or decide you do not want to place the order, pressing the <Esc> key in the upper left corner of your keyboard will clear the text.

Limit Order Shift Keys

Orders are entered by pressing the shift key and:

Shift Q—Limit buy one lot   **Shift P—Limit sell one lot**
Shift A—Limit buy closeout   Shift L—Limit sell closeout

After pressing one of the shift keys listed above, the top line of the Watcher screen will look something like:

$$\text{\$NB1000MSFT99 7/8}$$

The N indicates a limit order, the B means buy, followed by quantity, symbol, and price. Press <Enter> to enter the order, or press <Esc> to clear it. When pressing the above keys, Watcher will automatically price the order to buy one SOES lot on the current bid or sell one SOES lot at the current offer. You can accept the default order price and size by pressing <Enter>. Or you can modify it by using your arrow keys to change the price (control and arrows to change in $1/_{16}$) and the < or > to change the size (use the closeout keys if you are closing an odd lot) and the press <Enter> when you are ready to place the order.

How do all these Island participants see your order? On Watcher, unfilled limit orders will automatically be canceled after 3 minutes. *If you want to cancel the order earlier than that, press function key F6, select the order you wish to cancel with the up and down arrow keys, and then press the "\" key* (which is above the <Enter> key on most keyboards). Read the "F6 page" section, which follows, for more details.

If you try to place a limit order with a price outside the current marketplace that would be unfavorable for you if executed, you may see a message in the middle screen area that says:

TRIED TO SELL STOCK AT OR BELOW THE BID. USE .O TO
OVERRIDE

If you are certain that you want to place the order, just press .O and then the <Enter> key.

ISLAND ORDERS

An ECN (electronic communications network) such as Island (ISLD), Instinet (INCA), Bloomberg (BTRD), or Terranova (TNTO) allows customers to display bids and offers to both other customers and market makers. This is done by representing bids and offers entered on the ECN in the level 2 displayed quote. If the order is placed at the same price as the current quote, there will be no change to the inside market. If the order is priced inside the current market quote, the market will be changed to reflect this better bid or offer. All limit orders entered on Watcher are displayed on the Island and can be filled by anyone. If your order is the best bid or ask displayed in the quote, your order must be traded before the stock trades at a lower bid or higher offer according to the SEC order handling rules.

Island inside markets appear in green at the top of each quote window. They show price and quantity available on the Island system.

Remember that when you enter a NOW or market order and there is stock bid or offered on Island, your order will automatically be diverted to Island for instant execution. When your order is diverted, it will come up in the position window in your Watcher in an aqua color so that you don't miss it. This means that when you are offering or bidding stock on SelectNet, and subsequently the Island, your stock will be traded before another trader's order is routed to a market maker via SOES. This drastically improves your liquidity versus having your order eligible for execution on SelectNet alone.

PREFERENCE ORDERS

If you enter a preference order, you are sending an order to a specific market maker, which usually will be an attempt to buy stock on the offer or sell stock on the bid. When you preference a market maker at a price he is advertising, that market maker is obligated to trade with you unless he has just filled an order at that price. *If you choose to trade with an ECN (INCA, BTRD, or TNTO) other than Island, you will need to use a preference order* (these ECNS charge extra if you preference them). You can enter a preference order two different ways. Use the SelectNet keys and add the four market-maker letters before entering the order. Or:

Shift 0—Buy preference one lot   Shift 2—Sell preference one lot
Shift O—Buy preference closeout   Shift W—Sell preference closeout

These keys will preference market makers on the inside market. They will automatically preference ECNs first. Press the key again, and it will automatically bring up the next market maker. The order will not actually be sent until you press <Enter>. Keep in mind that you will have to wait 10 seconds before you can cancel a preference order.

Note: If the current market in the stock is 50 to $50^1/_2$, and you would like to buy stock at $50^1/_2$, you should use SOES or preference. If you would like to try and buy the stock at a price better than $50^1/_2$, you may display your bid on SelectNet or Island using the limit order keys.

KEYBOARD LOGIC

Knowing which keys to push is much easier than it looks. **B is for buy, and S is for sell** (NOW orders). The key above the B key (H) is for a market buy order, and the key above the S key (E) is a market sell order. If you are closing out a position and your position is something other than one SOES lot, use the key to the right of S (D) or the key to the right of B (N) and the machine will automatically enter an order with the number of shares you need to buy or sell to be flat (closeout). If you would like to offer one lot (a limit order entered via SelectNet/Island) at or near the offer, use the letter closest to the offer (P). If you want to bid for one SOES lot at or near the bid, then use the letter nearest to the bid (Q). The keys below the Q (bid) and A (offer) will show the exact amount that you would need to buy or sell to be flat. *Example:* You enter a NOW order by pressing shift B. Your order diverts to Island, and you get filled on 748 shares. The stock moves up two levels, and you want to offer the stock out on the offer—shift L offers 748 shares on the offer. Your order times out and you decide to lock in your profit, so you use the shift D key, which enters a NOW order to sell 748 shares.

Keys for buying or selling on the bid are on the left side of the keyboard, just as the bid is on the left side of the quote window. Keys for buying or selling on the offer are on the right side of the keyboard, just as the offer is on the right side of the quote window.

B is for buy. S is for sell. The letter near the ask offers. The letter near the bid bids. That is all you need to remember.

PAGES

The top area of the Watcher screen lets you look at different pages of information, such as a list of your positions or a scrolling stock ticker. The function keys across the top of the screen let you easily switch between pages. Simply press a function key to see a page.

Positions Page, F1

This page shows an alphabetical list of your positions and stocks that you have put on your ticker. You can scroll through the list with the up and down arrow keys, Page Up, Page Down, Home, or End. This page will show you how many shares you are long or short the stock, the price you bought or sold it, and other information.

$$2000 \text{ GEKA } 29\frac{1}{2}\ 30 \times 30\frac{1}{2}\ (2 \times 1)\ 12{:}21$$

For example, the above line on your positions page tells you that you have 2,000 shares of GEKA. $29\frac{1}{2}$ is the last price you traded GEKA at, and the current inside market is $30 \times 30\frac{1}{2}$, with two market makers at the inside bid and one at the inside ask price. The last tick in GEKA occurred at 12:21 P.M.

Note that the F1 page scrolls and all the information may not be listed on the page (so do the F3, F5, F6, F7, and F10 pages). Occasionally you may have to push the up or down arrow to view all your information. If unsure, "Pos" on your status bar tells you how many positions that you actually have.

Watching Stocks with the Ticker Page, F2

This page has two windows. The window on the left is called the TID and shows all inside market changes (actual changes in price). The window on the right shows any market-maker update in a stock that you have added to your ticker list.

The TID window shows stock price changes that affect the inside spread. A line in the TID window looks like:

$$9{:}58{:}56 \uparrow \text{NSCP } 99\frac{1}{4} \times 99\frac{1}{2} \uparrow +\frac{1}{4}$$

This tells you the time of the change, if the change is an uptick or downtick, the stock, the current inside spread, which side of the spread (either the bid or the ask) moved in which direction, and the net change.

Since the TID window will show you any inside spread change on any of 7,000+ NASDAQ stocks, it can become a very quickly moving window. There are two ways to modify which stocks appear in this window. One is to specify your default settings. This will let you eliminate an entire tier level. The other is to specify the range of stock prices that you are interested in seeing in your TID window. For example, you could have tier 2 stocks (those that you can only trade in 200-share lots) eliminated for your TID, only see tier 5 stocks if their bid price is above $5, and only see tier 10 stocks if their bid price is greater than $5 and their ask price is below $50. Since stock prices change and since new stocks are added, these settings are used to refresh your TID every day. You will need to call your account executive to make these changes.

Risers and Fallers Page, F3

This page lists stocks whose prices have changed the most for the day. Try not to stay on this page for very long because it can slow down your Watcher.

Locks Page, F4

This page shows stocks whose inside bid is equal to or above the ask price or vice versa. Try not to stay on this page for very long because it can slow down your Watcher.

Report Page, F5

This page lets you examine reports on your trades. You can review your transactions from the previous day. Or you can review a summary of your trades stock by stock for the previous day or for the month. You will also find information about your current equity and maximum buying power in these reports. **You should check your F5 Reports every day.** Use the up and down arrow keys to select the report you want to view (you can only view your own reports). Press F5 again to read the report. The up and down arrow, Page Up, Page Down, Home, and End keys, can be used to scroll through the report.

There is also a report called "Watcher News." This report has up-to-the-minute information that you need to know about the Watcher program and NASDAQ rule changes. *You should read Watcher News every day.*

Pending, Executed, Timed-Out, or Canceled Orders Page, F6

This page lets you view the status of all orders that you have entered except those that were diverted to Island (since these orders are immediate or cancel). Canceled or expired orders are listed in red, orders you have instructed NASDAQ to cancel are yellow, pending orders are white, and executed orders are green. A pair of blinking pink down arrows tell you that there are more orders below the bottom of the screen. Press the end or down arrow key to view the new orders. *Note:* Partially filled orders turn green, and the balance is indicated.

If you wish to cancel a pending order, use the up or down arrow key to select the pending order and then press the "\" key. This key is located above the <Enter> key on most keyboards. You will see * appear next to the order, and after a few seconds the white pending order will change to red, indicating the order has been canceled.

Recap Page, F7

This will show you all of your orders entered today as well as the inside market and number of market makers when you entered the order. Further, this window will show you the number of shares in your position and whether your executed orders were opening or closing a current position. Executed orders are listed in green, and canceled or timed-out orders are listed in red.

Message Page, F8

This will show the last few broadcast messages received. Broadcast messages are sent out to keep you up to date on late-breaking news—for example, when NASDAQ is having computer problems that could affect you. When a new message comes in, it will pop up in the middle of your screen to ensure that you see it. Press F8 to clear the pop-up message window.

News Page, F9

This page shows you the latest headlines that concerned a NASDAQ stock. These headlines are compiled from several sources. If news appears on a stock on your ticker, you will get a message in the middle area on your Watcher screen. The news page will only show you the headline of the story. *Note:* Your Watcher will only show you news stories in stocks that are on your ticker or in a symbol that you have typed in during that trading day.

Sometimes a news article will mention a stock, but the stock symbol will not appear in the headline. So do not be confused if your Watcher tells you that news came out on a stock, but you do not see the stock listed on the news page.

Ticker Page, F10

This page shows you the stocks and colors that are highlighted for the F2 page. All stocks in gray are stock issues that have been pulled up in an execution window but have not been added to the F2 page ticker. All stocks on this page are enabled for the F9 news feature on Watcher. *Note:* This page scrolls.

FYI, F11

This page shows you the latest SelectNet information on stocks enabled for FYI. You may enable a stock by typing the symbol of the stock followed by =.

Note: Watcher is frequently updated, and this guide can never be complete or 100 percent accurate. This guide is intended to give the reader a basic look at how Watcher operates. Online demonstrations are available through Broadway Consulting Group in New York.

Ticker Guide*

First in Business
Worldwide

2200 Fletcher Avenue
Fort Lee, NJ 07024
(201) 585-2622
Updated: May 30, 1997

HOW TO USE THE CNBC TICKER TO FOLLOW THE MARKET:

The Ticker is a continuous display of numbers and symbols that helps you understand the buying and selling activity of each business day.

The CNBC Ticker provides useful information about market indices, stock prices and commodity futures.

This guide will show you how to follow the Ticker's upper and lower bands, and what information you can find on a typical business day.

THE UPPER BAND:

8:00 a.m. to 9:30 a.m. (ET)

An alphabetical recap of New York Stock Exchange closing prices from the previous day's close. All stocks that have traded in the previous 20 days are included.

In addition, commodity futures quotes begin running at 8:00 a.m. and are shown at :01, :11, :21, :31, :41 and :51 after each hour, in real time. These prices run until 7:30 p.m. (ET).

---

*Reprinted with the permission from CNBC. Copyright 1997 CNBC, Inc.

9:30 a.m. to 4:00 p.m. (ET)

Display of stock prices, the change from the previous day's close and
volume data for selected trades on the New York Stock Exchange.

4:00 p.m. to 7:30 p.m. (ET)

An alphabetical recap of New York Stock Exchange closing prices
for all the stocks that traded that day with the amount of change
from the previous day's close. The commodity futures trading recap
also appears.

THE LOWER BAND:

8:00 a.m. to 9:30 a.m. (ET)

An alphabetical recap of American Stock Exchange and Nasdaq closing
prices from the previous day's close, punctuated by market summaries.
This recap displays all stocks that have traded at least once in the
previous 20 sessions.

9:30 a.m. to 9:45 a.m. (ET)

CNBC's real time market summary repeats uninterrupted for 15 minutes.

9:45 a.m. to 4:15 p.m. (ET)

CNBC's market summary reports continue along with American Stock
Exchange and Nasdaq stock trades. AMEX and Nasdaq trades are
delayed by 15 minutes.

4:15 p.m. to 7:30 p.m. (ET)

An alphabetical recap of issues that traded that day on the American
Stock Exchange and Nasdaq with their changes from the previous
day's close, punctuated by market summaries.

TYPICAL TRADES:

HAL 118 $+\frac{1}{4}$. HAL is the stock symbol, 118 is the price at which
the trade was made, $+\frac{1}{4}$ indicates the stock is up $\frac{1}{4}$ from the previous
day's composite close. (The "composite" close is the last trade of
the day on any of the nation's major exchanges, not necessarily the
stock's primary exchange.)

CDS 15s22 $-^3/_4$ .. CDS is the stock symbol, "s" stands for shares, so 15s designates the volume of the trade with the last two zeroes omitted (1500 in this example), 22 is the price, $-^3/_4$ indicates the stock is down $^3/_4$ from the previous day's close.

NCR 11.000s55 .. NCR is the stock symbol, 11.000s designates the volume of the trade (zeroes are not omitted if the volume is over 10,000 shares), 55 is the price.

Stock prices are expressed in U.S. Dollars and fractional parts of U.S. Dollars. For example, a stock price of 26-$^1/_2$ equals $26.50. Fractions are written out on the ticker except for sixteenths, which are designated using an apostrophe. For example, 2´3 + ´5 on the ticker equals 2-$^3/_{16}$, up $^5/_{16}$.

A "class" of a company's shares are indicated by a period and the letter corresponding to the class. Thus, VIA.B are the Class "B" shares of Viacom. (Some companies issue separate "classes" of stock with specific rights or characteristics. For example, different classes may have different voting rights.)

Preferred shares are designated with a PR after the symbol. For example, Fpr would be used for Ford's preferred shares. FprB indicates Ford's Class B preferred shares. (Preferred shares give their owner a claim ahead of common stockholders to a company's earnings and assets. They generally pay a fixed dividend that's determined when the shares are issued.)

The letters "WI" after a stock symbol indicates "when issued" trading. That's trading between the time a new security is announced and the time when certificates are actually issued.

Due to the large number of trades, the ticker is unable to show every transaction. Our computer selects which trades to show, based on factors including the number of shares and the movement in price from the previous trade. The larger the volume or the price movement, the greater the chances that the trade will be included on the ticker.

S&P 100 STOCKS AND SYMBOLS

AA	Aluminum Co. of America	HNZ	Heinz (H.J.)
AEP	American Electric Power	HON	Honeywell
AGC	American General	HRS	Harris Corp
AIG	American Int'l. Grop	HWP	Hewlett-Packard
AIT	Ameritech	IBM	International Bus. Machines
ALT	Allegheny Teledyne Inc	IFF	International Flav/Frag
AMP	AMP Inc	INTC	Intel Corp
AN	Amoco	IP	International Paper
ARC	Atlantic Richfield	JNJ	Johnson & Johnson
AVP	Avon Products	KM	Kmart
AXP	American Express	KO	Coca Cola Co
BA	Boeing Company	LTD	Limited, The
BAC	BankAmerica Corp	MAY	May Dept. Stores
BAX	Baxter International Inc	MCD	McDonald's Corp
BC	Brunswick Corp	MCIC	MCI Communications
BCC	Boise Cascade	MER	Merrill Lynch
BDK	Black & Decker Corp	MKG	Mallinckrodt Group Inc
BEL	Bell Atlantic	MMM	Minn. Mining & Mfg
BHI	Baker Hughes	MOB	Mobil Corp
BMY	Bristol-Myers Squibb	MRK	Merck & Co
BNI	Burlington Northern Sant	MSFT	Microsoft Corp
BS	Bethlehem Steel	MTC	Monsanto Company
C	Chrysler Corp	NB	NationsBank
CCI	Citicorp	NSC	Norfolk Southern Corp
CEN	Ceridian Corp	NSM	National Semiconductor
CGP	Coastal Corp	NT	Northern Telecom
CHA	Champion International	ORCL	Oracle Corp
CI	CIGNA Corp	OXY	Occidental Petroleum
CL	Colgate-Palmolive	PEP	PepsiCo Inc
COL	Columbia/HCA Healthcare	PNU	Pharmacia & Upjohn, Inc
CSC	Computer Sciences Corp	PRD	Polaroid Corp
CSCO	Cisco Systems	RAL	Ralston-Ralston Purina Group
DAL	Delta Air Lines	ROK	Rockwell International
DD	Du Pont (E.I.)	RTN	Raytheon Co
DEC	Digital Equipment	S	Sears, Roebuck & Co
DIS	Walt Disney Co	SLB	Schlumberger Ltd
DOW	Dow Chemical	SO	Southern Co
EK	Eastman Kodak	T	AT&T Corp
ETR	Entergy Corp	TAN	Tandy Corp
F	Ford Motor	TEK	Tektronix Inc
FCN	First Chicago NBD Corp	TOY	Toys R Us Hldg. Cos
FDX	Federal Express	TXN	Texas Instruments
FLR	Fluor Corp	UCM	Unicom Corp
GD	General Dynamics	UIS	Unisys Corp
GE	General Electric	UTX	United Technologies
GM	General Motors	WMB	Williams Cos
HAL	Halliburton Co	WMT	Wal-Mart Stores
HET	Harrah's Entertainment	WY	Weyerhaeuser Corp
HIG	Hartford Financial Svc. Group	XON	Exxon Corp
HM	Homestake Mining	XRX	Xerox Corp

NASDAQ 100 STOCKS AND SYMBOLS

AAPL	Apple Computer, Inc.
ADBE	Adobe Systems Incorporated
ADCT	ACD Telecommunications, Inc.
ADPT	Adaptec, Inc.
ADSK	Autodesk, Inc.
ADTN	ADTRAN, Inc.
AGREA	American Greetings Corporation
ALTR	Altera Corporation
AMAT	Applied Materials, Inc.
AMGN	Amgen Inc.
ANDW	Andrew Corporation
APCC	American Power Conversion Corp.
ASND	Ascend Communications, Inc.
ATML	Atmel Corporation
BBBY	Bed Bath & Beyond Inc.
BGEN	Biogen, Inc.
BMCS	BMC Software, Inc.
BMET	Biomet, Inc.
BOST	Boston Chicken, Inc.
CBRL	Cracker Barrel Old Country Store
CEFT	Concord EFS, Inc.
CEXP	Corporate Express, Inc.
CHIR	Chiron Corporation
CMCSK	Comcast Corporation
CNTO	Centocor, Inc.
COMS	3Com Corporation
COST	Costco Companies Inc.
CPWR	Compuware Corporation
CRUS	Cirrus Logic, Inc.
CSCO	Cisco Systems, Inc.
CTAS	Cintas Corporation
DELL	Dell Computer Corporation
DIGI	DSC Communications Corporation
EFII	Electronics for Imaging, Inc.
ERTS	Electronic Arts Inc.
FAST	Fastenal Company
FDLNB	Food Lion, Inc.
FISV	Fiserv, Inc.
FORE	FORE Systems, Inc.
GART	Gartner Group, Inc.
GEMS	Glenayre Technologies, Inc.
GENZ	Genzyme Corporation
GNCI	General Nutrition Companies, Inc.
HBOC	HBO & Company
HCCC	HealthCare COMPARE Corp.
IDXX	IDEXX Laboratories, Inc.
IFMX	Informix Corporation
INTC	Intel Corporation
INTU	Intuit Inc.
JJSC	Jefferson Smurfit Corporation

NASDAQ 100 STOCKS AND SYMBOLS

KLAC	KLA-Tencor Corporation
KMAG	Komag, Incorporated
LLTC	Linear Technology Corporation
MCAF	McAfee Associates, Inc.
MCCRK	McCormick & Company, Inc.
MCHP	Microchip Technology Incorporated
MCIC	MCI Communications Corporation
MLHR	Herman Miller, Inc.
MOLX	Molex Incorporated
MSFT	Microsoft Corporation
MUEI	Micron Electronics, Inc.
MXIM	Maxim Integrated Products, Inc.
NOBE	Nordstrom, Inc.
NOVL	Novell, Inc.
NSCP	Netscape Communications Corp.
NWAC	Northwest Airlines Corporation
NXTL	Nextel Communications, Inc.
OFIS	U.S. Office Products Company
ORCL	Oracle Corporation
OSSI	Outback Steakhouse, Inc.
OXHP	Oxford Health Plans, Inc.
PAGE	Paging Network, Inc.
PAIR	PairGain Technologies, Inc.
PAYX	Paychex, Inc.
PCAR	PACCAR Inc
PETM	PETsMART, Inc.
PHSYB	PacifiCare Health Systems, Inc.
PHYC	PhyCor, Inc.
PMTC	Parametric Technology Corporation
PSFT	PeopleSoft, Inc.
QCOM	QUALCOMM Incorporated
QNTM	Quantum Corporation
QTRN	Quintiles Transnational Corp.
ROST	Ross Stores, Inc.
RPOW	RPM, Inc.
SBUX	Starbucks Corporation
SIAL	Sigma-Aldrich Corporation
SNPS	Synopsys, Inc.
SPLS	Staples, Inc.
STEI	Stewart Enterprises, Inc.
SUNW	Sun Microsystems, Inc.
SYBS	Sybase, Inc.
TCOMA	Tele-Communications, Inc.
TLAB	Tellabs, Inc.
TYSNA	Tyson Foods, Inc.
VKNG	Viking Office Products, Inc.
WCLX	Wisconsin Central Transportation
WCOM	WorldCom, Inc.
WTHG	Worthington Industries, Inc.
XLNX	Xilinx, Inc.

COMMODITY FUTURES SYMBOL GUIDE:

The first two letters of a Commodity Symbol indicate the name of the Commodity. (There are a few commodities with one-letter symbols.) The third number indicates the month of the contract for that commodity.

S&P 500	SP	Silver	SI
S&P 400	MD	Platinum	PL
Russell 2000	RL	Palladium	PA
Dow Jones Ind. Avg	DJ	Copper	HG
Nasdaq 100	ND	Corn	C
Nikkei 225 Ind.	NK	Wheat	W
NYSE Index	YX	Soybeans	S
Value Line	KV	Soybean Oil	BO
T-Bonds	US	Soybean Meal	SM
T-Bills	TB	Oats	O
Eurodollars	ED	Live Cattle	LC
Federal Funds	FF	Feeder Cattle	FC
2-Year T-Note	TU	Goldman Sachs	GI
5-Year T-Note	FV	Commodity Index	
10-Year T-Note	TY	Live Hogs	LH
Libor 1-month	EM	Pork Bellies	PB
Muni-Bonds	MB	Cotton	CT
Dollar Index	DX	Lumber	LB
Swiss Franc	SF	Crude Oil	CL
Deutschemark	DM	Heating Oil	HO
Japanese Yen	JY	Unleaded Gasoline	HU
British Pound	BP	Natural Gas	NG
Canadian Dollar	CD	Sugar	SB
Australian Dollar	AD	Coffee	KC
CRB Index	CR	Cocoa	CC
Gold	GC	Orange Juice	JO

January	F	July	N
February	G	August	Q
March	H	September	U
April	J	October	V
May	K	November	X
June	M	December	Z

GLOSSARY OF MARKET SUMMARY COMPONENTS:

Stock Exchanges

New York Stock Exchange: The NYSE is also known as the Big Board. Listing more than 3,275 stocks, the NYSE generally lists the oldest, largest and best-known companies in the United States. Stocks are exchanged on a trading floor located on Wall Street in New York City.

The Nasdaq Stock Market: Includes the Nasdaq Stock Market and Nasdaq National Market, or NNM. There is no physical exchange where stocks are traded. Instead, prices are determined and trades are made on computer screens at brokerages around the country. The Nasdaq Stock Market is not synonymous with the over-the-counter market. The more than 5,000 Nasdaq-listed companies trade in a highly structured environment which has listing standards, real-time trade reporting, corporate governance requirements, affirmative obligations for market makers, execution services and automatic linkages with clearance and settlement facilities. This cannot be said of the approximately 5,000 OTC securities.

American Stock Exchange: Listing approximately 940 stocks, the AMEX lists smaller, younger companies. The AMEX trading floor is in New York City.

Futures Exchanges (Chicago)

Chicago Board of Trade (CBT):   Grains, bonds and short-term interest rates.

Chicago Mercantile Exchange (CME):   Livestock, currencies and stock index futures.

Futures Exchanges (New York)

The Commodities Exchange (COMEX):   Precious Metals, Copper and Aluminum

New York Cotton Exchange (NYCE): Cotton and Dollar Index

New York Mercantile Exchange (MERC):   Petroleum and Precious Metals

Coffee, Sugar and Cocoa Exchange (CSCE)

INDICES, AVERAGES AND OTHER MARKET INDICATORS IN THE CNBC

Market Summary

DJIA: The Dow Jones Industrial Average, also referred to as "The Dow." The Average is calculated using a formula and the common stock prices of 30 major U.S. industrial companies listed on the New York Stock Exchange.

TRAN: The Dow Jones Transportation Average is calculated using the prices of 20 airline, trucking and railroad company stocks.

UTIL: The Dow Jones Utility Average is a group of 15 gas, electric and power company stocks.

DJCOMP: The Dow Jones 65 Composite Average is calculated from the average of all the stocks in the Dow Jones Industrial, Transportation and Utility Averages.

S&P 500:   The Standard & Poor's 500 Index is calculated using the stock prices of 500 relatively large companies as measured by capitalization. (Capitalization is the value of a company as measured by the market price of its common shares multiplied by the total number of shares that have been issued.). The S&P 500 is widely used as an indicator of stock market trends and for futures trading strategies. The Index is market-weighted, which means the component stocks affect the Index in direct proportion to the dollar value of the shares outstanding. The components of the Index can change, as S&P adds or deletes stocks to reflect changing conditions.

The Standard & Poor's 500 is also broken down into smaller industry segments which are monitored separately. These segments are industrial (400 companies), transportation (20 companies), utilities (40 companies) and financial (40 companies).

PREM and FV: The PREM Value Index and Fair Value are useful in determining when computer driven "buy" or "sell" programs are likely. Through computer programs, traders take advantage of premiums or discounts between the current price of stocks and stock index futures. Comparing the actual index to the futures contract, a trader will quickly sell the more expensive of the two and buy the less expensive. This computer-based activity (known as "program trading") can often accentuate sudden swings in the price of certain stocks, or cause dramatic shifts in the entire market.

Fair Value is a figure calculated once each day. It's what traders believe is the "proper" or "fair" difference between the current price of stocks and futures, based on interest rates and other factors.

In general, when the PREM is significantly higher than the Fair Value, buy programs are likely to occur. When the PREM is significantly lower, sell programs are likely.

As a contract moves toward expiration, the difference between the future and cash price will diminish. As a result, the premium or discount needed for a buy or sell program will also get smaller.

30-YR YLD: The yield of the most recently issued 30-year U.S. Treasury Bond. This is widely used as a benchmark for long-term interest rates. Due to limited data availability, it is only shown between 9 a.m. and 3 p.m. Eastern.

XMI: The Major Market Index is a price-weighted index of 20 stocks. It is the basis for options traded at the AMEX and futures traded at the Chicago Board of Trade.

OEX: Known as the S&P 100, this is used by the Chicago Board Options Exchange to trade stock index options.

NYSE: The NYSE Composite Index, a capitalization-weighted index of all common stocks listed on the New York Stock Exchange, is the basis for options and futures traded on the New York Stock Exchange.

TICK: This is a very short-term trading indicator. It is the difference between the number of NYSE stocks trading at a price higher than the previous trade ("uptick") and the number of stocks trading at a lower price than the previous trade ("downtick"). That is, TICK=Number of stocks moving higher minus the number of stocks moving lower. A large positive tick (the number usually ranges between -900 and $+900$) generally means the market is attracting more buyers than sellers. The opposite is true of a large negative number. The direction of the tick is important. If it is moving in a positive direction, $(-100, 0, +150)$, it means the market is moving upward. If the tick is moving in a negative direction $(+100, 0, -150)$, it means the market is going down.

ARMS: This used to be called the Trin, or the short-term trading index. It is the ratio of the quotient of advancing issues divided by declining issues and up volume divided by down volume.

$$\frac{\text{Advancing Issues/Up Volume}}{\text{Declining Issues/Down Volume}} = \text{ARMS Index}$$

The direction of the ARMS Index is most important.   A falling ARMS signals a strong market, while a rising ARMS suggests weakness ahead. The normal range is from 0.5 to 2.0.

NY ADV: The number of stocks on the New York Stock Exchange that have increased in price from the previous day's close.

DEC: The number of NYSE stocks that have decreased in price from the previous day's close.

UNCH: The number of NYSE stocks trading at the same price as the previous day's close.

NY VOL UP: The number of shares that have been traded for NYSE stocks that have increased in price from the previous day's close.

DN: The number of shares that have been traded for NYSE stocks that have decreased in price from the previous day's close.

TOT: The total number of shares that have been traded in NYSE stocks during the current trading day.

VAL: The Value Line Index is an arithmetic average of 1700 stocks compiled by Value Line. It is the basis for options traded on the Philadelphia Board of Options Exchange.

MID: The S&P MidCap 400 Index is calculated using the price of 400 medium-sized U.S. companies.

WSX: The Wilshire Small Cap Index measures the performance of companies with relatively small capitalizations. It is a market-weighted index that includes 250 stocks, chosen on the basis of their market capitalization, liquidity and industry group representation. The Small Cap Index originates from the Wilshire Next 1750 Index, a benchmark for institutional investors in the small cap sector.

SOX: The Philadelphia Stock Exchange's Semiconductor Sector index measures the performance of some of the largest and most widely-held U.S. computer chip stocks. This price-weighted index is made up of 16 stocks, including Intel, Micron Technology and Texas Instruments.

MSH: The Morgan Stanley High-Technology 35 Index is designed to measure the performance of the electronics-based technology industry. Hewlett-Packard, IBM and Microsoft are among the 35 stocks in this equal-dollar weighted index.

BKX: The Philadelphia Stock Exchange/Keefe, Bruyette & Woods Bank Sector index is composed of stocks designed to represent national money center banks and leading regional institutions. It is a capitalization-weighted index. BancOne, Citicorp and Wells Fargo are among the 24 stocks in this index.

CRB: The Knight-Ridder Commodity Research Bureau Price Index tracks 17 commodities. A decline in the CRB indicates commodities prices are falling, which can signal lower inflation and interest rates, possibly leading to higher bond prices.

XOI: The AMEX Oil Index includes 16 oil stocks. An increase can indicate rising oil prices, which may lead to increased inflation.

XAU: The Gold and Silver Index is comprised of seven stocks on the New York and American Stock Exchanges. Some investors consider gold to be a "safe haven." As a result, its price often goes up in times of inflation, international finance crises and threats of war.

AMEX AND NASDAQ SUMMARIES:

These summaries provide information about each of these exchanges, including the number of advancing and declining issues and up and down volume.

AMEX: The American Stock Exchange AMEX Composite Index includes all common stocks listed on the American Stock Exchange.

NMS COMP: Nasdaq's National Market System Composite is an index of all issues traded over-the-counter on the Nasdaq National Market System.

Stock Indexes

CBOE Automotive Index

Symbol: AUX

Symbol	Name
C	Chrysler Corporation Holding Co
DCN	Dana Corp
ECH	Echlin Inc
ETN	Eaton Corp
F	Ford Motor Co
GM	General Motors Corp
GPC	Genuine Parts Co
GT	Goodyear Tire and Rubber Co
MGA	Magna International Inc
TRW	TRW Inc

CBOE S&P Banks Index

Symbol: BIX

Symbol	Name
BAC	Bankamerica Corp
BBI	Barnett Banks Inc.
BK	Bank of NY Company Inc.
BKB	BankBoston Corp
BT	Bankers Trust NY Corp
CCI	Citicorp
CFL	Corestates Financial Corp
CMA	Comerica Inc.
CMB	Chase Manhattan Corp
FBS	First Bank System Inc
FCN	First Chicago NBD Corp
FITB	Fifth Third Bancorp
FLT	Fleet Financial Group Inc.
FTU	First Union Corp
JPM	JP Morgan and Co Inc.
KEY	Keycorp
MEL	Mellon Bank Corp
NB	Nationsbank Corp
NCC	National Citicorp
NOB	Norwest Corp
ONE	Banc One Corp
PNC	PNC Bank Corp
RNB	Republic New York Corp
STI	Suntrust Banks Inc.
USBC	US Bancorp of Oregon
WB	Wachovia Corp
WFC	Wells Fargo and Co

CBOE S&P Chemicals Index

Symbol: CEX

Symbol	Name
APD	Air Prod and Chemicals Inc.
DD	Du Pont El De Nemours
DOW	Dow Chemical Co
EC	Engelhard Corp
ECL	Ecolab Inc.
EMN	Eastman Chemical Co
FMC	FMC Corp
GLK	Great Lakes Chemical Corp
GR	BF Goodrich Co
GRA	WR Grace and Co
HPC	Hercules Inc.
IFF	Int'l Flavors & Fragrances
MII	Morton Int'l Inc
MTC	Monsanto Corp
NLC	Nalco Chemical Co
PPG	PPG Industries Inc.
PX	Praxair Inc.
ROH	Rohm and Haas Co
SIAL	Sigma Aldrich Corp
UK	Union Carbide Corp

CBOE Software Index

Symbol: CWX

Symbol	Name
ADBE	Adobe Systems Inc.
ASFT	Artisoft, Inc.
BMCS	BMC Software Inc.
BORL	Borland Int'l Inc.
BROD	Broderbund Software Inc.
CA	Computer Assoc. Int'l
ERTS	Electronic Arts Inc.
IFMX	Informix Corp
MSFT	Microsoft Corp
NOVL	Novell Inc.
ORCL	Oracle Systems Corp
PMTC	Parametric Tech Corp
SSAX	System Sortware Assoc.
SYBS	Sybase Inc.
SYMC	Symantec Corporation

CBOE Environmental Index

Symbol: EVX

Symbol	Name
BFI	Browning Ferris Indust Inc.
CCC	Calgon Carbon Corp
LDW/B	Laidlaw Inc.
MLTN	Molten Metal Tech
OHM	Ohm Inc.
RWIN	Republic Indust Inc.
SK	Safety Kleen Corp.
UW	USA Waste Services Inc.
WMX	WMX Technologies Inc.
WTI	Wheelabrator Tech Inc.

CBOE Gaming Index

Symbol: GAX

Symbol	Name
AGY	Argosy Gaming Company
AZR	AZTAR CORP
CIR	Circus Circus Enterprises
DJT	Trump Casinos
GND	Grand Casinos Inc.
IGT	International Game Tech
J	Jackpot Enterprise Inc.
MGG	MGM Grand
MIR	Mirage Resorts Inc.
PLAY	Players Int'l Inc.
PRMA	Primadonna Resorts Inc.
HET	Harrahs Entertainment
RHC	Rio Hotel and Casino
SBO	Showboat Inc.
STN	Station Casinos Inc.

CBOE Gold Index

Symbol: GOX

Symbol	Name
AU	AMAX Gold Inc
ABX	Barrick Gold Corp
BMG	Battle Mountain Gold Comp
ECO	Echo Bay Mines Ltd
HM	Homestake Mining Comp
NEM	Newmont Mining Corp
PDG	Placer Dome Inc
PDU	Pegasus Gold Inc.
GLD	Sante Fe Pacific Gold Corp
TVX	TVX Gold Inc

CBOE S&P Health Care Index

Symbol: HCX

Symbol	Name
ABT	Abbott Laboratories
AGN	Allergan Inc
AHP	American Home Products
AMGN	Amgen Inc
AZA	Alza Corp
BAX	Baxter International Inc
BCR	CR Bard Inc
BDX	Becton Dickinson and Co
BEV	Beverly Enterprises Inc
BMET	Biomet Inc
BMY	Bristol Myers Squibb Co
BOL	Bausch and Lomb Inc
BSX	Boston Scientific Corp
COL	Columbia Healthcare Corp
GDT	Guidant Corp
HRC	Healthsouth Corp
HUM	Humana Inc
JNJ	Johnson and Johnson
LLY	Eli Lilly and Co
MDT	Medtronic
MKG	Mallinckrodt Inc
MNR	Manor Care Inc
MRK	Merck and Company
PFE	Pfizer Inc
PNU	Pharmacia and Upjohn Inc
SGP	Schering Plough Corp
STJ	St Jude Medical Inc
THC	Tenet Healthcare Corp
UNH	United Healthcare Corp
USS	US Surgical Corp
WLA	Warner Lambert Corp

CBOE Internet Index

Symbol: INX

Symbol	Name
AOL	America Online Inc
CSCC	Cascade Communications
CSCO	Cisco Systems Inc
CSRV	Compuserve Corp.
NETA	Network Associates
NETC	Netcom Online Comm Svcs
NETM	Netmanage Inc
NSCP	Netscape Comm Corp
ORCL	Oracle Corporation
PSIX	Psinet Inc
SDTI	Security Dynamics Inc.
SGI	Silicon Graphics Inc.
SPYG	Spyglass Inc.
SUNW	Sun Microsystems Inc.
YHOO	Yahoo! Inc.

S&P Insurance Index

Symbol: IUX

Symbol	Name
AET	Aetna Inc.
AIG	American Int'l Group Inc.
ALL	Allstate Corp
CB	Chubb Corp
CI	Cigna Corp.
CNC	Conseco Inc.
FG	USF & G Corp
GRN	General RE Corp
HIG	ITT Hartford Group Inc.
JP	Jefferson Pilot Corp
LNC	Lincoln National Corp Ind
LTR	Loews Corp
PVN	Providian Corp
SAFC	Safeco Corp
SPC	St Paul Companies Inc.
TA	Transamerica Corp
TMK	Torchmark Corp
TRV	Travelers Group Inc
UNM	Unum Corp
USH	USLife

The Morgan Stanley Cyclical Index

Symbol: CYC

Symbol	Name
ALD	Allied Signal, Inc.
AA	Aluminum Company of America
BS	Bethlehem Steel Corporation
CAT	Caterpillar, Inc.
CCI	Citicorp
CSX	CSX Corporation
DCN	Dana Corporation
DOW	The Dow Chemical Company
ETN	Eaton Corporation
F	Ford Motor Company
GP	Georgia-Pacific Corporation
GT	Goodyear Tire & Rubber Company
HWP	Hewlett-Packard Company
HON	Honeywell Inc.
IR	Ingersoll-Rand Company
IP	International Paper Company
KM	Kmart Corporation
KRI	Knight-Ridder, Inc.
MAS	Masco Corporation
MYG	Maytag Corporation
MEA	Mead Corporation
MOT	Motorola, Inc.
PH	Parker-Hannifin Corporation
PD	Phelps Dodge Corporation
PPG	PPG Industries, Inc.
ROAD	Roadway Services, Inc.
ROH	Rohm & Haas Company
R	Ryder System, Inc.
TGT	Tenneco Inc.
UTX	United Technologies Corporation

CBOE Oil Index

Symbol: OIX

Symbol	Name
AHC	Amerada Hess Corp
AN	Amoco Corp
ARC	Atlantic Richfield Co
BP	British Petroleum PLC
CHV	Chevron Corp
XON	Exxon Corp
KMG	Kerr McGee Corp
MOB	Mobil Corp
OXY	Occidental Petroleum Corp
P	Phillips Petroleum Co
RD	Royal Dutch Petroleum
TX	Texaco Inc
TOT	Total Inc
UCL	Unocal Corp Delaware
MRO	USX Marathon Group—Oil

CBOE Reit Index

Symbol: RIX

Symbol	Name
AHE	American Health Prop Inc.
AVN	Avalon Properties Inc.
CBL	CBL and Assoc Properties
DRE	Duke Realty Investment
EQR	Equity Residential Prop.
FRT	Federal Realty Investment
GGP	General Growth Prop Inc.
GRT	Glimcher Realty Trust
HCP	Health Care Property
HGI	HGI Realty Inc
KIM	Kimco Realty Corp
MHC	Manufactured Home Comm
MRY	Merry Land and Investment
NHP	Nationwide Health Prop
NPR	New Plan Realty Trust
PPS	Post Properties Inc.
PSA	Public Storage Inc.
PTR	Security Capital Pacific
SPG	Simon Property Group Inc.
SPK	Spieker Properties Inc.
TCO	Taubman Centers Inc.
UDR	United Dominion Realty
WRE	Washington Realty Estate
WRI	Weingarten Realty Invest

CBOE Telecommunication Index

Symbol: TCX

Symbol	Name
ADCT	ADC Telecomm Inc.
AIT	Ameritech Corp
ATI	Airtouch Inc.
BEL	Bell Atlantic Corp
BLS	Bellsouth Corp
CMCSA	Comcast Corp
CQ	Comsat Corp
DIGI	DSC Communications Corp
FON	Sprint Corporation
GTE	GTE Corp
MCIC	MCI Communications Corp
MTEL	Mobile Telecomm Tech
NYN	NYNEX Corp
QCOM	Qualcomm Inc.
SBC	Southwestern Bell Corp
T	AT&T Corp
TCOMA	Telecommunications Inc
USW	US West Communications
VCELA	Vanguard Cellular System
VIA	Viacom Inc.
WCOM	Worldcom

CBOE Technology Index

Symbol: TXX

Symbol	Name
AAPL	Apple Computer Inc
ADBE	Adobe Systems Inc
ADCT	ADC Telecommunications Inc
ADPT	Adaptec Inc
AMD	Advanced Micro Devices Inc
BAY	Bay Networks Inc
CA	Computer Associates
COMS	3Com Corp
CPQ	Compaq Computer Corp
CRUS	Cirrus Logic Inc
CS	Cabletron Systems Inc
CSC	Computer Sciences Corp
CSCO	Cisco Systems Inc
DEC	Digital Equipment Corp
DIGI	DSC Communications Corp
HWP	Hewlett Packard Co
IBM	International Bus Machines
INTC	Intel Corp
MOT	Motorola Inc
MSFT	Microsoft Corp
MU	Micron Technology Inc
NOVL	Novell Inc
ORCL	Oracle Corporation
PCTL	Picturetel Corp
PMTC	Parametric Tech Corp
SEG	Seagate Technology Inc
SGI	Silicon Graphics Inc
SNPS	Synopsys Inc
TLAB	Tellabs Inc
XLNX	Xilinx Inc

NASDAQ 100 Index

Symbol: NDX

Index

1	AKLM	Acclaim Entertainment, Inc.
2	ADPT	Adaptec, Inc.
3	ADCT	ADC Telecommunications, Inc.
4	ADBE	Adobe Systems, Inc.
5	ACCOB	Adolph Coors Company
6	AESC	AES Corp.
7	ALEX	Alexander & Baldwin, Inc.
8	ALTR	Altera Corporation
9	AMER	America Online, Inc.
10	AGREA	American Greetings Corp.
11	APCC	American Power Conversion Corp.
12	AMGN	Amgen, Inc.
13	ANDW	Andrew Corporation
14	AAPL	Apple Computer, Inc.
15	AMAT	Applied Materials
16	ASTA	AST Research, Inc.
17	ASAI	Atlantic Southeast Airlines
18	ATML	Atmel Corp.
19	ACAD	Autodesk, Inc.
20	SHLM	A. Schulman, Inc.
21	BNET	Bay Networks, Inc.
22	BGEN	Biogen, Inc.
23	BMET	Biomet, Inc.
24	BMCS	BMC Software, Inc.
25	BOBE	Bob Evans Farms, Inc.
26	CNTO	Centocor, Inc.
27	CHRS	Charming Shoppes, Inc.
28	CHIR	Chiron Corp.
29	CTAS	Cintas Corp.
30	CRUS	Cirrus Logic, Inc.
31	CSCO	Cisco Systems, Inc.
32	CMCSK	Comcast Corp.
33	CPWR	Compuware Corporation
34	CBRL	Cracker Barrel Old Country
35	DELL	Dell Computer Corp.
36	DIGI	DSC Communications Corp.
37	ERTS	Electronic Arts, Inc.
38	FFDNLB	Food Lion, Inc.
39	GATE	Gateway 2000, Inc.
40	GENZ	Genzyme Corp.
41	GIDL	Giddlings & Lewis, Inc.
42	GEMS	GlenayreTechnologies
43	HBOC	HBO Company

NASDAQ 100 Index (Continued)

Symbol: NDX

Index

44	HCCC	HealthCare Compare Corp.
45	MLHR	Herman Miller, Inc.
46	HONI	Hon Industries, Inc.
47	IFMX	Informix Corporation
48	INTC	Intel Corp.
49	INEL	Intelligent Electronics, Inc.
50	INTU	Intuit, Inc.
51	JBHT	J. B. Hunt Transport Services
52	KELYA	Kelly Services, Inc.
53	KLAC	KLA Instruments Corporation
54	LRCX	Lam Research Corporation
55	LLTC	Linear Technology Corporation
56	MCCRK	McCormick & Co.
57	MCIC	MCI Communications, Inc.
58	MFST	MFS Communications Co., Inc.
59	MFST	Microsoft Corp.
60	MTEL	Mobile Telecommunications Technologies Corp.
61	MOLX	Molex, Inc.
62	CALL	NEXTEL Communications, Inc.
63	NDSN	Nordson Corp.
64	NOBE	Nordstrom, Inc.
65	NWAC	Northwest Airlines
66	NOVL	Novell, Inc.
67	ORCL	Oracle Systems Corp.
68	OSSI	Outback Steakhouse, Inc.
69	PCAR	PACCAR, Inc.
70	PHSYB	PacifiCare Health Systems
71	PAGE	Paging Network
72	PMTC	Parametric Technology
73	PAYX	Paychex, Inc.
74	PRGO	Perrigo Company
75	PCCW	Price/Costco, Inc.
76	QCOM	Qualcom
77	QNTM	Quantum Corp.
78	RPOW	RPM, Inc.
79	SIAL	Sigma-Aldrich Corp.
80	SPLS	Staples, Inc.
81	SSSS	Stewart & Stevenson Services Inc.
82	STRM	StrataCom, Inc.
83	STRY	Stryker Corp.
84	STJM	St. Jude Medical, Inc.
85	SUNW	Sun Microsystems, Inc.
86	SYBS	Sybase, Inc.

NASDAQ 100 Index (Continued)

Symbol: NDX
Index

87	TECUA	Tecumseh Products Company
88	TCOMA	Tele-Communications, Inc.
89	TLAB	Tellabs, Inc.
90	COMS	Three Com Corp.
91	TYSNA	Tyson Foods, Inc.
92	USHC	U.S. Healthcare, Inc.
93	USRX	U.S. Robotics Corp.
94	VCELA	Vanguard Cellular Systems
95	VKNG	Viking Office Products, Inc.
96	WMTT	Willamette Industries, Inc.
97	WCOM	WorldCom, Inc.
98	WTHG	Worthington Industries, Inc.
99	XLNX	Xilinx, Inc.
100	YELL	Yellow Corporation

Note: Index components change frequently. As a result, this list may not be 100 percent accurate.

CBOE BioTech Index

Symbol: BTK

AMGN	AMGEN Inc.
BGEN	Biogen Inc.
BTGC	Bio Technology General Corporation
CGNE	Calgene Inc.
CHIR	Chiron Corporation
CNTO	Centocor Inc.
CPRO	Cellpro Inc.
CYTO	Cytogen Corporation
ENZN	Enzon Inc.
EPT	Epitope Inc.
GENZ	Genyme Corporation
GNSA	Gensia Inc.
IMMU	Immunomedics Inc.
IMNR	Immune Response Corporation
IMNX	Immunex Corporation
IVX	IVAX Corporation
LIPO	Liposome Company Inc.
NVX	North American Vaccine Inc.
XOMA	Xoma Corporation

Note: Index components change frequently. As a result, this list may not
be 100 percent accurate.

The Philadelphia Semiconductor

Symbol: SOX

ADI	Analog Devices
AMAT	Applied Materials
AMD	Advanced Micro Devices
CY	Cypress Semiconductor
IDTI	Integrated Device Tech.
INTC	INTEL
IRF	International Rectifier
LSCC	Lattice Semiconductor
LSI	LSI Logic
MOT	Motorola
MU	Micron Technology
NSM	National Semiconductor
NVLS	Novellus Systems
TER	Teradyne
TXN	Texas Instrument
VLSI	VLSI Technology

Note: Index components change frequently. As a result, this list may not
be 100 percent accurate.

Stocks by Groups—NASDAQ Only

Airline	ASAI
Airline	COMR
Airline	NWAC
Airline	VJET
Auto	VOLVY
Banks	CICS
Banks	BBNK
Banks	FITB
Banks	FATN
Banks	FSCO
Banks	HBAN
Banks	LISB
Banks	NTRS
Banks	PBKC
Banks	SUBN
Banks	USBC
Banks	WAMU
Beverages	WINEA
Bldg-Prod	WMTT
Bldg-Prod	FAST
Chemicals	SIAL
Comml Svcs	HMSY
Comml Svcs	RTSY
Comml-Svcs	AMMB
Comml-Svcs	APOL
Comml-Svcs	CKSG
Comml-Scvs	CMGI
Comml-Svcs	EFII
Comml-Svcs	HCCC
Comml-Svcs	PAYX
Consumer Agrea	AGREA
Finance	COFI
Finance	GNPT
Finance	MONE
Finance	TROW
Finance	UCFC
Finance-Equity	FLCO
Financial-Svcs	CACC
Financial-Svcs	MEDA
Financial-Svcs	PMTS
Food	TYSNA
Food-Prep	MCCRK

Funeral-Svcs	LWNGF
Graphics	INGR
Graphics	TRID
Insurance	PTREF
Insurance	SAFC
Laser	BEAM
Laser-Sys	VISX
Leisure-Gaming	CSDS
Leisure-Movies	PIXR
Leisure-Toys	RIDE
Leisure-Movies	REGL
Machinery	PRST
Mail-Order	MWHS
Med-Instrument	BMET
Media	EVGM
Media	NWCG
Media	LBTYA
Media	TCOMA
Media-Cable	CMCSA
Media-Cable	CHCSK
Medical	AGPH
Medical-Prod	ATLI
Medical Biomed	BGEN
Medical Drugs	JMED
Medical-Biomed	BCHXF
Medical-Biomed	CNTO
Medical-Biomed	CEPH
Medical-Biomed	CHIR
Medical-Biomed	CURE
Medical-Biomed	GENIZ
Medical-Biomed	GENZ
Medical-Biomed	GILD
Medical-Biomed	HGSI
Medical-Biomed	IDPH
Medical-Biomed	LIPO
Medical-Biomed	SMTG
Medical-Drugs	CHMD
Medical-Drugs	DURA
Medical-Drugs	FUSE
Medical-Drugs	IPIC
Medical-Drugs	MATK
Medical-Drugs	MDRX
Medical-Drugs	NXTR
Medical-Drugs	RPCX
Medical-Drugs	SEQU
Medical-Drugs	TEVIY
Medical-Drugs	WATS
Medical-Eqip	APLX

Medical-Health	CPDN
Medical-Health	CVTY
Medical-Health	FHPC
Medical-Health	MAXI
Medical-Health	OXHP
Medical-Health	PHSYB
Medical-Health	PCAM
Medical-Health	USHC
Medical-Home	LNCR
Medical-Home	MRNR
Medical-Home	PHTC
Medical-Hosp	QHGI
Medical-Instr	CORD
Medical-Instr	IDXX
Medical-Instr	OLGC
Medical-Instr	PHYS
Medical-Instr	STRY
Medical-Instr	VNTX
Medical-Prod	CYGN
Medical-Prod	GENZ
Medical-Prod	MSNS
Medical-Prod	NELL
Medical-Prod	NSIX
Medical-Prod	NFLD
Medical-Supp	MNTR
Medical-Supp	OCAI
Medical-Supp	PSSI
Medical-Supp	STR
Medical-Supp	TGE
Metal-Prod	WTGH
Movie Equip	AVID
Office-Equip	DSPC
Office Supp	SPLS
Office Supplies	OFIS
Office-Equip	INFS
Office-Suppl	VKNG
Oil Drilling	APGR
Oil Prod	SOLV
Oil Svcs	PGSA
Oil-Gas-Svcs	GLBL
Pollution-Svcs	UWST
Pollution-Equip	MLTN
Pollution-Svcs	RWIN
Retail	BSST
Retail	BBBY
Retail	GYMB
Retail	FEET
Retail	NOBE

Retail	PETM
Retail	PCCW
Retail	ROST
Retail	RAYS
Retail-Mail	WSGC
Retail-Office	CEXP
Retail-Rest	APSO
Retail-Rest	ACXM
Retail-Rest	BOST
Retail-Rest	STAR
Retail-Rest	OSSI
Retail-Rest	RAIN
Retail-Rest	SBUX
Tele-Cellular	COMMA
Tele-Cellular	ICEL
Tele-Equip	ACTI
Tele-Equip	ASPT
Tele-Equip	CELL
Tele-Equip	CDTC
Tele-Equip	CSCC
Tele-Equip	CDCO
Tele-Equip	CMVT
Tele-Equip	ECILF
Tele-Equip	ESOL
Tele-Equip	GEMS
Tele-Equip	GVIL
Tele-Equip	INTV
Tele-Equip	OCTL
Tele-Equip	PAIR
Tele-Equip	PCTL
Tele-Equip	PRMS
Tele-Equip	QCOM
Tele-Equip	TLAB
Tele-Equip	TRMB
Tele-Equipment	STRM
Tele-Svcs	APRA
Tele-Svcs	MCIC
Tell-Svcs	MFST
Tele-Svcs	MTEL
Tele-Svcs	PACE
Tele-Svcs	SPOT
Tele-Svcs	USLD
Tele-Svcs	WCII
Tele-Svcs	WCO
Textile	NAU
Transportation	FRTZ
Trucks & Parts	PCAR

NASDAQ Stocks in the S&P 500

American Greetings	AGREA
Amgen	AMGN
Andrew Corp	ANDW
Apple Computer	AAPL
Applied Materials	AMAT
ADSK	AUTODESK
Bay	BAY NETWORKS
Boatman's Bancshares	BOAT
Charming Shoppes	CHRS
Cisco Systems	CSCO
Comlast	CMCSK
Adolph Coors	ACCOB
DSC Communications	DIGI
Gidding & Lewis	GIDL
Intel	INTC
Intergraph	INGR
MCI Communications	MCIC
Microsoft	MSFT
Nordstroms	NOBE
Novell	NOVL
Oracle	ORCL
Paccar	PCAR
Price Costco	PCCW
Ryans Family Steakhouse	RYAN
Safeco	SAFC
Shared Medical	SMED
Sigma Aldrich	SIAL
St. Jude Medical	STJM
Sun Microsystems	SUNW
Telecommunications Class A	TCOMA
Tellabs	TLAB
US Bancorp	USBC
Willamette	WMTT
Worthington Industries	WTHG
Yellow Corporation	YELL

INDEX

Marc Friedfertig is the Managing Member of Broadway Trading LLC, a brokerage firm specializing in online trading. He has trained and worked with hundreds of successful day traders who are currently earning superior returns trading listed securities, NASDAQ securities, and equity options. He is now working with many very successful SOES traders on the Watcher system and listed traders on the DOT system. The firm's philosophy is "Broadway Trading is committed to constantly improving the tools it provides to its customers to assist them in achieving the results they desire. We look for long-term relationships with our customers. If they succeed, we succeed."

Marc is a graduate of the Columbia University Business School, having earned a master of business administration in finance. He did his undergraduate work at Tulane University, where he received a bachelor in science and management degree. He has worked for The First Boston Corporation and Morgan Stanley & Co., Inc. He was a member of the New York Futures Exchange, where he actively traded index futures. He was a member of the American Stock Exchange for 8 years, where he was considered one of the top traders and supervised and trained many other traders. Marc has had phenomenal success trading. In this book and in his lectures he shares his winning ideas and techniques with others.

George West is the President of Broadway Consulting Group as well as Managing Member of JGM Securities LLC. JGM Securities specializes in trading NASDAQ and listed securities. Broadway Consulting provides a book, a video, a training program, and online chats for day traders. Through these media George shares his expertise gained from extensive experience trading options and both listed and NASDAQ securities. He was an options market maker on the American Stock Exchange. He was also a trader at Spear, Leeds, & Kellogg, where he gained exposure to trading with large institutional clients. Both he and Marc Friedfertig have developed novel trading strategies for electronic day trading.

George West graduated from St. Lawrence University, majoring in political science. George is a top trader and regularly uses the strategies and technology described in this book.

George Pieczenik (Editor) is a professor of biochemistry and microbiology at Rutgers University. He has published with several Nobel laureates, including the discoverer of the structure of DNA. He has major patents in combinatorial recombinant chemistry and specializes in biotechnology securities, companies, and patents.

Dr. Pieczenik graduated from Harvard University and trained at the MRC Laboratory of Molecular Biology, Cambridge, England, and at Rockefeller University. George studies the market in his free time and has a passion for day trading.

COMPANY BACKGROUND

Broadway Consulting Group is a leading provider of day-trading educational services. The company offers books, videos, an online chat room, and a seminar that provides traders and others interested in trading a clear understanding of how day trading works. Broadway teaches techniques to choose the right stocks at the right time using the most advanced technology available. Through advanced training and superior technology, Broadway Consulting Group has succeeded in training traders with a wide variety of professional backgrounds including attorneys, computer consultants, advertising executives, and real estate developers, to name a few. Many of these traders are currently earning more than $20,000 per month.

Broadway Consulting Group is operated by day traders who boast more than 20 years of experience on Wall Street.

Part of what makes Broadway Consulting Group successful is its training philosophy. Broadway Consulting Group believes in creating long-term relationships with customers by sharing market knowledge, trading skills, and cutting-edge technology. Visit the company's website at www.electronicdaytrader.com.